D1036625

The Children
Hurricane Katrina
Left Behind

Now They're Wet

Hurricane Katrina as Metaphor for Social and Educational Neglect

GLORIA LADSON-BILLINGS

My first glimpse of Hurricane Katrina came from almost 6,000 miles away, as I attended a conference in London, England. I was even more of a news junkie than usual during this trip because London had recently experienced a terrorist attack on its transit system, and the university where my meetings were being held was located near the spot where one of the buses was bombed. However, little of what I saw on the BBC and CNN World News focused on terrorism or bombings. Instead, I saw the horror that was the aftermath of Hurricane Katrina, and those images left me sad, depressed, and angry. The more I watched, the more agitated I became. The e-mails I received from friends, family, and colleagues back in the States did little to alleviate my concerns. Things were worse, much worse, than they seemed on the news after

PETER LANG
New York • Washington, D.C./Baltimore • Bern
Frankfurt am Main • Berlin • Brussels • Vienna • Oxford

This article appeared in the Winter 2006 (Volume 40) issue of Voices in Urban Education: Equity After Katrina, published by The Annenberg Institute for School Reform at Brown University. Reprinted by permission. All rights reserved.

The Children Hurricane Katrina Left Behind

Schooling Context, Professional Preparation, and Community Politics

Sharon P. Robinson & M. Christopher Brown II, EDITORS

WITH A FOREWORD BY *Linda Darling-Hammond*
& AN AFTERWORD BY *Lynn Huntley*

Serving Learners

PUBLISHED FOR THE AMERICAN ASSOCIATION OF COLLEGES FOR TEACHER EDUCATION

PETER LANG
New York • Washington, D.C./Baltimore • Bern
Frankfurt am Main • Berlin • Brussels • Vienna • Oxford

Library of Congress Cataloging-in-Publication Data

The children hurricane Katrina left behind: schooling context, professional
preparation, and community politics / edited by Sharon P. Robinson,
M. Christopher Brown II.
p. cm.
Includes bibliographical references and index.
1. African American children—Education. 2. Discrimination in education—
United States. 3. Marginality, Social—United States. 4. Hurricane Katrina, 2005—
Social aspects. I. Robinson, Sharon P. II. Brown, M. Christopher.
LC2771.C45   371.829'96073—dc22   2006101454
ISBN 978-0-8204-9728-0 (hard cover)
ISBN 978-0-8204-8822-6 (paperback)

Bibliographic information published by **Die Deutsche Bibliothek**.
Die Deutsche Bibliothek lists this publication in the "Deutsche
Nationalbibliografie"; detailed bibliographic data is available
on the Internet at http://dnb.ddb.de/.

AACTE is sponsoring this publication to stimulate discussion, study,
and experimentation among educators. The findings, interpretations, and
conclusions presented herein are entirely those of the author(s) and do not
necessarily reflect the official position or policies of AACTE, nor does
sponsorship of this publication imply endorsement by AACTE.
Though AACTE and the author(s) have used their best efforts in preparing
this document, they make no representations or warranties with
respect to the accuracy or completeness of its contents and specifically
disclaim any implied warranties of merchantability or fitness for a particular
purpose. Neither AACTE, its Board of Directors, or officers, nor the
author(s) of this document shall be liable for any loss of profit
or any other commercial damages, including but not limited to
special, incidental, consequential, or other damages.

Cover design by Lisa Barfield

The paper in this book meets the guidelines for permanence and durability
of the Committee on Production Guidelines for Book Longevity
of the Council of Library Resources.

© 2007 Peter Lang Publishing, Inc., New York
29 Broadway, 18th floor, New York, NY 10006
www.peterlang.com

All rights reserved.
Reprint or reproduction, even partially, in all forms such as microfilm,
xerography, microfiche, microcard, and offset strictly prohibited.

Printed in the United States of America

LC2771
.C45
2007

077503969

■■■

To my beloved grandchildren,
Daniel and Emma,
for whom I wish a bright future filled
with quality teachers sensitive to their individual
learning needs; to my supportive daughter Kimberly
(and her husband Danny); to my sisters, Marie and Ellie,
and to my brother Woody; and in memory of my parents and sister Ferda.
I honor the legacies of my father and hero, Mr. Woodford R. Porter, Sr.,
and my mother, Harriett E. Porter, a woman much admired.
—spr

To William H. Gray III,
who taught me about leadership, vision, management,
fundraising, and commitment. Even more, Mr. Gray admonished
that in order for research to be good, it must be relevant;
to my mother, the Leo Lady;
to my aunts and uncles—Shirley, George,
Richard, Janice, Norman, Keren, Benita,
and Rodney—for their unwaverinig support;
and to all the "outlaws": Theodore, Earnestine, VaRhonda,
Wanda, Cynthia, Eddie, Michael, Tony, and Sonia.
May we always remember the life, living, and legacy of
Mrs. Evelyna Smith Brown.
—mcb2

9 percent and a white population of 91 percent. It has a 4 percent low-income student population. Philadelphia has a Black and Latino population of 79 percent, with a White and other racial/ethnic group population of 21 percent. The low-income student population of the Philadelphia schools is 71 percent of the school district. Any decent researcher knows that correlation does not equal causation. But the correlations between race (and class) and educational spending are troublesome.

How can it possibly be in the public interest to continue to keep poor children of color in a cycle of low achievement, low graduation rates, high levels of unemployment and underemployment, and compromised futures? How much of this do we imagine people will continue to accept? How soon will it be before we see the civil and social unrest that characterized the 1960s? Indeed, what we are talking about is no longer just about social and civic responsibility. It is about moral responsibility. We cannot call ourselves a moral people in the midst of this aggressive neglect.

I term what we are doing "aggressive neglect" because, at the same time we are experiencing unprecedented poverty, some segments of our society are experiencing an incredible bonanza of wealth. The growing income disparity makes it difficult for many Americans to experience empathy with those who do not have. We blame and demonize the poor and, more pointedly, we isolate them. We do not see them, we do not acknowledge their existence. They are both out of sight and out of mind. However, then Hurricane Katrina hit and we were shamed in the presence of our fellow Americans and before the entire world.

The Lengths to Which Communities of Color Must Go

Communities of color could not wait for us to hear their anguished cries. They have tried desperately on their own to get high-quality education for their children. Just how desperately? Well, in some cases they are desperate enough to opt out of the system altogether. In Milwaukee and Cleveland, families of poor Black and Brown children are eagerly participating in voucher programs. Like a committed public school advocate (I sent all of my children to public schools), but I cannot insist that these parents select public schools when they have other choices.

Perhaps the most extreme example of desperation was made apparent to me in a *New York Times* review of the documentary film *The Boys of Baraka*. Stephen Holden (2005) begins with a disturbing but familiar statistic—"76 percent of Black male students in Baltimore city schools do not graduate from high school." In what White middle-class community would that be an acceptable piece of data? However, the film describes the extraordinary lengths to which some families will go to address that shameful statistic: they send their children in an experimental program to school in

Table of Contents

Part Two: Preparing Professionals for the Possible

destruction of this hurricane cut across racial and economic lines. [...] and satellite maps concluded that poor Black residents of New Orleans were disproportionately displaced and suffered the greatest loss. Hence, Hurricane [...] symbol of what can happen when a nation systematically and [...] the most vulnerable.

[...] not want to [...] ramifications on the poor. When [...] uals or members of organized groups responded to Hurricane [...] ous donations of money, service, sympathy and incalculable acts of kindness [...] citizens and individuals, we should all be proud of these [...] those [...] need. However, there are financial, emotional, and physical [...] uals' and groups' ability to sustain altruism over time. In fact, [...] the hurricane, the *Houston Chronicle* (Spencer & Radcliffe, 20[...]) [...] school employees were experiencing "compassion fatigue" [...] [...] Katrina students enrolled in Houston's schools. When "compassion [...] some individuals applaud their generosity, decompartmentalize [...] on with their own lives. I believe that the images of desperate [...] ple literally drowning under the weight of poverty were too [...] for the average person because watching bore an acknowledgement [...] responsibility to act.

Still others struggled with "compassion fatigue" by blaming [...] predicament—reproaching them for the dire circumstances [...] themselves. Often the popular media exploited this perception [...] as ignorant, lazy, welfare-dependent people who did not heed [...] uate, or worse, looters and criminals who took advantage of the [...] published stories about evacuees using FEMA and Red Cross [...] expensive clothes and alcoholic beverages.

Compassion fatigue and victim blaming were predictable [...] Katrina because individual donations and the work of volunteers [...] be a substitution for or a distraction from focusing on identi[...] tions to poverty and racism at the larger societal level. Michael [...] accurately observed that "Episodes of goodwill and compassion [...] for structural change." [...] Charity can never be a substitute [...]

Structural changes are required if the poverty rate is to [...] The U.S. Census Bureau (Kryter, 2005) reported that the poverty [...] last year with 1.1 million more individuals living in poverty [...] America's poverty rate is the highest among developed nations [...] alent to the population of Canada (Adler, 2005). Some of the [...] United States reside in Mississippi, Louisiana, and Alabama. [...] ple in each of these states who earn less than $40,000 a year [...]

FOREWORD

Countering Aggressive Neglect

Creating a Transformative Educational Agenda in the Wake of Katrina

LINDA DARLING-HAMMOND

There are events of such enormous historical importance that a single word takes on symbolic meaning: "Watergate" connotes political corruption. "Brown" has come to denote a commitment to equality. And "Katrina" has come to signify both governmental neglect and institutional racism. The disaster revealed not only what Gloria Ladson-Billings here calls "aggressive neglect" of Black families during the hurricane itself but also brought to light the tragically inadequate health, housing, employment, and education these families experienced long before Katrina hit. Jacqueline Jordan Irvine observes that, "Hurricane Katrina is a symbol of what can happen when a nation systematically and unabashedly abandons the most vulnerable."

Less discussed has been the aggressive educational neglect that also character-izes the education of most African American and Latino children in cities across the United States. Eboni Zamani-Gallaher and Vernon Polite note that Katrina "is but a metaphor for the calamity that commonly faces African American students in urban school settings." Indeed, the situation in New Orleans "should not be misconstrued as an anomaly; the 'storms' of centuries of educational neglect and failed social policies have been as catastrophic as the woefully deplorable federal, state, and local response to Hurricane Katrina and its victims." The essays in this volume speak powerfully and poignantly to that neglect, and to what we can and must do about it.

The immediate tragedy of Katrina played out on rooftops as people called unsuccessfully for help to helicopters overhead; in attics as the rising water inched steadily up helpless ankles, legs, waists, and torsos; in the stadium as families begged for water, food, and health care for the sick and elderly. More than 1,000 people died as the international community looked on, in shock that the so-called richest nation in the world could not / would not take care of its own citizens in dire need. Just as Selma and other Civil Rights marches shocked unsuspecting Americans who watched on their home televisions as peaceful marchers were attacked by dogs, clubs, and water hoses, Katrina brought into the living rooms of a sleeping nation the raw, unvarnished racism that has been made increasingly invisible to those beyond its reach. If every tragedy carries with it the potential for change, this may have been the blessing of Katrina—to make it brutally clear just how dispensable this government has considered those who are poor, Black, and marginalized.

In the flurry of activity since, it is difficult to know whether the nation has grasped and will respond to the longer-term tragedy brought to light by Katrina. The educational neglect made visible by the diaspora of nearly 375,000 students who scattered from New Orleans to other school systems has been the stuff of headlines in the local papers of cities that took them in. As Kassie Freeman, former Education Dean of historically Black Dillard University in New Orleans, points out, in the same way that African American students of the "Great Migration" from the South were described as academically behind when they reached the North, New Orleans children now in schools in Texas, Georgia, and other states are characterized as far behind their peers. Only about half of the elementary-age evacuees, for example, were able to pass reading tests in Texas that more than 80% of Texas students pass and that are known nationally as being very low-level tests of basic skills.

This should not have been news. The sorry state of education for Blacks in Louisiana in general and in New Orleans in particular—where 96% of students were African American—has been known by those paying attention for a very long time. M. Christopher Brown, T. Elon Dancy, and James Earl Davis report chilling statistics about the inadequate educational expenditures, teachers' salaries, and graduation rates of Louisiana schools, where well under half of 9th graders are able to graduate 4 years later. As Ladson-Billings notes, education was not working for children in New Orleans long before the streets were flooded and the roofs were blown away. The fact that the schools were nearly entirely African American means that most White children were sent to private schools—schools that for some time the state and city sought to publicly fund, as did many parts of the South when desegregation was mandated.

The public schools were, as Jacqueline Leonard reports here from her discussions with teacher colleagues, "plagued by corruption and scandal." Classes were conducted in buildings that had leaks, poor plumbing, and paint peeling off the ceilings and walls. Large proportions of teachers were unprepared and uncertified, providing a revolving door of marginally competent instructors who left as fast as they entered.

The allocation of expert teachers is as racialized as the distribution of aid during Katrina. Typical is the story told by a young recruit from Teach for America who recounted how she met a veteran teacher with more than 10 years' experience who had applied for the job she received. The veteran, who was not hired in the all-Black public school system because she would have cost several thousand dollars more than the untrained TFA recruit, went to teach instead in the all-White private school nearby. When the young recruit resigned part-way through her first year, a certified teacher was hired for her position that afternoon. It was then that she realized that "teacher shortages are not defined by lack of people but by lack of money," and that the students were denied access to the experienced teachers they needed because they were not considered worthy of the investment.

Hurricane Katrina raised to attention the educational neglect that children in New Orleans experienced for many years, as well as the lack of adequate employment, health care, housing, and other basic needs. It is an open question whether the new system that could be envisioned to take its place will emerge from the steps now being taken to replace the public school system with charter schools and incentives for privatization.

Changing historic patterns will take greater foresight than is generally exercised in addressing crises that affect the poor and disenfranchised. The extent to which history can repeat itself when band-aids are substituted for needed investments is brought home in two essays that remind us of floods that preceded Katrina. Linda Schaak Distad recalls that in 1965, Hurricane Betsy had covered 80 percent of New Orleans' 9th ward when the levees were overwhelmed, leaving more than 80 people dead and hundreds homeless. For years before that episode and in the years since, the Army Corps of Engineers had known that it was only a matter of time before the inadequate levees would be overtaken and the surrounding areas would be devastated. P. Rudy Mattai and Jacqueline M. Williams go back even further to the Great Mississippi Flood of 1927, which similarly overwhelmed the known-to-be-inadequate infrastructure for flood control in the Delta, and led W. E. B. Du Bois to say about Blacks in Mississippi, " . . . Let them ride, run and crawl out of this hell. There is no hope for the black man there today. . . ."

Like these natural disasters, the educational disasters that are inflicted on African Americans are known; they are structural; and their effects can be predicted. What is essential for rebuilding urban schools in both New Orleans and the nation is that we recognize, first, that the problems are woven into the warp and woof of our educational infrastructure; second, that the task is to envision and enact a transformative agenda for change—not merely a collection of marginal reforms; and third, that the foundations for this work must include new approaches and renewed commitments to a revolutionary perspective in the education of those who will do the work.

Institutional Racism: Structuring Educational Inequality

The shock that most Americans experienced as the lessons of Katrina came to light is a sign that the structural nature of ongoing institutionalized racism is poorly understood. Just as the assault on affirmative action is built on the false presumption that education for "minorities" has been equalized, the conditions that were brought to light by Katrina are inaccurately viewed by many as unique and anomalous. Though it is true that educational conditions in New Orleans have been particularly dreadful, it would be a mistake to think that they are rare or even unusual for low-income African American students today.

From the time southern states made it illegal to teach an enslaved person to read until the present, African Americans, along with Mexican Americans and Native Americans, have faced de jure and de facto exclusion from educational opportunities across the nation. International assessments reveal that America's schools continue to be the most unequal in the industrialized world in terms of spending, curriculum offerings, teaching quality, and outcomes, and are nearly as inequitable today as when Arthur Wise wrote *Rich Schools, Poor Schools* more than three decades ago. In fact, these differentials are highly correlated with race. Indeed over the last few years, lawsuits in at least a dozen states have pointed out that inadequate education funding combined with acute segregation has produced apartheid schools for Black and Latino students that lack even the most rudimentary building blocks for an education: safe facilities, textbooks, and qualified teachers.

The level of neglect experienced by students in what Dianne Smith calls "the new Jim Crow schools" takes a long time to accumulate, and it is a hidden cancer that is ravaging our nation. As Arthur E. Wise and Jane A. Leibbrand point out in their chapter, it consigns thousands of children each year to schools where they are taught by a parade of untrained teachers who do not know how to teach them to read or to become proficient in the disciplines. These same children are then at risk for failing state tests, being retained in grade, dropping out, and joining the school-to-prison pipeline that has contributed to ballooning prison populations, which have tripled in the last two decades, causing prison expenditures to increase by 600%, now rivaling state spending for higher education.

Indeed, according to the Justice Policy Institute, between 1980 and 2000, three times as many young African American men were added to the nation's prison systems as were added to colleges. In 2000, an estimated 791,600 African American men were in prison or jail, while 603,000 were in higher education. The public costs of this wastage, in addition to the human tragedies it represents, are not only the $30,000 annual costs for each inmate—almost a year's tuition at an Ivy League school—but the costs of health and human services, lost wages and taxes. Irvine notes the economic costs of low achievement in this country include $192 billion lost each year to the economy as a result of young people who never complete high school.

Increased incarceration—and its disproportionate effects upon the African American community—is not only a function of discriminatory criminal justice practices, but also of the lack of access to education that could lead to literacy, needed skills, and employment. More than half the adult prison population has literacy skills below those required by the labor market, and nearly 40 percent of adjudicated juvenile delinquents have treatable learning disabilities that went undiagnosed and untreated in the schools. This is substantially, then, an educational problem associated with inadequate access to the kinds of teachers and other resources that could enable young people to gain the skills that would make it possible for them to become gainfully employed.

In 1991 Jonathan Kozol documented the effects of these disparities in *Savage Inequalities,* contrasting schools like Goudy Elementary School serving an African American student population in Chicago, using "15-year-old textbooks in which Richard Nixon is still president," offering "no science labs, no art or music teachers . . . [and] two working bathrooms for some 700 children," with schools in the neighboring town of New Trier (more than 98% White), where students had access to "superior labs . . . up-to-date technology . . . seven gyms [and] an Olympic pool." In 2005, when Kozol recorded the tenacity of America's commitment to educational inequality in *The Shame of a Nation,* school spending in New Trier, at nearly $15,000 per student, still far exceeded the $8,500 per student available in Chicago for a population with many more special needs—a pattern found in urban / suburban comparisons across the country. Furthermore, as Brown, Dancy, and Davis describe, city school systems are charged to serve needy populations amid increasing poverty rates, eroding tax bases, aging and costly facilities, and complex, racialized politics that make education more expensive than it is elsewhere.

The students notice the results. As one New York City 16-year-old told Kozol of his school, where holes in ceilings expose rusty pipes and water pours in on rainy days:

> If you . . . put white children in this building in our place, this school would start to shine. No question. The parents would say: "This building sucks. It's ugly. Fix it up." They'd fix it fast—no question. . . . People on the outside may think that we don't know what it is like for other students, but we visit other schools and we have eyes and we have brains. You cannot hide the differences. You see it and compare. . . .

Lest we think the educational conditions in New Orleans are exceptional for students of color, here is one of several descriptions of California schools serving African American and Latino students included in a recent equity lawsuit complaint:

> At Luther Burbank School, students cannot take textbooks home for homework in any core subject because their teachers have enough textbooks for use in class only . . . . For homework, students must take home photocopied pages, with no accompanying text for guidance or reference, when and if their teachers have enough paper to use to make homework copies. . . . Luther Burbank is infested with vermin and roaches and students routinely see mice in their classrooms. One dead rodent has remained, decomposing, in a corner in the gymnasium since the beginning of the school year. The school library is rarely open, has no librarian, and has not recently been updated. The latest version of the encyclopedia in the library was published in approximately 1988. Luther Burbank classrooms do not have computers. Computer instruction and research skills are not, therefore, part of Luther Burbank students' regular instruction. The school no longer offers any art classes for budgetary reasons. . . . Two of the three bathrooms at Luther Burbank are locked all day, every day. . . . Students have urinated or defecated on themselves at school because they could not get into an unlocked bathroom. . . . When the bathrooms are not locked, they often lack toilet paper, soap, and paper towels, and the toilets frequently are clogged and overflowing. . . . Ceiling tiles are missing and cracked in the school gym, and school children are afraid to play basketball and other games in the gym because they worry that more ceiling tiles will fall on them during their games. . . . The school has no air conditioning. On hot days classroom temperatures climb into the 90s. The school heating system does not work well. In winter, children often wear coats, hats, and gloves during class to keep warm. . . . Eleven of the 35 teachers at Luther Burbank have not yet obtained regular, nonemergency teaching credentials, and 17 of the 35 teachers only began teaching at Luther Burbank this school year (*Williams et al., v. State of California,* Superior Court of the State of California, Complaint, filed June, 2000, pp. 22–23).

This description vividly confirms the point made by M. Jayne Fleener, Jerry Willis, Sister Judith Brun, and Kristy Hebert in this volume. They note that, while "there may be something comforting about exporting the problems of poverty, poor health care, poor educational opportunities, and limited job possibilities to a group of countries we can call Third World, if we look out our windows, we can often find all the characteristics of the Third World right here at home." They challenge academics to recognize and redress institutionalized racism, suggesting that, "Often, while those of us in research university colleges of education are searching for The Answers, we keep our heads down and try not to look out our windows. That is because the view often spotlights the problems and needs of children, schools, and parents right down the street."

These needs, as Vivian Gadsden and Susan Fuhrman remind us, are not situated in schools and school systems alone. Furthermore, addressing them "will not happen naturally. . . . (I)t is perhaps an unnatural act, given the range and severity of needs of families and the comparably limited resources." If productive action is to occur, we will need to engender *aggressive attention* to counter the aggressive neglect that has gotten us where we are today. As Jacqueline Jordan Irvine argues, "Schools and society have to be *transformed,* not merely *reformed.*"

Envisioning and Enacting an Educational Transformation

Mary Hatwood Futrell frames the choice clearly: "We can simply provide makeshift services, or we can use this as an opportunity to build a model system of education that provides a quality education for every child. . . ." In her essay in this volume, Dianne Smith quotes Ella Baker on the nature of the transformation that is needed:

> In order for us as poor and oppressed people to become a part of a society that is meaningful, the system under which we now exist has to be radically changed. This means that we are going to have to learn to think in radical terms. I use the term *radical* in its original meaning—getting down to and understanding the root cause. It means facing a system that does not lend itself to your needs and devising means by which you change the system.

Changing the system starts from a different conception of the problem than fighting to save one child at a time or even one school district at a time. Irvine uses a powerful metaphor to describe the difference between educators' behavior when they think of themselves as fighting on behalf of individuals against the system and when they conceptualize their work as system transformation. She describes a boy who devotes his mornings to throwing starfish back into the sea, one at a time, even though they wash back up on the shore the next night. Despite his devotion, his approach is much less effective than if he were to use his energy to develop more systemic solutions to prevent the starfish from washing ashore. She notes that the same shortsightedness occurs when educators and school reformers think of themselves as starfish throwers. Rather like "engineers designing the new levees after Hurricane Katrina—

building category 3 levees for category 5 hurricanes to come, (t)hey work diligently with outdated plans and inadequate funding to build an adequate structure. School transformers, on the other hand, are committed and trained to design schools that tackle the big educational hurricanes—racism, classism, sexism, heterosexism, and religious intolerance."

We need to pay aggressive attention to these "big educational hurricanes" and to the structural conditions that hold them in place. Irvine's argument that educators in K-12 and higher education should re-define their role as school transformers committed to eliminating structural inequality is echoed by other authors. Wise and Leibbrand suggest, "In spite of desegregation rules, busing, demonstration projects, and some equalization of property tax structures, children in inner cities are trapped just as surely as were the hurricane victims. They can't get out. Just as occurred in the aftermath of Katrina, new resources must be brought to where these children are, and a structure for these resources must be built into the districts where the children reside." That structure includes a system to ensure well-prepared teachers—that is, teachers prepared to teach all students well—in every classroom.

Developing such a system requires a transformative vision of what is possible. Ira Lit and Jon Snyder start with the process of developing those images: "Close your eyes," they command. "Imagine a classroom. Envision a school." Beyond whimsical ideas of what might be possible, they point to the systemic elements of what is needed to enact these visions. They suggest that we pay aggressive attention to what it is that matters most in successful teaching: how we can recruit and retain talented people into the profession who are capable of doing what matters most; how we successfully prepare and support teachers to do these things; how we can organize schools so that teachers can do what matters most; and how we can productively reward teachers for doing what is most important for student learning. That constructing a system of education might even be plausible is suggested by recent polling data, cited in Wise and Leibbrand, revealing that most members of the public are willing to invest more in public education, particularly if funds are used to enhance teacher quality.

Developing Change-Agents
for Equitable Schools and Teaching

Sharon Robinson and Penny Engel see Katrina as a potential catalyst for this work, arguing that "New Orleans' rebirth can serve to escalate the transformation of teacher preparation for the good of the entire nation. What is needed is known, but not yet widely practiced. We know the critical importance of the teacher. We know what constitutes exceptional teachers and how they can be developed. And we know the essential elements of accelerated preparation. Now is the time to put that knowledge to work."

To move this understanding to the profession as a whole from individual practitioners who successfully teach African American and other "minority" students and from individual preparation programs that currently prepare extraordinarily effective new teachers requires thinking systemically about teacher education as well. It means paying aggressive attention to the recruitment, induction, licensing, accreditation, and certification policies that can construct both pressure and support for radical transformations of teacher preparation practice. It means envisioning and enacting a day when strong incentives to enter teaching and supports for high quality preparation attract highly talented, committed, and diverse individuals, fully reflective of the students in our schools, to carefully designed, coherent programs that deftly interweave theory and practice. In well-conceptualized courses that model effective pedagogy wrapped around carefully constructed clinical placements that model effective teaching of students of color, these programs should produce both deep understanding of children from different communities, cultures, and language backgrounds and a sophisticated repertoire of teaching skills guided by expert judgment attentive to how students learn.

A key to developing programs that will produce powerful teachers is recognizing that such programs must engender moral commitments and understandings that match the technical skills they provide to enable students to learn. Teacher educators Pamela Smith and Pat Williams-Boyd advocate "a fundamental shift in our work and in our ways of looking at the world" that is not narrowly focused only on "meeting the cognitive demands of methodology while ignoring the affective demands of caring through which community is built." To accomplish this, they argue that teacher educators and prospective teachers must leave the "tidy confines of their classrooms and enter the messy social arenas that provide them with opportunities to act upon moral imperatives informed by social need."

They need to learn through praxis, as Arthur E. Levine suggests, the lesson of "tikkun olam"—that they have an obligation to improve the human condition. They also need to be armed with the skills to do so. For it is not enough to develop commitments without the abilities to act upon them effectively. In order to hold onto the belief that all children can learn it is essential to have the skills to enable them to learn. Effective action in difficult situations requires deep knowledge of children—their development, families and culture, and the learning process—and the curriculum—its demands and possibilities, as well as how to structure access to powerful ideas and support particular students' progress in making this knowledge their own.

Furthermore, such programs must themselves be clear about their moral purpose. Linda Schaak Distad points out that, as Paulo Freire contended, education is never neutral; it is either an instrument of conformity or of "the practice of freedom," which enables people to participate in the transformation of their world. Distad suggests that "the challenge before us is to determine how to transform our teacher preparation programs in light of our understandings of the 'new normal,' a normal in which being neutral or deliberately naïve is not tolerated." She argues for preparation that enables educators to pay aggressive attention to the causes and manifestations of institutional racism.

I would suggest as well that the nature of the education teachers are prepared to offer matters greatly. In the early days of the Civil Rights Era, W. E. B. Du Bois argued strenuously not only for access to schools, but for the kind of education that would enable students to think critically and take control of the course of their own learning, to determine their own fate, and to lead their own people:

> Of all the civil rights for which the world has struggled and fought for 5000 years, the right to learn is undoubtedly the most fundamental. . . . The freedom to learn . . . has been bought by bitter sacrifice. And whatever we may think of the curtailment of other civil rights, we should fight to the last ditch to keep open the right to learn, the right to have examined in our schools not only what we believe, but what we do not believe; not only what our leaders say, but what the leaders of other groups and nations, and the leaders of other centuries have said. We must insist upon this to give our children the fairness of a start which will equip them with such an array of facts and such an attitude toward truth that they can have a real chance to judge what the world is and what its greater minds have thought it might be.

Access to this kind of empowering education that has animated the African American quest for more than 300 years will not be produced by a parade of under-prepared teachers managed by a scripted curriculum. It will require the dedication of knowledgeable, culturally competent, and revolutionary teachers committed to the long-term struggle for serious learning and liberation. Temporary band-aids are not an adequate response to Katrina and what it represents. As Michael Eric Dyson has observed, "Episodes of goodwill and compassion are no replacement for structural change . . . Charity can never be a substitute for justice."

Instead, as Mary Hatwood Futrell argues, "The United States must transform its infrastructure, especially its education system, so that at every level we are providing each American with the educational foundation to fulfill his or her responsibilities, as well as to realize their dreams as a citizen of this country and of the world." This volume describes what it will take to ensure that these dreams are realized and justice is done.

■|■|■

PART ONE

Education and School Contexts

■|■|■

CHAPTER I

Crossing the Waters

Katrina and the Other Great Migration—Lessons for African American K-12 Students' Education

KASSIE FREEMAN

After crossing the waters, I thought my dream was just around the corner. Instead, I found a wasteland.

(Bruce Wilkinson, *The Dream Giver*)

Many great African American artists, historians, and writers (Toni Morrison, Jacob Lawrence, as examples) have captured the events of the "Great Migration" of African Americans from the South to the North and West (Harrison, 1991). However, there has been little, if anything, written about how the "Great Migration" affected past and current educational dilemmas confronting African American K-12 students. Hurricane Katrina triggered the most recent migration, and, although it was involuntary, it has provided a unique opportunity to compare outcomes from these migratory events of enormous proportions and to contrast and assess the implications both occurrences have had and will have on the education of African American students. This comparison is enormously important because often examinations of educational dilemmas begin without a context, particularly an historical and/or a cultural context.

As defined by Adero (1993), migration is a mass movement. Although the first "Great Migration" constituted the largest internal migration (mass movement) in U.S. history with over 5 million African Americans migrating (Harrison, 1991), in the case of Hurricane Katrina, it is historic because of the cause, conditions, and numbers, particularly of African Americans, forced to move because of a natural disaster. As such, the guiding questions of this examination are as follows: How do mass movements impact on the educational outcomes of students, in this case African Americans? What role does location of migrants play in the educational achievement of students? Are there similarities and differences in the effects of the previous "Great Migration" and the migration caused by Hurricane Katrina on the educational outcomes of African American K-12 students? What lessons can be learned from the "Great Migration" and Hurricane Katrina migration to assist in the current education of African American students, particularly those students from New Orleans? These students, like students from the previous migration, as indicated by Wilkinson in *The Dream Giver,* instead of finding their dream, are likely to find a wasteland.

Although many historians describe two African American migrations from the South to the North prior to the Hurricane Katrina migration, with some describing the first migration beginning in the late 1800s and ending between 1914 and 1916 and the second migration occurring from 1940 to 1970 (Harrison, 1991; Marks, 1991; Sherman, 1970), this research is based on the work of those historians who describe one continuous "Great Migration," beginning in approximately 1915 and continuing to the 1970s. The more specific start year of the "Great Migration," according to Marks (1991), was "the spring of 1916" (p. 36). In essence, regardless of the starting point whether in the late 1800s or early 1900s, there was a long and continuous movement of African Americans from the South to the North and West, creating the "Great Migration," so named because it was the largest internal migration in U.S. history (Sherman, 1970).

Many may wonder why one should bother to examine an historic event that happened so long ago and compare it to the aftermath of Hurricane Katrina. This research suggests that there are commonalities between occurrences during the Great Migration and that there are lessons from it that can set the foundation for better understanding the educational phenomena that are currently occurring and are likely to be faced by African American students of the Katrina migration. This examination will provide the unique opportunity to enhance researchers' and policymakers' understanding of the link between history and culture in the educational outcomes of African American students and, in the process, fill a huge gap in the literature regarding the influence of the previous Great Migration on the current status of education for African American students. In reviewing and assessing the link between the Great Migration and educational outcomes for African American students, there are lessons for better understanding the current educational dilemma of these students.

Historical Overview of the Past and Current Migrations

According to Harrison (1991), the study of the Great Migration is as important to understanding African American history as are the Civil War and the civil rights movement. According to him, almost all African Americans have in some way been touched by the events of the Great Migration, be it directly or through relatives and friends. The stories of the experiences have been passed down from generation to generation (Adero, 1993). As further stated by Harrison (1991), "The psyches and ethos of black Americans, accordingly, with no exception that matters, have been formed and dominated by an American environment" (p. xiii).

The Great Migration has often been described as the search for the "Promised Land" and had its own challenges for African Americans who moved. The cities that were the recipients of the largest numbers of African Americans during this movement were New York, Chicago, Detroit, Philadelphia, and, to the West, Los Angeles. However, as pointed out by Marks (1991), the opportunity to move was not necessarily an equal opportunity. That is, the advantages went to those who already had some resources (who could pay their own transportation costs), and the general pattern of out-migration was highest among literate groups. In other words, according to Marks, it was not easy to get to where people perceived to be the Promised Land (p. 45).

The African Americans who most often migrated tended to be the most literate and frequently, would seek better educational opportunities for their children. However, once in the North, those who out-migrated found segregated housing and schooling, though both were often better than what was available to them in the South. Thus, it is safe to surmise that the segregated housing practices and White flight once African Americans moved in led to inner-city schools. Though they relocated in the North, African Americans experienced unequal distribution of education. It is necessary to understand this Great Migration phenomenon that caused the creation of inner-city schools to better comprehend one of the potential outcomes of the Katrina migration.

Although the causes of the migrations are different, according to an article written in the *Dallas Express* in August 1917 (Adero, 1993), in the case of the first migration(s) as with Katrina, Blacks did not want to leave. The article reported the following: "But the Negro would prefer to remain in the South. There are under-developed resources down here, mills and factories are yet to be built. The geographical division is more inviting to him than the North. And the Negro's motives for migrating North are but natural and they are similar to those which incite the foreigner to immigrate to America—the Negro is simply seeking to better his condition" (p. xix). Similarly, with the Katrina migration, African Americans did not want to migrate, but they were forced to because of the conditions created by the hurricane.

Interestingly, according to Carter G. Woodson (cited in Adero, 1993), one primary cause of the Great Migration, beginning with the exodus during the war, was floods associated with weakened levees—the same reason that triggered the migration after Hurricane Katrina. Woodson stated that in addition to the search for employment and better schooling, the mass movement of Blacks was caused by "floods aggravated by the depredations of the boll weevil" (p. 2). He summed it up in this way:

> Although generally mindful of our welfare, the United States Government has not been as ready to build levees against a natural enemy to property as it has been to provide fortifications for warfare. . . . There are now 1,538 miles of levees on both sides of the Mississippi from Cape Girardeau to the passes. These levees, of course, are still inadequate to the security of the planters against these inundations. Carrying 406 million tons of mud a year, the river becomes a dangerous stream subject to change, abandoning its old bed to cut for itself a new channel, transferring property from one State to another, isolating cities and leaving once useful levees marooned in the landscape like old Indian mounds or overgrown entrenchments. This valley has, therefore, been frequently visited with disasters which have often set the population in motion. The first disastrous floods came in 1858 and 1859, breaking many of the levees, the destruction of which was practically completed by the floods of 1865 and 1869. (pp. 2–3)

Although written in 1918, Woodson captures the similar events that caused the Flood of 1927. In that flood, because of weakened levees, over 14 million acres were flooded in Mississippi, Arkansas, and Louisiana and more than 600,000 individuals were displaced. Interestingly, the City of New Orleans was spared because portions of the river were bombed to divert water away from the city (Daniel, 1977). Both of the previous floods coincided with the movement of African Americans in the Great Migration and enhanced and/or continued their migration beyond their homeland.

In a similar scenario to those previous floods in conjunction with the Great Migration that caused the mass movement of African Americans, the Hurricane Katrina migration caused the largest rapid movement of individuals in history due to a natural disaster, over 1 million people, with over 300,000 mostly African Americans from New Orleans displaced (Edmondson, 2006). The insufficient levees, ignored by the U.S. government for years, essentially since the 1800s, as described by Woodson, caused the largest natural disaster in U.S. history and once again set the African American population in motion.

In the same way, the migration caused by Hurricane Katrina has also impacted on the lives of African Americans in historic proportion that is sure to cause families to pass down stories about survival for generations to come. Just as the "Great Migration" helped to reshape the complexion of African American education, the effects of Hurricane Katrina will certainly also have tremendous influence on African American students' education now and in the future.

Similarities and Differences of Previous Migration and Katrina on Education

To better understand the current plight of education for African American students displaced by Hurricane Katrina and to make projections about the long-term effects of this disaster, it is important to understand the similar and different characteristics of the Great Migration and the migration caused by Hurricane Katrina as it relates to education. From the Report of the National Advisory Commission on Civil Disorders (as cited in Sherman, 1970), during the "Great Migration," African Americans followed three major routes from the South: One ran along the north along the Atlantic Seaboard toward Boston; another ran north from Mississippi toward Chicago, and the third ran west from Texas and Louisiana toward California (p. 14). Based on the routes, it is possible to see and understand the pattern of feeder states. For example, African Americans who migrated to New York typically came from North Carolina, South Carolina, Virginia, Georgia, and Alabama. Those migrating to Chicago most often came from Mississippi, Tennessee, Arkansas, Alabama, and Louisiana, with Mississippi contributing approximately one-third. While those migrating to Los Angeles most often came from Texas and Louisiana, some also came from Mississippi, Arkansas, and Alabama (p. 14).

Due to the urgency of the necessity of their movement due to Hurricane Katrina, the pattern of individuals' movement to states was decidedly in the South, although there were individuals in every state. The states where the largest populations settled were Louisiana, Texas, Mississippi, Arkansas, and Georgia. Although the locations of dispersion were different, the Great Migration to the North and West, and Hurricane Katrina primarily to the South, there were similarities in the patterns of treatment of African American families and students, particularly related to students' educational experiences.

The Great Migration and Education

The Great Migration caused three unique circumstances that impacted on African American students' schooling and that still have devastating consequences for the educational outcomes of these students: first, housing segregation that led to inner-city urbanization; second, complications in race relations; third, unequal distribution of educational opportunities and/or experiences. These events are interrelated in ways that have compromised African American students' schooling historically and currently.

As is pointed out by the pattern of migration of Blacks during the Great Migration, most migrants moved to large urban cities. However, as they moved to cities, as Sherman (1970) indicated, they mostly moved to "older sections of the central city because the lowest cost housing was located there, friends and relatives were likely to be living there" (p. 16). However, even when they could afford to live in other parts of the city, their exclusion was accomplished through various discriminatory practices, some obvious and overt, others subtle and hidden (Sherman, p. 16). These discriminatory housing practices coincided with the exodus of Whites from central cities to suburbs, leaving behind obsolete housing for new and more attractive housing and better schools. As Sherman stated, "The rapid expansion of all-Negro residential areas and large-scale white withdrawal have continued a pattern of residential segregation that has existed in American cities for decades" (p. 16).

No one would deny that it has been residential segregation that has led to the current state of urbanization that has persisted today and was such a part of the housing dilemma that confronted African Americans in New Orleans. Such segregation is largely responsible for the pattern of schooling conditions/experiences of African American students. It is widely known that urban school districts are largely attended by African American students and have the least funding. The very development of these school districts can be traced back to the pattern of movement of African Americans during the Great Migration.

Aside from the housing segregation, the Great Migration also further complicated race relations. Whites in the South were concerned about losing cheap labor while in the North and West employers were looking for laborers. These same employers, though, were increasingly concerned about allowing too many "Negro" residents. For example, according to Haynes (1993), there were "race riots in and outrages in East St. Louis, Omaha, Chicago and Washington that paralyzed the city" (p. 81). Haynes discussed a further example of how a small town spent an entire evening deliberating how they could control "the adjustment of Negroes in the community with some fairness and yet not make it favorable enough to attract additional numbers" (p. 82). The Great Migration, while providing better economic opportunities for African Americans, nonetheless complicated race relations in that African Americans were not treated as equal participants but were used in different ways for the needs of employers as they had been in the South. Consequently, instead of facing overt racism, African Americans in their new cities faced covert racism.

Third, the Great Migration continued, in a different way from the South, the unequal distribution of educational opportunities/experiences for African Americans. Finding better schooling opportunities was one of the motivators for African Americans migrating. As Sherman (1970) indicated, "An important attraction of the city for some of the Negro migrants was the prospect of finding decent schools for their children" (p. 63). However, their hopes were only partially fulfilled. Sherman stated, "While urban schools did have facilities that were not available in much of the rural South, they were often ill-equipped to meet the challenges presented by the rapid increase in Negro population. . . . As the central city became more and more black, the neglect of the schools by remote public officials resulted in the deterioration of plant, equipment, and standards until the educational system in some cities was reduced to a condition of endemic crisis" (p. 63). E. Franklin Frazier (cited in Sherman, 1970), who wrote a summary in 1957 about public schools in northern cities, illuminated the plight of schooling during the Great Migration for African American students similarly. He summarized the conditions in this way:

> The mass migrations of Negroes from the rural South naturally created educational as well as social problems. There was the problem of acquainting the Negro children with the physical school plants in the northern city. Then there was the problem of inducting them into the routine which has become a part of the organization and functioning of urban schools. However, the most important problem was that of adjusting the Negro children to the curriculum of the school in the northern city. (p. 67)

Thus, although African American parents thought that their dreams for a better education for their children were just around the corner, they, instead, found a wasteland where segregated housing, complicated race relations, more covert than in the South but nonetheless just as harmful, began the current pattern of limiting educational opportunities for African American students.

Summarizing this dilemma in the 1960s, Sherman (1970) stated the following: "The frustrations of black parents in the 1960s, who are desperately trying to improve the schools for their children by gaining local control, contrasts sadly with the hopes that were expressed several decades earlier" (p. 63). Almost like a bad dream, the history of what happened during the Great Migration regarding the impact on African American students' educational opportunities/experiences was sadly expressed again in the aftermath of Hurricane Katrina.

Hurricane Katrina Migration and Education

The only flood-caused migration that was even close to the devastation caused by Katrina was the mass movement caused by the Flood of 1927. Both Hurricane Katrina and the Flood of 1927 were unique in the large number of forced rapid migrants that they caused. Where as in the Great Migration, although larger in number of individuals moved, the movement was by choice and over a more expansive time period.

Following the events of Hurricane Katrina when families were displaced to largely Southern states, the evacuees were largely African American and poor, particularly from New Orleans. Understandably, such rapid movement created enormous challenges, especially for school children. As Redliner (2006) described the situation, school officials estimated that there were more than 125,000 children from Louisiana alone. As he indicated and was highlighted from televised reports, most of the families were living in poverty before the hurricane, and he said, "If you thought that the government's response to last year's response to Hurricane Katrina was a shocking display of mismanagement and incompetence, you should see what's happening to the displaced children of families" (p. 1). If parents had any notion that all students would be treated equally, they now know that was not the case.

Now we know that more than 372,000 students were displaced by Hurricane Katrina, with Louisiana (47,000), Texas (40,200 students), and Georgia (10,300) accepting the largest number of students in their school districts (Cook, 2006). In fact, according to Klein (2006), there were students attending school in every state except Hawaii. We also know that once again race played a role, not only in students' placement in schools but also in the kind of facilities and curricula to which they were exposed. Three similar patterns emerged during Katrina: African American students' schooling experiences can be directly correlated to African American students' educational experiences during the Great Migration: first, the same language was used to describe students' academic achievement; second, there was unequal distribution of educational experiences, and there were segregated schooling experiences; third race relations were complicated.

Similar to how students in the Great Migration were described as academically behind, student victims of Hurricane Katrina in schools in Texas and Georgia have been described as lagging behind their counterparts (Steinhauser, 2006). The press has been filled with reports about the academic deficiencies of students, particularly African American students from New Orleans. As an example, DeParle (2006) reported, "Texas officials have estimated that Katrina students, on average, lag their new classmates by at least a full grade," and standardized tests revealed that a student displaced in Georgia was "reading two years below his grade level, even though he got A's and B's back home" (p. 8). Similarly, Cook (2006) stated, "And a large number of students—especially those from New Orleans—have played academic catch-up in their new schools. The fact that the same language has been used to describe the academic standing of African American students from the Great Migration and the academic standing of African American students from the Katrina migration, is indicative that the reason to use the same language has to do with something more than the students themselves. Indeed such a long-standing educational dilemma (more than 70 years old) is reason to be alarmed.

Even if students are underprepared, given such findings, one would assume that Katrina students would then be placed in the best schools with the best teachers. That has not been the case. The same pattern of placing African American students in the worst schools that confronted African American students during the Great Migration confronted students during the Katrina migration. For example, Cook (2006) reported on the tale of two students, both from metropolitan New Orleans, one White and one Black. The White student evacuated from the suburbs and the Black student from the city of New Orleans and, as Cook indicated, where the two currently live and attend school since being displaced reflects, in part, their backgrounds. The White student attends one of the highest performing schools in a suburb, and the Black student attends a predominantly Black school with less facilities. DeParle (2006), citing Orfield, reported on one warning sign: "evacuee schools looked worse than evacuee neighborhoods. They have more low-income students than schools regionwide, more minorities and lower test scores. That is worrisome because "the schools resegregate first and the neighborhoods tend to follow" (p. 8.).

Both the language used to describe students' achievement and the placement of students in lower performing schools are indicative of a continuous pattern of complicated race relations. Just as African Americans were welcomed, on the one hand, as this research has indicated, they were welcome on a limited basis. As DeParle (2006) pointed out, "Mayor Bill [in Texas] White led a welcoming effort, but public sentiment is turning against evacuees" (p. 8). These sentiments have also been played out in the schools with what has been described as cultural tensions and turf wars (Cook, 2006; DeParle, 2006).

In addition to the similarities of the educational experiences African American students faced in the Great Migration and Katrina migration, however, Katrina caused different types of educational experiences that have and will prove problematic for African American students, such as the following: first, dropout rates of students living at FEMA trailer parks, and, second, prospects of educational experiences at their home schools.

At a trailer park located in Baker, Louisiana, Dewan (2006) reported that, "of the 560 children who are evacuees and enrolled in the school districts in mid-September, only 190 were still attending when the school year ended on May 19"

(p. A16). Such a dilemma, naturally leads to many important questions, as Dewan suggested. Will these students return to school? If so, how many will return? Will there be a continuous high dropout rate of students who migrated? What programs should be implemented now to address such a dilemma?

Students also face another difficulty when they return to their home schools. For example, in New Orleans will there be schools to accommodate the students? Will they have access to better schooling than when they left? How will housing and educational facilities be coordinated to ensure that educational outcomes are better linked to students' neighborhoods? The questions regarding the dropout rates of Katrina students coupled with the prospect of schooling once students return to their home schools have extremely important consequences for educational outcomes, particularly of African American students. Based on the information from the Great Migration, if these questions are not addressed now, we will be looking forward to 50 years or more of under-achievement of African American students.

Lessons for African American K-12 Students' Education

When one has a concept of the cultural and historical context of the Great Migration, the largest internal migration in U.S. history, and of the lessons that can be learned for African American students' education from that event for the Katrina migration demonstrates how important it is to examine the aftermath of Hurricane Katrina from an historical and a cultural context. There are currently many research projects under way on the migration caused by Katrina that do not offer a context. While it is true that there is no road map to understanding such a catastrophic event, there are certainly trends and patterns that can be projected from such a mass movement.

Looking back at the events of the Great Migration can set the foundation for the types of questions educators and policymakers should be asking about the current educational experiences that are confronting African American students. Looking back can also predict future outcomes based on past behaviors of mass movements.

As this research demonstrates, it is clear that the patterns of behavior and outcomes are similar. Addressing the current educational needs of African American students who have been severely affected by Hurricane Katrina cannot be accomplished without acknowledging that many of these problems have continued since the Great Migration.

It is clear from comparing the two greatest mass movements of African Americans in history that there are similarities of the impact on African American students' outcomes. Unfortunately, more than 80 years later, the issues are still the same. After crossing the water, there was no dream waiting around the corner for African

American students. Whether they return to their homes or stay in new locations, African American students will be facing a wasteland. It is up to researchers and policymakers to help these students find and live their dreams.

REFERENCES

Adero, M. (1993). *Up South: Stories, studies, and letters of this century's Black migrations.* New York: The New Press.

Cook, G. (2006, April). Schooling Katrina's kids. *American School Board Journal,* pp. 18–26.

Daniel, P. (1977). *Deep'n as it come: The 1927 Mississippi river flood.* New York: Oxford University Press.

DeParle, J. (2006, April 23). Katrina's tide carries many to hopeful shore. *The New York Times,* pp. 1–12.

Dewan, S. (2006, June 1). For many, education is another storm victim. *The New York Times,* p. A16.

Edmonson, B. (2006). American diaspora. http://www.epodunk.com/top10/diaspora/index.html.

Frazier, E. F. (1970). Problems and advantages of public schools in northern cities: A tentative summary. In R. B. Sherman (Ed.), *The Negro and the city.* Englewood Cliffs, NJ: Prentice-Hall, Inc.

Harrison, A. (1991). *Black exodus: The great migration from the American South.* Jackson, MS: University Press of Mississippi.

Haynes, G. E. (1993). Negro migration: Its effects on family and community life in the North. In M. Adero (Ed.), *Up South: Stories, studies, and letters of this century's Black migrations.* New York: The New Press.

Klein, A. (2006, April 5). Schools get Katrina aid, uncertainty. *Education Week,* p. 1.

Marks, C. (1991). The social and economic life of southern blacks during the migration. In A. Harrison (Ed.), *Black exodus: The great migration from the American South.* Jackson, MS: University Press of Mississippi.

Redliner, I. (2006, May). Orphans of the storm. National Center for Disaster Preparedness at Columbia and the Children's Health Fund.

Sherman, R. B. (1970). The Negro and the city. Englewood Cliffs, NJ: Prentice-zHall.

Steinhauser, J. (2006, April 20). Storm evacuees placing strains on Texas hosts. *The New York Times,* pp. 1–4.

Wilkinson, B. (2003). *The dream giver.* Sisters, OR: Multnomah Publishers, Inc.

■|■|■

CHAPTER 2

Now They're Wet

Hurricane Katrina as Metaphor for Social and Educational Neglect

GLORIA LADSON-BILLINGS

My first glimpse of Hurricane Katrina came from almost 4,000 miles away as I attended a conference in London, England. I was even more of a news junkie than usual during this trip because London had recently experienced a terrorist attack on its transit system, and the university where my meetings were being held was located near the spot where one of the buses was bombed. However, little of what I saw on the BBC and CNN World News focused on terrorists or bombings. Instead, I saw the horror that was the aftermath of Hurricane Katrina, and those images left me sad, depressed, and angry. The more I watched, the more agitated I became. The e-mails I received from friends, family, and colleagues back in the States did little to alleviate my concerns. Things were not only as bad as they seemed on the news; they were worse. By about the third day of the catastrophe, a Londoner at my hotel

*   *This article appeared in the Winter 2006 (Number 10) issue of* Voices in Urban Education: *"Equity After Katrina," published by The Annenberg Institute for School Reform at Brown University. Reprinted by permission. All rights reserved.*

asked, "What in the world is happening in your country?" It was then that I had a painful insight and remarked to the questioner, "Actually, the only difference between the people you are seeing on television today and their status two weeks ago is now they're wet!" My cynical comment addressed the just-below-the-surface frustration I have been living with for many years. The hurricane was not just about government breakdowns in the face of a natural disaster. It was about the failure of government (and, by default, much of the nation) to take seriously the plight of the poor and disenfranchised. It was about the kind of nation we have created and how we can continue to live as we have for many years.

Glaring Inequities, Long Before Katrina

My first visit to New Orleans was in the mid-1980s. I went with a dear friend and colleague to give a paper at a conference. We arrived in the city late on the night of Mardi Gras. By the time we arrived at our hotel, the New Orleans police had done their final sweep of the French Quarter; all the revelers were off the street, and the city coffers were filled with the profits from another Fat Tuesday. However, in the light of the Wednesday morning, the Big Easy did neither look festive nor easy.

After giving our paper, my colleague and I decided to explore the city. We traveled through the city's Garden District with its beautiful Victorian mansions and the lovely campuses of Tulane University and Loyola University. We wanted to visit Xavier University. We had read about a wonderful program in mathematics education that the university had pioneered. We also knew that Xavier was one of the more successful historically Black Universities—known for its high rate of sending African American students to medical, pharmaceutical, and veterinary programs.

When we arrived at Xavier, though, we were unprepared for what we saw. We were surprised by how much deferred maintenance there was. (It is important to note that in the 1990s, Xavier, like a number of historically Black colleges and universities, embarked on some much-needed capital improvements.) The landscape was shabby, and nothing of its environs suggested the beautiful grassy knolls and stately quads of the Tulane and Loyola campuses. Even more disappointing was the "cutting-edge" mathematics education program we came to see. Tucked away in a small building, we found an elderly nun who took us through boxes and boxes of old materials that represented the mathematics program. Both my colleague and I were working in a Catholic university in California at the time, and we knew that the church prided itself on its support of education. But how could it justify the clearly differential treatment of Xavier—the only Black university among the 253 Catholic colleges and universities in the United States—compared to Loyola?

Xavier was not the only example of inequity we witnessed in New Orleans some twenty years ago. Although we ate many meals in the French Quarter and downtown areas, we ventured into more traditionally African American communities for some outstanding meals. Unfortunately, going into those areas reminded us of the stark contrasts between the good-time, party city of tourism and debauchery and the extremely poor, hard lives of much of the city's African American residents—the people who live in what the rest of the world learned was the Ninth Ward.

Citizenship Denied

Well before the devastation of the hurricane, New Orleans was suffering from neglect. Chief among the neglected aspects of the city were its schools. Before Katrina, the statistics on Orleans Parish painted a grim picture of life for many of its citizens (portions of this section are adapted from Ladson-Billings, forthcoming).

According to the U.S. Census Bureau (2000), New Orleans had a population of 484,674 before the hurricane, and 67 percent of that population was African American. Almost a fourth—23.7 percent—of the total population and 35 percent of the African American population lived below the poverty line. Over 40,000 New Orleans residents had less than a ninth-grade education and 56,804 residents had between ninth- and twelfth-grade educations without diplomas. A telling statistic is that 96.1 percent of the public school population was African American, which meant that most of the White families with school-aged children sent their children to private schools.

Education clearly was not working for those in New Orleans who depended on public schools. It was not working long before the streets were flooded and the roofs were blown away. A well-known Norman Rockwell painting from the early 1960s depicts a little African American girl walking between federal marshals on her way to school. The girl in the painting, Ruby Bridges, was the first African American to integrate New Orleans schools. The painting, though, does not tell the whole story. White communities bordering New Orleans fiercely resisted allowing African American students to enter their schools (Wells, 2004). Out of 137 African American students who applied to attend formerly all-White schools, only four, including Ruby, were selected. When Ruby enrolled in the William Frantz Elementary School, all of the White students boycotted the school. Only one teacher, a White woman from New York, was willing to teach Ruby. Then, as a consequence of Ruby's attending the previously all-White school, her father was fired from his job and her grandparents were evicted from their tenant farm.

For most of us, the story of Ruby Bridges is one of courage and heroism. However, the deeper story is how America's fatal flaw—racism—continues to distort and destroy the promise on which the nation claims to be founded. The history of New Orleans school desegregation is a part of a larger history—not just of *educational access* denied, but of *citizenship* denied. The same mentality that allowed White citizens to barricade themselves from school desegregation in the 1960s is present among White citizens who armed themselves to prevent desperate Black citizens of New Orleans in the midst of the hurricane disaster from seeking refuge from the floodwaters. What kind of "public" official (in this case, a sheriff) points a gun at destitute evacuees, says, "You're not coming in here," and leaves them to wither on a freeway overpass (Glass, 2005)?

Limiting education is but one of the ways to create second-class citizenship. However, it is one of the more effective ways; once people are mis-educated or undereducated, the society can claim the need to use "merit" as the standard by which postsecondary decisions (e.g., college admission, job placement) will be made. New Orleans is a municipality where people were *systematically* excluded from social benefits—housing, health, employment, and education. Hurricane Katrina brought to the surface the horror that has existed in New Orleans for more than a century.

"Aggressive Neglect" in Our Nation's Urban School Districts

So, now that we have all seen the huge economic and social chasm that exists in New Orleans, what will be our response? One of the dangers of witnessing such a tragedy is to presume that the conditions of life for poor people of color in New Orleans are unique. Rather than think of New Orleans as an example of a larger phenomenon, we have a tendency to isolate it and think of it as something out of the ordinary. Unfortunately, Jonathan Kozol's book, *The Shame of the Nation: The Restoration of Apartheid Schooling in America* (2005) reminds us that the condition of schooling in New Orleans is a regular and commonplace occurrence for students in far too many of the nation's largest public school districts.

As a native Philadelphian, I looked up the data on Philadelphia. The 2002–2003 per pupil expenditure for students in the Philadelphia School District was $9,299. That same year, the per-pupil expenditure for the Lower Merion School District (which is almost across the street from Philadelphia) was $17,261—a difference of almost $8,000. What makes the children of Lower Merion worth almost twice as much as their urban neighbors? Lower Merion has a Black and Latino population of about

9 percent and a white population of 91 percent. It has a 4 percent low-income student population. Philadelphia has a Black and Latino population of 79 percent with a White and other racial/ethnic group population of 21 percent. The low-income student population of the Philadelphia schools is 71 percent of the school district. Any decent researcher knows that correlation does not equal causation, but the correlations between race (and class) and educational spending are frightening.

How can it possibly be in the public interest to continue to keep poor children of color in a cycle of low achievement, low graduation rates, high levels of unemployment and underemployment, and compromised futures? How much of this do we imagine people will continue to accept? How soon will it be before we see the civil and social unrest that characterized the 1960s? Indeed, what we see in our cities is no longer just about social and civic responsibility. It is about *moral* responsibility. We cannot call ourselves a moral people in the midst of this aggressive neglect.

I term what we are doing "aggressive neglect" because, at the same time we are experiencing unprecedented poverty, some segments of our society are experiencing an incredible bonanza of wealth. The growing income disparity makes it difficult for many Americans to experience empathy with those who do not have. We blame and demonize the poor and, more pointedly, we isolate them. We do not see them; we do not acknowledge their existence. They are both out of sight and out of mind. However, then Hurricane Katrina hit and we were shamed in the presence of our fellow Americans and before the entire world.

The Lengths to Which Communities of Color Must Go

Communities of color could not wait for us to hear their anguished pleas. They have tried desperately on their own to get high-quality education for their children. Just how desperately? Well, in some cases they are desperate enough to opt out of the system altogether. In Milwaukee and Cleveland, families of poor Black and Brown children are eagerly participating in voucher programs. I am a committed public school advocate (I sent all of my children to public schools), but I cannot insist that these parents select public schools when they have other choices.

Perhaps the most extreme example of desperation was made apparent to me in a *New York Times* review of the documentary film *The Boys of Baraka*. Stephen Holden (2005) begins with a disturbing but familiar statistic—"76 percent of Black male students in Baltimore city schools do not graduate from high school." (In what White middle-class community would that be an acceptable piece of data?) However, the film describes the extraordinary lengths to which some families will go to address that shameful statistic; they send their children in an experimental program to school in rural Kenya. There, on a 150-acre ranch, without television or a consistent source of electricity, twenty middle school boys from Baltimore experience a two-year academic program that successfully prepares them for Baltimore's most competitive high schools. The program's recruiter tells the parents of the prospective students that their sons' futures have three possibilities—an orange jumpsuit and bracelets (prison), a black suit and a brown box (early death), or a black cap and gown with a diploma. Who wouldn't take the last option?

How ironic is it that children from the wealthiest, most powerful nation in the world have to go to one of the poorest nations to experience academic and personal success? What does this say about the kind of communities we have created for poor children?

The Need for "Aggressive Attention"

The tragedy of Katrina is not only what happened, but also that it is so quickly fading from our consciousness. We are now consumed with worsening news of the war in Iraq, an escalating gasoline and fuel-oil crisis, and massive job cuts at our major automobile manufacturers. The victims of Katrina have melted into the fabrics of cities like Houston, Atlanta, Los Angeles, and Memphis. We have moved on to new crises. Discussions about rebuilding New Orleans regularly omit the poor. Indeed, several conversations discuss a notion of a new city without the return of the poor. The schools that are being reopened are unlikely to be those in the Lower Ninth Ward.

Katrina may be fading from our national consciousness, but Katrina remains ever present in my mind. I know that what happened on August 29, 2005, and the days following are not just about a natural disaster. It is about how we have systematically neglected the poorest, most vulnerable members of our society. There are plenty of potential Katrina scenarios in the United States, and we must acknowledge that it will take a concentrated and focused effort to reverse them. We have to be committed to ensuring that we do not have another group of people who end up without adequate homes, jobs, health care, and education. The children in all of our cities deserve our aggressive attention—whether they are dry or wet.

REFERENCES

Glass, I. (Ed.). (2005). After the flood. *This American Life,* WBEZ Chicago, Episode #296 (September 9). Download available from <www.thislife.org>.

Holden, S. (2005, November 30). Goodbye city streets, Hello African wilderness. *New York Times.*

Kozol, J. (2005). *The shame of the nation: The restoration of apartheid schooling in America.* New York: Crown.

Ladson-Billings, G. (Forthcoming). Introduction. In G. Ladson-Billings & W. F. Tate (Eds.), *Education research in the public interest.*

United States Census Bureau. (2000). Search by city on the Web at <www.census.gov/index.html>.

Wells, A. (2004). Good neighbors? Distance, resistance, and desegregation in metropolitan New Orleans. *Urban Education* 39: 408–427.

■|■|■

CHAPTER 3

What Hurricane Katrina Uncovered About Schooling in America

JACQUELINE JORDAN IRVINE

My perspectives on America's educational system changed dramatically on August 29, 2005. This was the day Hurricane Katrina devastated Louisiana and other parts of the Gulf Coast. Before I witnessed the horrors of this event, I had always considered myself a progressive teacher, educator, and researcher committed to the reformation of schools in order to provide equal educational opportunities for all students, but particularly low income and African American and Latino students. However, as I watched the national response to this disaster grow more shameful each day, I was convinced that the reformation of schools was not enough. Schools and society have to be transformed, not merely reformed.

Why did the worst natural disaster recorded in U.S. history change how I thought about schools? Unlike other natural disasters of the past, Katrina came ashore and uncovered what many Americans preferred not to see—poverty, racism, classism, arrogance of power, and decades of neglect. Although the damage and destruction of this hurricane cut across racial and economic lines, FEMA data and satellite maps concluded that poor Black residents of New Orleans were disproportionately displaced and suffered the greatest loss. Hence, Hurricane Katrina is a symbol of what can happen when a nation systematically and unabashedly abandons the most vulnerable.

I do not want to be misunderstood on this point. Most Americans, as individuals or members of organized group, responded to Hurricane Katrina with generous donations of money, service, sympathy, and incalculable acts of kindness. As American citizens and individuals, we should all be proud of these efforts to help those in need. However, there are financial, emotional, and physical limitations to individuals' and groups' ability to sustain altruism over time. In fact, only two months after the hurricane, the *Houston Chronicle* (Spencer & Radcliffe, 2005) reported that school employees were experiencing "compassion fatigue" as 21,000 Hurricane Katrina students enrolled in Houston's schools. When "compassion fatigue" happens, some individuals applaud their generosity, decompartmentalize, detach, and then move on with their own lives. I believe that the images of desperate and abandoned people literally drowning under the weight of poverty were too heavy a burden to bear for the average person because watching bore an acknowledgment and ultimately a responsibility to act.

Still others struggled with "compassion fatigue" by blaming the displaced for their predicament—reproaching them for the dire circumstances in which they found themselves. Often the popular media exploited this perception by portraying the poor as ignorant, lazy, welfare-dependent people who did not heed the warning to evacuate; or worse, looters and criminals who took advantage of the disaster. Newspapers published stories about evacuees using FEMA and Red Cross debit cards to purchase expensive clothes and alcoholic beverages.

Compassion fatigue and victim blaming were predictable responses to Hurricane Katrina because individual donations and the work of volunteer groups can never be a substitution for or a distraction from focusing on identifying causes and solutions to poverty and racism at the larger societal level. Michael Eric Dyson (2006) accurately observed that "Episodes of goodwill and compassion are no replacement for structural change . . . Charity can never be a substitute for justice" (p. 152).

Structural changes are required if the poverty rate is to decline in this country. The U.S. Census Bureau (Kristof, 2005) reported that the poverty rate rose again last year with 1.1 million more individuals living in poverty than a year earlier. America's poverty rate is the highest among developed nations. The numbers are equivalent to the population of Canada (Adler, 2005). Some of the poorest people in the United States reside in Mississippi, Louisiana, and Alabama. There are 90,000 people in each of these states who earn less than $10,000 a year (Dyson, 2006).

Any documentation of long-term and consistent attention to the issues of poverty are absent from the record. Some progress was made during President Johnson's War of Poverty in the 1960s. Since the early 1960s, policy makers have known about the deleterious effects of single-parent families, low wages, unemployment, lack of health care benefits, and prenatal care, poor nutrition, lead poisoning, and high mobility. Research data are convincing about the value of parental education and pre- and after-school programs. However, the war on poverty ended as a resounding defeat as politicians waved the "white flag of surrender" signaling a retreat from the poor and the defenseless.

Perhaps the most painful Katrina experience for me was to watch what happened to the children. What do we know about these children? According to the Children's Defense Fund (2005), each day in America:

- 2,447 babies are born into poverty
- 77 babies die before their first birthdays.
- 367 babies are born to mothers who received late or no prenatal care.
- 1,154 babies are born to teen mothers.
- 1,701 babies are born without health insurance.
- 2,252 babies are born to mothers who are not high school graduates.
- 3,879 babies are born to unmarried mothers.

These data on poverty cannot be disconnected from issues of race and racism. There is a strong relationship between the two. In an informative piece, *The Hidden Cost of Being African American,* Shapiro (2004) states that the "average African American family holds 10 cents of wealth for every dollar that Whites possess" (p. x). Making the distinction between wealth and income, Shapiro noted that the income gap (primarily based on job salaries and wages) actually narrowed in 2000 when the average Black family earned 64 cents for every dollar earned by white families. But wealth is another issue. The primary sources of wealth are home ownership, home equity as well as stocks, bonds, and savings that are passed on from generation to generation. This wealth, as contrasted to income, is called a transformative asset. The most recent analysis (1999) that looked at wealth, rather than salaries, revealed that 26% of White children grew up in asset-poor homes compared to 52% of Black and 54% of Hispanic children.

These discouraging race and poverty data are related to larger and more systemic issues of school inequality. Two examples serve to illustrate this point—segregation and the test score gap.

Segregation

The Civil Rights Project (Orfield, Frankenberg, & Lee, 2002/2003) and the Educational Testing Service (Laoso, 2001) provide some sobering statistics on segregation. Segregation has been on the rise in the last decade despite rapid increases in the number of ethnically and culturally diverse students. Census Bureau data indicate that the White population is declining and the percentage of ethnic groups is increasing. Currently, 40% of students in our nation's schools come from ethnically diverse backgrounds and in our largest school districts half or more of the students are diverse. More than one-half of all students in the South and the West are Black and Latino and in some states (California, Hawaii, Mississippi, Texas, and New Mexico) these students represent the majority of student populations (Orfield, Frankenberg, & Lee, 2002/2003).

However, this growing diversity does not foretell growing integration. The average African American attends a school that is 67% African American, and 75% of Latinos attend mostly so-called minority schools. Of note is the finding that White students remain the most isolated group in this country. The average White student attends a school that is 80% White (Orfield & Lee, 2006). Interestingly, there is no national discussion about the fact that the vast majority of White students will be ill prepared to participate in an increasingly diverse society.

Credible research has documented that school segregation is a result of residential segregation that has been supported by decades of reversals of school bussing cases, particularly in medium to large urban areas. The other contributing factor to school segregation is the increase in private school enrollment by White students. Studies by Reardon and Yun (2002) and Kozol (2005) found White private school enrollment today is comparable to the percentages reported in 1968 (about 13%).

The Test Score Gap

The fact that our nation's schools are still segregated is disturbing enough. More troubling is the fact that far too many African American and Latino students in mostly segregated schools are performing poorly. This test score gap is revealed in the fact that White students, on average, score 20 to 30 points higher than their Black and Hispanic peers. Seventeen-year-old Black and Hispanic students have skills in reading, mathematics, and science that are similar to those of a 13-year-old White student (Haycock, Jerald, Huang, 2001). This finding has remained stable over time. Interestingly, the test score gap exists even when researchers control for social class. In other words, when middle and upper-middle income African American students are compared to their social class counterparts, the gap persists.

Hence, low school achievement caused by segregation and the test score gap are essentially related to more profound issues of structural inequality and have major implications for the economic survivability of this nation. Researchers (e.g., Richards, 2005) have estimated the economic costs of low achievement in this country. They found that:

- A high school dropout earns $260,000 less over a lifetime than a high school graduate, and hence pays less taxes and Social Security.
- The economy loses $192 billion with each cohort of 18-year-olds who never complete high school.

Given these data on the nature of structural inequality, why are there limited conversations and initiatives in education that focus on larger systemic issues related to the causes of low achievement of low income and African American and Latino students? Why do educators choose instead to focus on individual students in their schools and classrooms? The subsequent story about teachers addresses this predicament. Anthropologist Loren Eiseley (1979) calls the story *The Starfish Thrower.*

Once upon a time there was a famous writer who walked the beach each day before he began his work. One day as he was walking along the shore, he saw a young boy picking up something and very gently throwing it into the ocean. As he got closer he called out, "Good morning! What are you doing?"

The boy replied, "Throwing starfish in the ocean." The writer responded: "Why are you throwing starfish in the ocean?" The boy said: "The sun is up and the tide is going out. And if I don't throw them in, they'll die."

"But, young man," said the writer, "don't you realize that there are miles and miles of beaches with starfish all along them. You can't possibly make a difference!"

The young man listened politely. Then bent down and picked up another starfish. He threw it into the sea, past the breaking waves and said—"It made a difference for that one." The story ends with the adage that teachers are like the boy in the story, starfish throwers, making a difference—one child at a time.

This inspirational story about making a difference, one child at a time, has some inherent limitations. I am not convinced that the boy's plan to save starfish is the best strategy to employ. I admire the boy's hard work, his concern, and his commitment. However, the man and the boy should find the space and time to find out why so many starfish wash ashore and die. The solutions require the work of coalitions in the community, like the expertise of climatologists, ecologists, marine biologists, educators, and ordinary citizens.

Concomitantly, there are fundamental problems when educators just think of themselves as mainly starfish throwers. What happens to the other students in a teacher's class while the starfish thrower is saving the one student who needs help? How many starfish throwers are needed to make a lasting and significant difference in society?

School reformers are like the starfish throwers. They remind me of the engineers designing the new levees after Hurricane Katrina—building category 3 levees for category 5 hurricanes to come. They work diligently with outdated plans and inadequate funding to build an adequate structure. School transformers, on the other hand, are committed and trained to design schools that tackle the big educational hurricanes—racism, classism, sexism, heterosexism, and religious intolerance.

I am proposing here that educators in K-12 and higher education should re-define their role as school transformers, not reformers, committed to eliminating structural inequality that fosters low quality schools and low achievement. I offer a few strategies for a broader and more systemic vision for educational change. I believe that we cannot move the equity agenda forward in K-12 schooling until we address the primary questions: Who makes the critical decisions about education? Who controls the curriculum, the assessments, the policies, and the money? Although the federal government has no constitutional powers over education, its role has dramatically increased over the past decade. I believe educators should act collectively to gain control of the educational agenda so that all children can have access to an education that not only leads to academic achievement but also prepares them to be decision makers, critical thinkers, and advocates for social change.

Specifically, I recommend the development of new coalitions, new models for school funding, new curriculum models, and new models of teacher education.

New Coalitions

We cannot make long-term differences by "saving one starfish" at a time. Our work is as much about politics as it is about pedagogy. We have to forge multiracial and multiethnic coalitions with social activists in areas such as housing, health, employment, environment, and criminal justice.

New Models for School Funding

The property tax as a source for school funding leaves poor children in substandard schools with limited resources. The Education Trust (2005) concluded that we spend about $900 less per pupil on students in our poorest districts when compared to students in wealthier districts. This is yet another example of how we provide less for children who need the most.

New Curriculum Models

In a book called *Culturally Responsive Teaching* (Irvine & Armento, 2001), Armento and I argue that the demographic changes in today's schools demand new ways of organizing and implementing instruction. Diverse students bring a range of cultural and everyday lived experiences that may be different from the teacher's knowledge, beliefs, and views, and certainly different from the dominant norms of the school. Such differences should motivate educators to think about ways to maximize instruction for diverse students. As part of meaningful instruction, educators must consider the language and textbooks we use to represent concepts and ideas, and find better ways to connect with the realities students know and live in order to help them understand the instruction.

New Models of Teacher Education

One sobering finding in multicultural teacher education that keeps surfacing is that teacher education programs may have some short-term effect on changing our pre-service teachers' beliefs and attitudes about diversity, but our long-term influence is probably minimal. We need to find ways to identify candidates in teacher education who are persistent, open-minded, reflective, complex thinkers, and risk takers. Goodman (2000) observed that the people who are more likely to be committed to multiculturalism come from marginalized groups, people from ethnic groups, people with strong moral and spiritual orientations for social justice, and people who have experienced injustices in our society. Colleges of education need to find ways to attract more teachers of color but also find ways to motivate and educate people from other groups and from mono-cultural backgrounds to teach in culturally diverse settings. Teacher educators should encourage their students to see themselves as social reconstructivists who dismantle systems of racism, inequality, and oppression and advocate for those who cannot advocate for themselves.

Finally, teacher educators should make teachers aware that vulnerable and hopeless students, like the displaced students of Hurricane Katrina, are in classrooms all over this nation. We have to prepare teachers to help these students achieve. How? Not by rescuing one drowning child at a time, but by tackling issues of structural inequality and building impenetrable levees and caring shelters that protect all children. We must act hastily on these urgent educational issues because the hurricanes of apathy, ignorance, and prejudice continue to destroy the aspirations and achievement of America's most neglected students.

REFERENCES

Adler, J. (2005, September 19). The other America. *Newsweek,* pp. 42–48.

Children's Defense Fund. (2005). *Each day in America* [On-line]. http://www.childrensdefense.org/data/eachday.asp.

Dyson, M. E. (2006). *Come hell or high water: Hurricane Katrina and the color of disaster.* New York: Basic Books.

Education Trust. (2005). *Funding 2005: Most states shortchange poor and minority students.* Washington, DC: Author.

Eiseley, L. (1979). *The star thrower.* New York: Harcourt Brace & Co.

Goodman, D. J. (2000). Motivating people from privileged groups to support social justice. *Teachers College Record,* 102(6),1061–1085.

Haycock, K., Jerald, C., & Huang, S. (2001). *Closing the gap: Done in a decade.* Washington, DC: The Education Trust.

Irvine, J. J., & Armento, B. J. (2001). *Culturally responsive teaching.* Boston: McGraw-Hill.

Kozol, J. (2005). The shame of the nation. *Rethinking Schools, 20*(1), 22–30.

Kristof, N. (2005, September 7). A nation lets down its most vulnerable. [On-line]. Available: http://www.ajc.com.

Laoso, L. M. (2001). *The new segregation.* Princeton, NJ: Educational Testing Service.

Orfield, G., Frankenberg, E. D., & Lee, C. (2002/03). The resurgence of school segregation. *Educational Leadership,* 60(4), 16—20.

Orfield, G., & Lee, C. (2006). *Racial transformation and the changing nature of segregation.* Cambridge, MA: The Civil Rights Project, Harvard University.

Reardon, S., & Yun, J. T. (2002). *Private school racial enrollments and segregation.* Cambridge, MA: The Civil Rights Project, Harvard University.

Richards, A. (2005, November 2). Researchers tally cost of educational failings. *Education Week,* 25(10), 6–7.

Shapiro, T. (2004). *The hidden cost of being African American.* Oxford: Oxford University Press.

Spencer, J., & Radcliffe, J. (2005, October 18). Learning to cope with stress. [Online]. Available: http://www.HoustonChronicle.com.

■|■|■

CHAPTER 4

Hurricane Katrina

Catastrophe or Opportunity?

JACQUELINE LEONARD

On August 25, 2005, Hurricane Katrina came ashore in Florida and then made her way to the Gulf Coast on August 29, 2005, leaving a path of destruction that will be felt for years to come. While the damage was widespread, a great deal of attention was placed on the city of New Orleans, Louisiana, aka The Big Easy. While not intentionally trying to neglect the impact of Hurricane Katrina on other areas, I choose to focus my attention on her impact on The Big Easy for two reasons. First, I attended no less than four research conferences in the city from 2000 to 2004, including the American Educational Research Association, Research Association of Minority Professors, and Teaching Teachers with Technology. Second, I have two friends who lived in New Orleans and were teachers there before Hurricane Katrina hit. Their lives have been forever changed by the political and geographic landscape. Some of the comments I make in this chapter are the result of listening to their conversations and seeing New Orleans before and during the aftermath of Hurricane Katrina through their eyes and my own. Before I begin my formal treatise, I will briefly reflect on the way things were in New Orleans prior to the hurricane.

Before the Storm

On September 2, 2005, an editorial in *USA Today* entitled "Hurricane exposes issues of class, race" shows a poignant photograph of Sheila Dixon and her 18-month-old daughter as they awaited evacuation (p. A20). The author reported Census Bureau statistics, which stated that the number of Americans living in poverty rose to 12.7% in 2004, but the rate of poverty in New Orleans before Hurricane Katrina was almost double the national rate with 40% of the city's predominantly African American children, living in poverty. The ravages of Hurricane Katrina exposed the two faces of American life to the world at large. W. E. B. Du Bois (1995) vividly described two Americas one Black and one White in his text *The Souls of Black Folk.* He further described the double consciousness that blacks have as a result of living in a country that is defined by race and class. Nowhere is that consciousness more evident today than in New Orleans, Louisiana.

According to my teacher colleagues, whom I met in Dallas, Texas, when I taught for the Dallas Independent School District, Orleans Parish was plagued by corruption and scandal. I was told that the superintendent mismanaged funds, leaving students in one of the nation's poorest cities to attend classes in buildings that had leaks, poor plumbing, and paint peeling off the ceilings and walls. As a conference attendee, who often walked to and from five star hotels in the financial district, I never saw these schools. However, Louisiana fourth- graders were tied with Mississippi to rank third lowest on National Association of Educational Progress (NAEP) in reading in 2003 (scaled score 205) (NCES, 2004). Only students in New Mexico and the District of Columbia scored lower (203 & 188, respectively). At the eighth-grade level, reading scores were tied with Alabama, ranking fourth lowest in the nation (scaled score 253) (NCES, 2004). Only Nevada, California, and District of Columbia students ranked the same or lower (253, 251, & 239, respectively).

In addition to my lack of knowledge about school achievement in Orleans Parish, I was oblivious to the poor. My eyes were blind to many of the poor residents who lived in the city. My one trip to the emergency room at Tulane University Hospital when I got ill on my last visit to The Big Easy caused me a two-hour wait in the middle in of the night in March 2004, but somehow I managed to miss seeing all of those indigent patients at the city hospital across the street who were the last to be evacuated after the hurricane. The hurricane helped to open my eyes to the reality that school children and poor adults faced in The Big Easy on a daily basis.

The Mis-Education of African American Students

Challenged by a poignant address by Gloria Ladson-Billings on Palm Sunday, April 9, 2006 at the Annual Meeting of the American Educational Research Association in San Francisco, I have been thinking more deeply about the achievement gap, which Dr. Ladson-Billings characterized more accurately as the "education debt." Briefly outlining the history of education, Ladson-Billings stated that educational opportunities are not up to par for students of color even after rulings such as *Plessey vs. Ferguson,* which called for "separate but equal education" of Black and White children, and *Brown vs. Boardof Education,* which sparked a movement toward "desegregation" that was never actually realized. We were challenged to take our expertise and resources to places where the need was most dire, such as New Orleans, Louisiana, where recovery from the aftermath of Hurricane Katrina is still ongoing. Given that the annual meetings of the AERA were held in New Orleans in 2000 and 2002, the images portrayed in a slide show at the conclusion of Ladson-Billings's address were surreal. It left me asking the questions: What can be done to bridge the achievement gap and level the playing field for students of color who are underachieving in America's schools? What can be done to enhance schooling and educational opportunity for those who remain in Orleans Parish?

When I think of educational opportunity, I cannot help but relate it to mathematics. The ability to know and do mathematics is the key to gaining access to higher education and lucrative jobs (Leonard, 2004; Martin, 2000; Moses & Cobb, 2001). Even so, more than a decade of rhetoric about mathematics equity has not led to equity for many students of color and poor White students (Martin, 2003). Unequal resources, lack of high quality teachers, and tracking have a negative impact on standardized test scores and contribute to low achievement in mathematics (Gamoran & Weinstein, 1998). However, educational inequities, tracking, and lack of cultural relevance do not explain why some African American children achieve despite these adverse circumstances (Martin, 2000; Ogbu, 2003).

African American Students
and Mathematics Achievement

The underachievement of students of color in mathematics is a national dilemma. From early childhood to secondary educational settings, schools have failed to provide students of color with high-quality instruction in mathematics (Martin, 2003; Rousseau & Tate, 2003). According to Martin (2003), students of color in the class of 2002 have done no better in mathematics despite the fact that these students started kindergarten when the first standards document was published by the National Council of Teachers of Mathematics (NCTM, 2000). African American students have consistently lagged behind their White counterparts in mathematics achievement (NCES, 2004). Research continues to show underachievement among African American students even when socioeconomic status (SES) is controlled (Tate, 1997). Results of 2003 NAEP data show 46% of fourth- and 61% of eighth-grade African American students scored below the basic expectations in mathematics compared to 13% and 20% of White students at respective grade levels (NCES, 2004). Despite gains on the NAEP over the past ten years, less than 1% of Black fourth- and eighth- graders achieved at advanced levels in mathematics (NCES, 2004). As a result, these students begin to disappear from the mathematics pipeline as early as elementary school (Martin, 2000). In addition to the achievement gap, the technology gap in the level of computer ownership and Internet access has increased between racial groups (Songer, Lee, & Kam, 2002). Data show that 20.52% of White students have Internet access compared to 14.18% of black students, and 11.76% of Hispanic students (Swain & Pearson, 2003). Such disparities in access to technology contribute to the achievement gap.

A recent study of predominately African American and Latino high school dropouts in the federal Job Corps program revealed that mathematics difficulties were the primary cause of student dropouts (Viadero, 2005). In addition to limited resources, poor instruction, unchallenging work, and tracking into low-level classes, a primary reason for student disaffection and poor performance in mathematics has been the disconnection between the curriculum and students' cultural orientations (Ladson-Billings, 1994; Malloy & Malloy, 1998). Given these compelling factors, as well as their grave practical consequences (lack of access to jobs, high school attrition, poor literacy rates, and so on), there is a need for programming to address the needs of underserved students outside of the traditional education system. Programs such as the Job Corps have been successful in helping high school dropouts to find jobs as unskilled laborers.

While some want to limit underachievement in mathematics to lower socioeconomic minority groups, the achievement gap in mathematics is also prevalent among middle-class students (Tate, 1997). Ogbu (2003) conducted a study of African American students in Shaker Heights, Ohio, an affluent suburb. While black students had superior performance in comparison to other black students around the country, there was still a Black-White achievement gap in Shaker Heights. Ogbu (2003) found that African American students did not work up to their potential and were highly disengaged in the learning process. A myriad of reasons were given by students for the "low-effort syndrome" described in the study (Ogbu, 2003, p. 17). Reasons cited by students for underperformance included the following:

- norm of minimum effort;
- "it's not cool" to work hard or show you are smart;
- boring or uninteresting courses;
- lack of motivation;
- poor study habits;
- poor teachers.

School practices such as low teacher expectations, leveling, and disproportionate representations of blacks in special education, reinforce the belief that black students are simply not as intelligent as whites. Perceiving black students who perform well as "exceptional" continues to reinforce the stereotype that being black and smart is abnormal (Ogbu, 2003, p. 85).

In another study, Martin (2000) used qualitative case study methodology to examine the mathematics identity and mathematics socialization of teachers, parents, and students. He defines mathematics identity as "the participants' beliefs about (a) their ability to perform in mathematical contexts, (b) the instrumental importance of mathematical knowledge, (c) constraints and mathematical opportunities in mathematical contexts, and (d) the resulting motivations and strategies used to obtain mathematics knowledge" (Martin, 2000, p. 19). Mathematics socialization is defined as "the processes and experiences by which individual and collective mathematics identities are shaped in sociohistorical, community, school, and intrapersonal contexts" (Martin, 2000, p. 19). Martin (2000) asked, "Why is it that despite increased demands for those who possess mathematics-related skills and knowledge, significant advances in educational theory, and calls for higher educational standards, African-Americans continue to experience their mathematics educations in ways that place them at or near the bottom on all measures of achievement and persistence?" (p. 9). To answer this question, Martin interviewed a number of parents and students about their school experiences. After interviewing four parents, Martin (2000) found that socioeconomic and educational experiences caused two participants to diminish the value of mathematical knowledge in their own and their children's lives. In the other two cases, parental experiences were a motivating factor to revisit obtaining mathematical knowledge for their own as well as their children's benefit. One African American male whom Martin interviewed provides a poignant but telling commentary about the perception of mathematics education among some African Americans:

> "I only indulged myself in my studies to the degree that I was satisfied that I could do math up to multiplication and division of fractions and decimals and that was good enough for me for what I was going to do. I wasn't going to be doing any math. To be a laborer, all it's going to require is to run a piece of machinery." (p. 42)
>
> "We don't have no industry out there and the industry that is out there, they're not

targeting the Black community and saying, "If you go and get more math, then I can guarantee you this." (p. 45)

"I have hopes. My expectation is that (my son) will graduate from high school. If he doesn't, it's no big deal. . . . My expectation for him is to probably be no worse than I was. Just to pass." (p. 46)

Clearly, there is a culture that has shaped the attitudes and values of this African American male. The norm of minimum effort and the low-expectation syndrome described by Ogbu (2003) are evident in the parent's response to questions about his effort in school and his hopes for his son. However, the comment about industry providing incentives is an interesting one. While there are some incentives such as Inroads and other programs that target African Americans to pursue careers in engineering, the message is not getting out to the community that African Americans can fill the 1.3 million high-tech jobs that largely go unfilled (Moses & Cobb, 2001). Moses and Cobb (2001) argue that a culture of mathematics literacy needs to operate in the African American community to the same extent as church culture does.

Martin (2000) believes negative community beliefs about mathematics send students mixed messages about the importance of learning mathematics and as a result impact mathematics achievement and persistence (Martin, 2000). In the aforementioned qualitative study, he found male and female middle school students in Oakland, California, who persisted in mathematics and were succeeding in advanced mathematics courses. However, all of these students were taunted and ridiculed by peers who perceived that academic engagement and persistence in mathematics was "nerdy" behavior or "acting White" (Martin, 2000, p. 167). Moreover two out of four parents interviewed were not sending their children the right message about attaining mathematical knowledge because of their own negative experiences and lack of socioeconomic opportunity. Thus, the African American community must examine its values and beliefs about mathematics in order to change these perceptions. In order to do this, mathematics must be seen for its liberating power and the message of acquiring mathematical knowledge must become the mantra of those who have the power to effect change in the community.

The foregoing studies and statistics as well as the comments of my colleagues from New Orleans, who have since relocated to San Antonio, Texas, imply that Orleans Parish, the 39th largest school district in the United States in 2003, and other large urban school districts are not meeting the needs of their most precious resource: children. With no plans to return to New Orleans in the next four years, my colleagues consider themselves blessed. They have been able to find jobs and build a new home in the suburbs of San Antonio where their daughter will attend high school. However, for those less fortunate and those who remain in New Orleans the hurricane provides researchers and educators with an opportunity to improve conditions, which were appalling by most standards.

It Takes a Village

The African American community can promote the development of mathematics identity and mathematics socialization in a myriad of ways. First, we can embrace mathematics as part of our history. Students should know that Benjamin Banneker excelled in mathematics. He used his genius to create the first wooden clock and to design plans for the city of Washington, DC. Women were also pioneers. Bessie Coleman was the first African American to earn an international pilot's license. She certainly knew how to use mathematics to accomplish such a magnificent feat. From the cradle to the school house door, from the pulpit to the pew, everyone in the African American community must send children the message that it is okay to be black and to be literate in mathematics. African American religious, business, and social institutions must collaborate to change the belief that achieving in mathematics is "acting White" (Martin, 2000; Ogbu, 2003).

The Black Church can play an integral role in mathematics socialization by "mathematizing" Sunday school lessons whenever the opportunity presents itself. There are numerous texts in the Bible that lend themselves to mathematics questions. For example, Jesus fed 5,000 men with five loaves (biscuits) of bread and two fish (Mk. 6:38). The Bible says that all were filled and 12 baskets of food fragments were left over. While not minimizing the miracle, it can be understood in mathematical terms. If one thought of the problem with the fish and the loaves as an exponential function, the following questions could be raised around this text: we know how many people could be fed with 5 loaves and 2 fish. How many loaves and fish would it take to feed 100 times as many people? 1,000 times? 5,000 times? 10,000 times? Not only would the children be intrigued by the mathematics, but they would also understand the depth of the miracle involved. In John 2:6, we are presented with another miracle where Jesus turned water into wine. Jesus used mathematics to convey meaning and so should the Black Church.

In addition, beauty salons and barber shops are stable businesses in the Black community with which African American children can identify. Mathematics can be seen in hair braiding (cornrows and extensions) and designer hair cuts. The patterns and designs that are formed from braiding and cutting hair can be examined from a geometric perspective to help children learn terms such as *point, ray, angle, line segment, line, parallel,* and *perpendicular*. The menu of prices found in barber shops and beauty salons provides teachers and parents with a source to develop culturally relevant mathematics problems for children to solve.

Moreover, mathematics can be found in music and art. Some African American children easily learn the words to complicated and intricate rap and hip-hop lyrics; they should also learn the mathematics involved in the music itself. Students are doing mathematics when they understand how to use the signature of the music to *count* the number of beats. Understanding of *fractions* is also enhanced by learning the value of notes (eighth note, quarter note, half note, whole note, and so on). Further, mathematics and art can be integrated by teachers to help children to observe different geometric patterns that can be found in artifacts such as sculpture, paintings, and prints (Leonard, 2001). Students can use patterns and shapes to create their own *tessellations* (artistic patterns often found in tile and mosaics). These activities are not only fun but help students to value and develop their artistic talent while understanding the importance of mathematics.

Furthermore, literacy in mathematics and reading are not necessarily mutually exclusive. Anderson, Anderson, and Shapiro (2004) found that parents and children shared a variety of discourses in mathematics during shared storybook reading. Results suggest that particular books elicit different kinds of mathematics interactions in diverse families. African American parents can read multicultural stories with their children and solve mathematics problems simultaneously (Strutchens, 2002). *The Patchwork Quilt* (Flournoy, 1985), *The Black Snowman* (Mendez, 1989), and *Sadako and the Thousand Paper Cranes* (Coerr, 1993) are a few examples of multicultural texts that can be used to develop problem solving.

Finally, mathematics can be learned by participating in games, like dominoes (Nasir, 2002) and chess (Thomas-El, 2003), as well as sports. The game of dominoes, which appeals to both children and adults, is complex, and players must learn to handle *addition* and *multiplication* to keep track of scoring. The participants' identity is shaped by the shared history and experience of the players (Nasir, 2002). Moreover, the game of chess requires the knowledge of hierarchical roles (i.e., bishops, rooks, and knights) as well as *logic* to win. Players develop an identity as they demonstrate their ability to challenge and compete with others. Likewise, baseball requires the use of *statistics, reasoning,* and *strategy* to learn how to score against an opponent. Identity is developed among players who call themselves "ballers" (Nasir, 2002). Track and field events contain plenty of mathematics as well. Students learn the value of *decimals* as they experience how *tenths* and *hundredths* of a second make the difference in winning or losing a race. From these and all of the foregoing examples, we can begin to understand how mathematics is part of the social milieu of African American life.

In conclusion, the voice of one sixth-grade African American male captures the importance of mathematics literacy:

> "I feel that [learning mathematics] is an achievement because math is all around. It teaches us how to work. If you can do no math, you can't do anything. You couldn't make a building. You couldn't do anything. I am learning something that will help me in the future." (Leonard, 1997, p. 154)

Indeed, mathematics is found in every aspect of life. Children model the beliefs and values of their parents, peers, and community. Thus, the entire community must take responsibility for helping African American children to develop mathematics identity and mathematics socialization.

Knowledge is power and mathematical literacy opens the door of opportunity. The demand for workers with high-tech skills in 2006 is expected to be more than 1.3 million (Moses & Cobb, 2001). These jobs require knowledge of mathematics and technology. Persons in high-tech fields earn 82% more than people in other industries (Moses & Cobb, 2001). Achieving in mathematics increases the likelihood that African Americans will get some of the technology jobs that will become available. Recently CEOs from Fortune 500 companies visited New Orleans to become involved in resurrecting the city's financial district. They, too, have a role to play in ensuring that persons of color will have job opportunities and in ensuring the success of school children in Orleans Parish. Mathematics literacy leads to higher education and economic access. Development of mathematics identity and socialization will result in high mathematics achievement and economic parity for students of color in New Orleans and other cities. In the spirit of Ladson-Billings's address, let us strive as educators, researchers, and business leaders to resurrect one of America's great cities by providing high quality mathematics education for *all* of its children.

REFERENCES

Anderson, A., Anderson, J., & Shapiro, J. (2004). Mathematical discourse in shared storybook reading. *Journal for Research in Mathematics Education, 35*(1), 5–33.

Coerr, E. (1993). *Sadako and the thousand paper cranes.* New York: Dell Yearling.

Du Bois, W. E. B. (1995). *The souls of black folk.* New York: New American Library. (Original work published 1903).

Flournoy, V. (1985). *The patchwork quilt.* New York: Dial.

Gamoran, A., & Weinstein, M. (1998). Differentiation and opportunity in restructured schools. *American Journal of Education, 106*(3), 385–415.

Hurricane exposes issues of class, race. (2005, September 2). *USA Today,* A20.

Ladson-Billings, G. (1994). *The dreamkeepers: Successful teachers of African American children.* San Francisco: Jossey-Bass.

Leonard, J. (1997). Characterizing student discourse in a sixth-grade mathematics classroom. (Doctoral Dissertation, University of Maryland at College Park, 1997). *Dissertation Abstracts International, A: 58/09,* p. 3450.

Leonard, J. (2001). Integrating art and mathematics: Using art to teach math concepts. *The Journal of the New England League of Middle Schools, 14*(1), 36–39.

Leonard, J. (2004, September). *Still not saved: The power of mathematics to liberate the oppressed.* Paper presented at Frederick D. Patterson Institute Conference: Still Not Equal, Washington, D.C.

Malloy, C. E., & Malloy, W. M. (1998). Issues of culture in mathematics teaching and learning. *The Urban Review, 30*(3), 245–257.

Martin, D. B. (2000). *Mathematics success and failure among African American youth: The roles of socio-historical context, community forces, school influence, and individual agency.* Mahwah, NJ: Lawrence Erlbaum.

Martin, D. B. (2003). Hidden assumptions and unaddressed questions in *Mathematics for All* rhetoric. *The Mathematics Educator, 13*(2), 7–21.

Mendez, P. (1989). *The black snowman.* New York: Scholastic.

Moses, R. P., & Cobb, Jr., C. E. (2001). *Radical equations: Math literacy and civil rights.* Boston: Beacon Press.

Nasir, N. (2002). Identity, goals and learning: Mathematics in cultural practice. *Mathematical Thinking and Learning,* (2&3), 211–245.

National Center for Educational Statistics. (2004). *The nation's report card.* Retrieved August 22, 2004, from http://nces.ed.gov/nationsreportcard/mathematics/results2003/raceethnicity.asp

National Council of Teachers of Mathematics. (2000). *Curriculum and Evaluation Standards for School Mathematics.* Reston, VA: The Council.

Ogbu, J. U. (2003). *Black American students in an affluent suburb: A study of academic disengagement.* Mahwah, NJ: Lawrence Erlbaum.

Rousseau, C., & Tate, W. F. (2003). No time like the present: Reflecting on equity in school mathematics. *Theory into Practice, 42*(3), 210–216.

Songer, N. B., Lee, H., & Kam, R. (2002). Technology-rich inquiry science in urban classrooms: What are the barriers to inquiry pedagogy? *Journal of Research in Science Teaching, 39*(2), 128–150.

Strutchens, M. E. (2002). Multicultural literature as a context for problem solving: Children and parents learning together. *Teaching Children Mathematics, 8*(8), 448–454.

Swain, C., & Pearson, T. (2003). Educators and technology standards: Influencing the digital divide. *Journal of Research on Technology in Education, 34*(3), 326–333.

Tate, W. F. (1997). Race-Ethnicity, SES, gender, and language deficiency trends in mathematics achievement: An update. *Journal for Research in Mathematics Education, 28*(6), 652–679.

Thomas-El, S. (2003). *I choose to stay: A black teacher refuses to desert the inner city.* New York: Kensington Press.

Viadero, D. (2005). Transition mathematics project. Retrieved August 12, 2005 from: http://www.transitionmathproject.org/marketingarticle.asp

Warren, B., Ballenger, C., Ogonowski, M., Rosebery A. S., & Hudicourt-Barnes, J. (2001). Rethinking diversity in learning science: The logic of everyday sense-making. *Journal of Research in Science*

Teaching, 38(5), 529–552.

Wiest, L. R. (2003). The current status of male teachers of young children. *Educational Forum, 68*(1), 62–70.

■|■|■

CHAPTER 5

Still Waters Run Deep

Cracks in the Educational Pipeline for African American Students Post-Hurricane Katrina

EBONI M. ZAMANI-GALLAHER & VERNON C. POLITE

History will undoubtedly record not only the devastation of Hurricane Katrina but also how well and how quickly the American public responded to the challenges and needs of its fellow countrymen—the time to respond is now! Akin to the terrorist attacks of September 11, 2001, United States citizens and the world grappled with the distressing impact of Hurricane Katrina in Alabama, Florida, Mississippi, Texas, and Louisiana, with the greatest attention focused on the ravaging effects on the City of New Orleans and its residents. Unfortunately, the hurricane is but a metaphor for the calamity that commonly faces African American students in urban school settings. Hence, the aim of this chapter is to examine the peril, paradox, and prevalence of educational struggles facing the Gulf Coast area. Additionally, it is the goal of the authors to parallel the losses that encumber African American youths in the context of schooling. While the obvious challenges confronting African American students who struggle, daily, in the urban enclaves of this nation are not equivalent to the present issues of the children of Katrina, our public school systems' lackadaisical response to everyday disenfranchised students at-risk is quite damaging, if not equally disastrous.

The Great Deluge for African Americans: Man-made or Natural Disaster?

> Instead of being a remnant from the past, the social hierarchy based on race is a critical component in the organization of modern American society. The subordination because of the color of one's skin is a primary determinant of people's position in the social structure. Racism is the structural relationship based on the subordination of one racial group by another. Given this perspective, the determining feature of race relations is not prejudice towards blacks, but rather the superior position of whites and the institutions—ideological as well as structural—which maintain it. (Wellman, 1977, as cited in Wilson, 1991, p. xv).

It is not uncommon for people to readily accept as well as follow socially defined positions based on their race, gender and/or class. As culture imposes rules on its members, there are patterns of behavior that have been institutionalized based on individuals' ascribed characteristics and with regard to their status in the social order. There is a biological and social significance to race and gender, and these constructs frequently fall short of mitigating the effects of poverty and the position of African Americans in society.

One could argue that high water is ever present when it comes to the state of African Americans in the United States of America. Historically, the educational disadvantages, sociopolitical disregard, status quo positioning, and economic disparity that were the impetus to enact legislation to collapse an undemocratic social order are still a part of the experiences of many African Americans in contemporary society. Ironically, the title of this text *The Children Hurricane Katrina Left Behind* could not be closer to the truth as the nexus and adverse effects of the interaction between race, gender, and class are often exacerbated for African American students. However, the relevance of this current event should not be misconstrued as an anomaly; the "storms" of centuries of educational neglect and failed social policies have been as catastrophic as the woefully deplorable federal, state, and local response to Hurricane Katrina and its victims.

Although Hurricane Katrina (and Hurricane Rita) wreaked havoc in cities across five Delta states, clearly New Orleans is encumbered with residual damage of historic proportions. The largest numbers of citizens displaced due to Hurricane Katrina are Louisiana natives who are scattered across the United States. In fact, it is projected to cost $5.9 billion and may take more than 25 years to rebuild New Orleans (Jordan, 2006). What demographic shifts and cultural influences will the city reflect in the future? Given the refugee status of those left to combat yet another blow that widens the gulf between the haves and have-nots, will low-income Katrina survivors get to reenter New Orleans or systematically remain displaced, further reinforcing mainstream hegemony? The travesty of addressing the post-Katrina challenges of reconstruction, poverty, and racial discord is flanked by the stark similarity in the social and economic needs affecting the disenfranchised centuries ago.

The victims of Hurricane Katrina are representative of people of all walks of life— cutting across the color lines, dollar signs, ability levels, generations, and gender gaps. We are not interested in political blame shifting. In an effort to explore the implications of the crisis, we have to unframe the significance of the storm, stress, and disproportionate imprint of Katrina on African Americans, particularly in reference to the crumbling educational plight of African American students within urban centers. In attempting to completely understand the social context of pervasive inequality prior to the catastrophe, the next segment will underscore the crisis and context of Black placement in the United States, more explicitly New Orleans.

Reviewing the Damage: Civil Rights Challenges Before and After the Storm

Following Katrina's aftermath, we are bearing witness to the next pattern in African American population migration. Unlike the vast majority of Americans who voluntarily immigrated to the United States, the history of African Americans in the United States originated through the forced movement of Africans to America. However, the other major population movement of Black people occurred after the Civil War as most African Americans who remained in the South as sharecroppers or tenants were confronted daily with the many indignities of de facto Jim Crow segregation. Drawn by what was perceived as better educational opportunities, manufacturing jobs and fewer legal restrictions, African Americans began to leave the South migrating to Northern cities where they still faced restricted opportunities in schooling, housing/voting rights, and employment opportunities (Bennett, 1988). By 1920, 450,000 Blacks had relocated to the North from the South. During the 1990s, many African Americans left the "rust belt" cities, returning to what is considered a "revitalized" or "the new" South (e.g., Atlanta, Birmingham, Charlotte, and New Orleans) with numerous and varied job opportunities, affordable housing possibilities, and distinctive African American cultural influences in art, food, and music (Encarta, 2001; Piazza, 2005).

At one point, New Orleans was the third largest metropolitan area but has suffered a residency decline since the 1960s. It is estimated that the city has sustained a loss of 10 residents per day for the last 45 years (Duke University, 2006). The racial/ethnic demographics of New Orleans have shifted considerably over the last century. Well-known for its blending of cultures such as Spanish, French, and African, New Orleans has historical roots in slavery. The city began to "Blacken" following the Civil War with increasing 'White flight' to the outskirts of the metropolitan area by the mid-to-late 1960s (Dyson, 2005; Polite, 1993). New Orleans was not alone in the trend of Whites leaving the city to move to the suburbs following the push of civil rights during the 1960s. To a great extent, many urban quarters across the nation also witnessed the pattern of White exodus in favor of suburban residency with African Americans segregated in large metropolitan areas (e.g., Chicago, Cincinnati, Cleveland, Detroit, Indianapolis, New York, Philadelphia, Pittsburgh, and St. Louis).

According to Fontenot (2005), well over two-thirds of New Orleans residents were African American at the turn of the new millennium in contrast to 37 percent in 1960. Also worthy of note is the correspondence of financial disparities with regard to racial and ethnic profiles in New Orleans. The majority of Blacks affected by Katrina were residents of the Ninth Ward, 36% of whom live beneath the poverty line. New Orleans ranks seventh out of 290 large counties in the United States. for poverty. In his text *Come Hell or High Water,* Michael Eric Dyson notes, "As the city got blacker, it got poorer" (2005, p. 7).

At a national level, an estimated 12 million children live below the federal poverty line. Even though Whites make up three quarters of the total population, they comprise less than eight percent of those living underneath the poverty line (U.S. Census Bureau, 2000). In comparison, African Americans make up 12.5 percent of the populace yet nearly one-quarter (twice as many) live in poverty. In the state of Louisiana, 31.5 percent of the population is African American yet Black youths account for 69 percent of the children in poverty (Dyson, 2005).

Table I. Racial/Ethnic Distributions of Persons under the Poverty Line

Race/Ethnicity	Percent under the poverty line
White	7.9
African American	24.8
Native American/Alaska Native	26.1
Asian American/Pacific Islander	11.6
Hispanic/Latino	24.2

Source: U.S. Bureau of the Census 2000

Given the concentration of most African American families' in urban centers, the Katrina crisis is indicative of not only racial neglect by elected officials but also fizzling attention to the depth of inner-city poverty. Poverty is most likely a condition of persons of color, women, full-time working poor, the illiterate, and the young. People with disabilities are also disproportionately affected by poverty; twenty-three percent of New Orleans residents are people with disabilities (National Council on Disability, 2005). Ten percent of Hurricane Katrina survivors are K-14 students and young adults (i.e., 5 to 20 years old) facing multiple marginalities and compounded loss.

What we do know about children and poverty in the United States is that as a nation we boast egalitarian values and act as if education were the absolute panacea. In reality, though, poor students most often have the novice teachers, lowest achievement outcomes, higher per-student-ratios, aged materials, declining facilities, weaker curricula and the least human/fiscal resources (Kozol, 1991; Payne, 2005). Correspondingly, many urban educators have expressed the impact of injurious institutional patterns as contributing to the prevalent school failure among African American students within inner-city school districts (Polite, 2000).

The immediate needs of the students of Katrina are obvious. As educational personnel, teachers and leaders surely we should be at the forefront in culturally responsive rescue and recovery for the students who have suffered because of Katrina, but that same immediacy and responsiveness are needed for all students who live at the margins of society and experience widespread educational neglect and foiled opportunities to learn and grow.

Assessing the Educational Pipeline: The K-16 Katrina Context

Given the profound changes in the racial/ethnic and gender composition of the U. S. citizenry, issues of access and the role of education are of great importance. Paradoxically, while racial/ethnic minorities and women are among the most visible subgroups in America, members of each group have struggled to move from the margins to the mainstream of societal thought and into the full participation (Zamani, 2003). Amidst solid numbers enrolled in K-12 education, little increase has occurred in higher education attendance (Anderson, 2002; Sedlacek, 1999). Considering that matriculation toward the collegiate years is predicated on K-12 success, it is hard to ignore that the frailty of Louisiana's school system and students' educational progression will be impacted beyond this academic year.

Some critics would contend that the public school system in New Orleans was disastrous before the hurricane hit (Voices for Katrina's Children, 2006). The repercussions of the Katrina aftermath include a sharp decrease in the local tax base supporting the schools with space at a premium and swelling enrollments in the educational settings least affected. Schools in a half dozen Louisiana parishes were destroyed or incurred significant damage, leaving nearly 300,000 school-age children displaced (The George Lucas Educational Foundation, n.d.). However, the federal government has given $21 million in grants in an attempt to revamp the New Orleans school system with the goal of reopening and expanding existing schools as well as creating several new charter schools (Voices for Katrina's Children, 2005).

As the 2005–2006 academic year began, many families sought refuge in states across the country with most children made homeless by the hurricane entering schools in nearby states such as Florida and Texas. Approximately 38,000 kids impacted by Hurricane Katrina are enrolled in Texas schools (Weber, 2006). Making the learning context more intricate and difficult to navigate for Katrina's students are the chilly school climates that, in some cases, have been less than inclusive, thus further problematizing issues of adjustment, transition, and matriculation. For instance, one burden surfacing is a gap in school readiness for early childhood learners due to family displacement and instability because of the storm or preexisting conditions exacerbated by Katrina (e.g., impoverished home/community).

Despite the emotional damage and in some cases academic delays due to the storm, there is an intolerance of Katrina's victims. Case in point are headlines such as the one from the Associated Press on March 29, 2006, that read, "Katrina evacuees wear out stay in Houston" or "Katrina's latest damage: Houston wants Katrina evacuees to move on" in the March 13, 2006, issue of *Newsweek.* Not helping matters are the recent standardized test scores of Katrina's kids on the Texas Assessment of Knowledge and Skills. Only 46 percent of fifth-grade evacuees passed the reading portion in contrast to 80 percent of all students and 89 percent of all third-graders passed the reading segment compared to 58 percent of Katrina's students. School board official Larry Marshall stated "We've got kids who are coming into our secondary system and cannot read" (as cited in Weber, 2006). About 2,000 evacuees failed the test, and many according to the Texas Education Agency (TEA) were academically a few years behind.

TEA approximates that as much as $350 million of additional revenues will be needed yearly to educate the children of Hurricane Katrina (Weber, 2006). Voicing concern over the learning gap and number of evacuees swamping Texas, former first lady Barbara Bush donated funds to Houston schools for Ignite Learning software programs. Her generosity has been overshadowed with questions regarding her concern for the fledgling academic performance of many evacuee students in Houston's school system versus an agenda to pay for instructional technologies produced by son Neil Bush's company with monies raised for evacuees through the Bush-Clinton

Katrina Fund (Garza, 2006). In sum, the achievement gap between students affected by Katrina in comparison to their counterparts with indistinguishable challenges has surfaced in Texas and other states, suggesting a systemic problem for ensuring college readiness in our knowledge-based economy.

While Hurricane Katrina is sure to present additional challenges to African American students who are transitioning to postsecondary institutions, nationally college and university figures remain relatively unchanged, reflecting stratified participation and persistent barriers to educational advancement of Blacks. Alabama, Florida, Louisiana, Mississippi, and Texas all are states with affected college campuses. However, because of the many needs and call for greater numbers of African American postsecondary participants, greater consideration should be paid to the implications for Louisiana higher education as the state sustained the greatest amount of damage, particularly the institutions of higher learning that are historically Black colleges and universities (i.e., HBCUs—Dillard, Southern, and Xavier).

The higher education environment is made up of nearly 4,100 two- and four-year publicly and privately controlled colleges and universities. Within the larger landscape of postsecondary institutions lie 105 HBCUs, including 40 public four-year, 49 private four-year, 11 public two-year and five private two-year colleges that enroll 14 percent of all Black students in higher education though representing just three percent of postsecondary education (*The Chronicle of Higher Education,* 2005a; White House Initiative on HBCUs, 2006). HBCUs account for roughly one-quarter of all African American students enrolled in four-year colleges, confer 24 percent of all baccalaureate degrees earned by African Americans nationwide, and award master's degrees and first-professional degrees to about 1 in 6 African American men and women (White House Initiative on HBCUs, 2006).

While there are 16 historically black community colleges, predominantly White two-year institutions register the preponderance of African American community college attendees. Further, greater numbers of African American faculty and staff are found at HBCUs in contrast to those employed at predominantly White institutions (Fleming, 1985). Ideally, collegiate faculty and support staff would mirror the overall student body. Unfortunately, the faculty units of the three HBCUs in New Orleans have been most adversely affected in contrast to their neighboring PWIs. Suffering the devastation along with the students, clusters of faculty members have been unpaid, laid off temporarily, or simply released without reinstatement. AAUP reports that over 25 percent of Southern University at New Orleans faculty and roughly 60 percent of Dillard University's full-time faculty was placed on furlough (J. E. K., 2006). Additionally, Xavier University of Louisiana released 73 of their 246 faculty members. CampusRelief.Org offers campus-to-campus disaster assistance and currently has online employment resources for faculty and staff affected by the hurricanes.

As faculty members of Louisiana institutions look for reinstatements or reassignments, it is clear that a reorganization of Higher Education, is underway in New Orleans. The restructuring of K-16 schooling in Louisiana was badly needed prior to Katrina according to the Commissioner of Louisiana higher education who announced dividing the state's 40 technical schools into nine regions, some of which will be headed by community colleges. According to E. Joseph Savoie, "The window's open and we're going to run as far and as fast as we can till somebody shuts it" (Dyer, 2006, p. 11) Walter Bumphus, president of the Louisiana Community and Technical College System (LCTCS), expressed, "We couldn't do business as usual, and it [Katrina] gave all of us an opportunity to think about what we wanted to look like 10 years out" (Dyer, 2006, p. 11).

As community colleges have often been the only postsecondary option for many first-generation low-income students, the rebuilding of higher education that is affordable and accessible in Louisiana will prove vital given the serious financial implications of Katrina for numerous displaced collegians. Many professional groups and foundations understand the importance of special population colleges and seek to provide aid in the recovery efforts. The Teagle Foundation is providing a $500,000 grant to Dillard University as it was hit the hardest by the storm. Similar support has been offered by the Lumina Foundation for Education which granted $2 million dollars to the American Association of Community Colleges (AACC) to offer monetary assistance to part-time and full-time two-year students affected by Katrina in Louisiana and Mississippi (*The Chronicle of Higher Education,* 2005b). AACC intends to distribute stipends up to $1,000 to low-income students adversely impacted by Hurricane Katrina toward tuition, books, fees, and other educational expenses. Additionally, Lumina is giving a $1 million grant to Scholarship America to provide disaster relief funds for postsecondary students enrolled in four-year institutions that have been impacted by the hurricane, and Sally Mae is offering $1,000 Katrina relief loans (*The Chronicle of Higher Education,* 2005b*).*

Many state colleges are also responding with generosity by expediting paperwork for displaced collegians, seeking to minimize costs, providing housing, and scholarships for tuition/fees. There are over 800 colleges across the nation registered on Katrina relief college databases such as CampusRelief.Org and/or elearners.com. The offering of institutional help will also be needed in training responsive school counselors and teacher-leaders committed to assisting African American students to self-actualize along the educational pipeline. Likewise, institutional culture and climate are gravely important in attracting, retaining, and advancing African American faculty and administrators who affirm the presence of African American collegians within Louisiana's colleges post-Katrina.

Theoretical Perspectives for Examining Psychodynamics of Post-Hurricane Katrina

Few of us will ever experience the crisis of the children and families of Hurricane Katrina. The above sections highlighted the schooling contexts and politics of community composition in New Orleans. As educators, we must be cognizant of the services necessary to provide Katrina's students with academic and social support that will sufficiently aid them in managing this traumatic series of events. Furthermore, it is our duty to adequately train educational professionals by underscoring the importance of teacher education preparation programs that encompass empathetic, culturally congruent, and competent approaches for working with children in crisis.

Post-Traumatic Stress Disorder

According to Breslau and colleagues (1998), over 60 percent of individuals experience a severe traumatic event that leads to Post-Traumatic Stress Disorder (PTSD). The changes from the events of Hurricane Katrina were sudden but will not be short-lived. It is estimated that 45,182 youths in Louisiana have or will develop PTSD in the months following the storm (Voices for Katrina's Children, 2006). PTSD involves experiencing a life threatening event that evokes intense fear, helplessness, horror, nightmares, flashbacks, feelings of recurrence that provoke a loss of interest in activities, startled responses, estrangement from others and difficulty concentrating or sleeping (Daneker, 2005). None of those individuals who wish that the evacuees would just "move on" as the headlines read has a clue. Now imagine being a child that has had life as he or she knows it disrupted in the worst way. Imagine the shock of being removed from your family, home, community, and familiarity of your school context. What relative comfortable balance you experienced prior to the hurricane no longer exists. Hence, the types of social interaction, level of comfort, cognitive processes, and emotional aspects (e.g., anger, despair, low self-esteem) you have are at this point being filtered through the pain of processing Katrina's trauma. Many students are emotionally not free to learn or strive given the trauma and upheaval recently experienced in their lives.

Coping

Being affected by the storm is sure to be seen as a deficit for some, while others in an effort to cope will alter their perception of this life-changing event to see the disruption as a meaningful intervention. Survivors of traumatic experiences move from the deficit model, exemplify resilience to create manageable ways of coping and moving on in spite of how their lives have been negatively affected. When considering the variation in cultural contexts, the refugee status of Katrina's students indicates the value of introducing coping strategies for displaced African American students. Research by Plybon and associates (2003) has indicated that urban, female middle school students have positive perceptions of self and community that directly and positively impacted their increased feelings of self-efficacy, which in turn contributed to earning higher grades and use of adult support coping.

One of the techniques for measuring coping has been with *Kidcope,* which is a checklist of 10 coping strategies designed by Spirito, Stark, and Williams (1988). In an attempt to distinguish the coping strategies of students of color, Clark and Marcon (1997) utilized *Kidcope* with inner-city minority students. In contrast to the White teens in Spirito and colleagues' sample, Clark and Marcon found African American inner-city African American eighth-graders to use more coping strategies with few gender differences in coping. Thus, the extant research suggests that African American adolescents are capable of using problem solving strategies more often when they perceive that a situation is controllable versus adaptive coping that employs more emotion-focused strategies when they feel they have no control over a situation.

Hope Theory

It is important for educational and counseling personnel to foster a sense of agency for post-Hurricane Katrina students, particularly African American students who overall have unique psychosocial needs and must generate coping strategies that are essential to their overall functioning (i.e., academically/cognitively, emotionally, socially). The Katrina catastrophe is yet another stressor that for some is race-related in terms of the prolonged waiting for rescue and lack of responsiveness from government entities. The ways and means by which young African American children and adolescents cope may vary considerably from the coping conditions of adults.

Turning attention to adult learners, Danoff-Burg, Prelow, and Swenson (2004) explored the effects of hope and coping with race-related stress on the life satisfaction in Black college students. The results of their study illustrate that increased coping efficacy and African American students with high hope employed more problem-focused coping strategies. However, for students exhibiting high hope, there was less use of active coping strategies in association with life satisfaction and race-related stress. Hope theory suggests that individuals exhibiting high hope have reduced levels of emotional exhaustion and higher levels of satisfaction (Sherwin et al., 1992; Snyder, 1995, 1996). In view of that, hope theory may be a useful framework for examining the unconscious and overt means by which Katrina's students try to process the psychological impact of the hurricane, adapt their new school and community environments, and *in time* master living by not rendering themselves helpless under these conditions but by finding a new norm.

Conclusions and Implications for Practice

Whether it is the disaster of a hurricane or the climate of man-ordained ruin, African American urban poor are more vulnerable to the suffering of the storms that so often surge. However, being poor and from the poorest neighborhoods does not rob one of human dignity or erase the legacies of inaction and indeterminate policy. This chapter explored the landscape of Hurricane Katrina as it pertains to the implications for K-16 education. In this segment, we looked through the lens of a number of areas with race, gender, and class at the intersection of recognizing that the tragedy on the Gulf Coast raises many sociopolitical issues that our public policies have not adequately addressed as the previous and current results rendered leave little to be desired.

Apparently as a nation, we still have a difficult time embarking on courageous conversations. The constructive dialogue has only just begun as it pertains to facing our history as we make history in our approaches to racial/gender disparities, poverty, educational inequities, immigration, and so on. While as tragic as Katrina was, we have also seen another side to this human tragedy and that is our collective response. Hundreds of thousands showed up to help and excelled in their generosity and volunteerism. Our churches and educational organizations have poured support in the form of dollars, service-learning initiatives and action on the scene. Our "Project Back Pack" at Eastern Michigan University is one of a myriad of undertakings to assist Katrina's youngsters in some fashion.

Even supposing the Bush administration did not wish to subvert rescue efforts for the poorest victims of Katrina who did not have the means to escape what was inevitable, historical evidence (e.g., Hurricane Betsy of 1965) coupled with the current disaster is sure to conjure multiple traumas of the compounded effects of racism, classism, and the educational neglect of urban African American students. According to Hawkins (2005), there is a need of the dominant group/mainstream society to understand "the long enduring stigma in the Black community . . . coupled with the mistrust of government, makes counseling and psychological intervention an additional challenge in the wake of Katrina." In closing, the effects of Hurricane Katrina will be experienced by its victims for a long time. As educators, we should step up to the plate in augmenting our curriculum in teacher education and educational administration preparation programs to include cultural competency training that can assist Katrina survivors. We should take advantage of our classrooms to clear up any questions, present the reality of this natural disaster and awareness of the long-term impact (e.g., 70 percent of evacuees that fled the flooding in New Orleans are Black). Finally, for all of us watching from a distance, while we may be several states away from the Gulf Coast, keep in mind that there are Katrina survivors who need assistance and reassurance in your neck of the woods. Our children are our future, and Katrina's kids have been impacted by unnecessary hardship. Find ways to take action and help; each one, reach one and teach one!

REFERENCES

Anderson, J. D. (2002). Race in American higher education: Historical perspectives on current conditions. In W. A. Smith, P. G. Altbach & K. Lomotey (Eds.), *The racial crisis in American higher education: Continuing challenges for the twenty-first century* (pp. 3–21). Albany, NY: State University of New York Press.

Bennett, L. Jr. (1988). *Before the Mayflower: A history of Black America.* (6th ed.). New York: Penguin Books.

Breslau, N., Kessler, R. C., Chilcoat, H. D., Schultz, L. R., Davis, G. C. & Andreski, P. (1998). Trauma and posttraumatic stress disorder in the community: The 1996 Detroit area survey of trauma. *American Journal of Psychiatry, 55,* 626–632.

The Chronicle of Higher Education (2005a, August). The almanac.

The Chronicle of Higher Education (2005b, December 7). Announcements from affected colleges and from associations and government agencies. Retrieved on April 25, 2006 from http://chronicle.com/katrina/?rss=1.

Clark, D., & Marcon, R. A. (April 1997). *Coping strategies of inner-city adolescents: Response to recent personal conflicts.* Presented at the annual meeting of the Southeastern Psychological Association, Atlanta, Georgia.

Daneker, D. P. (April 2005). *The body, mind, and soul of trauma: Putting the pieces together.* Paper presented at the Annual Meeting of the American Counseling Association, Atlanta, GA.

Danoff-Burg, S., Prelow, H. M., & Swenson, R. . (2004). Hope and life satisfaction in Black college students coping and race-related stress. *Journal of Black Psychology, 30*(2), 208–228.

Duke University (2006). *Future look of New Orleans.* Retrieved on April 25, 2006 from http://dukenews.duke.edu/2005/09/katrinanewstips.html

Dyer, S. (May 4, 2006). Louisiana higher education officials to reorganize state's technical colleges. *Diverse, 23*(6), 11.

Dyson, M. E. (2005). *Come hell or high water: Hurricane Katrina and the color of disaster.* New York: Basic Civitas Books.

Encarta, (2001). *United States history.* Retrieved on August 25, 2003 from http://encarta.msn.com/encyclopedia_1741500824_6/United_States_(People).html#p114

Fleming, J. (1985). *Blacks in College: A comparative study of students' success in black and white institutes.* San Francisco: Jossey Bass Publishers.

Fontenot, A. (September, 2005). *How to rebuild New Orleans.* Retrieved on April 2, 2006 from http://www.salon.com/news/feature/2005/09/30/rebuild_reaction

Garza, C. L. (March 23, 2006). Former first lady's donation aids son. *Houston Chronicle.* Retrieved on April 4, 2006 from http://chron.com/disp/story.mpl/headline/metro/3742329.html

The George Lucas Educational Foundation (n.d.). *When calamity invades the classroom.* Retrieved on April 25, 2006 from http://64.233.179.104/search?q=cache:uYsmF81-YVMJ: www.edutopia.org/php/print.php

Hawkins, D. (2005). *The road to psychological recovery: Psychologist group says cultural competency training is needed to aid Black Katrina survivors.* Cox, Matthews & Associates. Retrieved on April 25, 2006 from http://www.findarticles.com/p/articles/mi_m0WMX/is_18_22/ai_n15950865/print

J. E .K. (March-April, 2006). AAUP responds to Katrina's impact on New Orleans universities. *Academe, 10–14.*

Jordan, L. J. (March 30, 2006). *Official: New Orleans recovery could take 25 years.* Associated Press. Retrieved on April 4, 2006 from http://www.blackamericaweb.com/ site.aspx/headlines/powe11331

Kozol, J. (1991). *Savage inequalities: Children in America's schools.* New York: HarperPerennial.

National Council on Disability. (September 2, 2005). Hurricane Katrina: Its impact on people with disabilities. Retrieved on April 25, 2006 from http://www.nod.org/

Payne, R. K. (2005). *A framework for understanding poverty,* 4th edition. Highlands, TX: aha! Process, Inc.

Piazza, T. (2005). *Why New Orleans matters.* New York: Regan Books.

Plybon, L. E., Edwards, L., Butler, D., Belgrave, F. Z. & Allison, K. W. (2003). Examining the link between neighborhood cohesion and school outcomes: The role of support coping among African American adolescent girls. *Journal of Black Psychology, 29*(4), 393–407.

Polite, V. C. (1993). Educating African American males in suburbia: Quality education? Caring environment? *Journal of African American Male Studies, 2*(1), 1–25.

Polite, V. C. (2000). When "at promise" Black males meet the "at risk" school system: Chaos! In M. C. Brown II and J. E. Davis (Eds.), *Black sons to mothers: Compliments, critiques, and challenges for cultural workers in education* (pp. 193–215). New York: Peter Lang.

Sedlacek, W. E. (1999). Black students on White campuses: 20 years of research. *Journal of College Student Development, 40,* 538550.

Sherwin, E. D., Elliott, T. R., Rybarczyk, B. D., Frank, R. G., Hanson, S., & Hoffman, J. (1992). Negotiating the reality of care giving: Hope, burnout, and nursing. *Journal of Social and Clinical Psychology, 11,* 129–139.

Snyder, C. R. (1995). Conceptualizing, measuring, and nurturing hope and beyond. *Journal of Social and Clinical Psychology, 8,* 130–157.

Snyder, C. R. (1996). To hope, to lose, and to hope again. *Journal of Personal and Interpersonal Loss, 1,* 1–16.

U.S. Census Bureau (2000). *Projections of the resident population by race, Hispanic origin and activity: Middle series, 2050 to 2070.* Washington, DC: U.S. Census Bureau, Population Projections Program, Population Division.

Voices for Katrina's Children (2005a, November 29). *New Orleans is likely to be the largest charter-school city in the country.* Retrieved on April 2, 2006 from http://katrina.voices.org/

Voices for Katrina's Children (December 14, 2005b). *Over 35% of children exposed to one traumatic event will develop serious mental health problems.* Retrieved on April 4, 2006 from http://katrina.voices.org/

Voices for Katrina's Children (2006 January 5). *Getting to the root of the problem.* Retrieved on April 2, 2006 from http://katrina.voices.org/

Weber, P. J. (2006, March 23,). *Young Katrina evacuees score lower on standardized test.* Retrieved on April 4, 2006 from http://www.blackamericaweb.com/site.aspx/headlines/evacuees324

The White House Initiative on Historically Black Colleges and Universities (2006). The Tradition Continues: New Successes and New Challenges. 2006 Conference Brochure. Retrieved on May 26, 2006 from http://www.ed.gov/about/inits/list/whhbcu/edlite-index.html

Wilson, A. N. (1991). *Black-on-black violence: The psychodynamics of black self annihilation in service of white domination.* New York: African World Infosystems.

Zamani, E. M. (2003). African American women in divergent institutions. *New Directions for Student Services, 104,* 5–18. San Francisco, CA: Jossey-Bass.

■|■|■

CHAPTER 6

Drowning Beneath the Rising Tide

The Common Plight of Public Schools, Disadvantaged Students, and African American Males

M. CHRISTOPHER BROWN II, T. ELON DANCY II
& JAMES EARL DAVIS

On Monday, August 29, 2005, at 6:10 A.M. CDT, a fluctuating category 4 tropical storm designated Hurricane Katrina made landfall on the southernmost coast of the Mississippi Delta in Buras, Louisiana. Massive devastation would follow in the hours, days, weeks, and months thereafter. Unlike the many hurricanes that have come ashore over the last decade, the cause of devastation was not fierce winds, torrential rains, or sporadic tornados. The horrors of disruption, death, and disaster resulted from the rising flood waters of the ocean, rivers, and canals due to breached levees and rising tides. In some morbidly sadistic and ironic fashion, the physical flooding of New Orleans, Louisiana, served as a metaphor for what was already happening in the city's schools, as well as schools across the nation.

Twenty-three years have passed since the National Commission on Excellence in Education (1983) report, *A Nation at Risk,* asserted that K-12 schools in America were drowning under the "rising tide of mediocrity" (p. 5). While millions of

American children have been and are afforded substandard education and poorly trained teachers, many of America's economically and educationally privileged families send their children to the types of high-quality schools that enable them to secure power, status, and varied forms of capital (i.e., social, cultural, economic). Social position, place, and privilege thus provide these children with a lifeboat of opportunistic refuge when the tides of competition and hegemony loom near, threatening to violently rise and crash. These privileged students are thereby conditioned and enabled to maintain the ongoing system of exclusion while their economically underprivileged and academically disadvantaged counterparts are deluged by the tides of social and financial deprivation. This latter group of students is not given a lifeboat when the nation-state ignores their need for meaningful education reform. Indeed, in many cases they are set adrift to flounder in the turbulent pools of ignorance and poverty on their own.

Despite the passage in 2001 of the No Child Left Behind Act (NCLB), governments at the local, state, and federal levels are failing to ensure that equitable and comparable education is provided to all of the nation's children today. NCLB, the cornerstone of current President George W. Bush's educational policy, has been touted as an educational reform framework that can supply underachieving American children with a quality education. It mandates that America's elementary and secondary schools be held accountable for their underachieving students as well as for devising ways that student performance will improve. NCLB incorporates the following principles and strategies:

- increased accountability for states, school districts, and schools;
- greater choice for parents and students, particularly those attending low-performing schools;
- more flexibility for states and local educational agencies in the use of Federal education dollars;
- a stronger emphasis on reading, especially for the nation's youngest children. (Hess & Petrilli, 2006)

Purported to address deficiencies in both student achievement and accountability measures, NCLB has instead ensured that school and student performance are increasingly correlated to socioeconomic class. Many states are abandoning tests for promotion and graduation because they recognize that tests affect large numbers of disadvantaged students negatively and disproportionately (Steinberg, 2000). In Chicago, for example, the policy of retaining students who failed tests mandated by NCLB has led to the disproportionate retention of students from minority backgrounds (Gamoran, 2004; Moore, 1999). The plight of these students is not much different from those in other urban centers such as New Orleans, whose students' academic futures in the post-Katrina climate appear uncertain indeed.

The educational tides are still rising in the United States of America. As the nation gears up for the reauthorization of the NCLB legislation in 2007, acknowledgment is growing of the widening chasm of economic assets across social classes and the ways in which this trend both correlates and coagulates along racial lines. The adage—"a rising tide raises all boats"—may indeed be true, but it fails to address the issue of what happens to those without boats. Further, it does not account for the occasioned phenomenon of a rising tide that becomes a flood. Arguably under such conditions, the un-named and ignored may drown in torrents of indifference while more privileged and prepared persons are able to rise above the currents and sail forward.

The unprecedented natural disaster of Hurricane Katrina amplified enough realities of social inequality to disgust the sensibilities of any American who embraces idealized notions of democracy, access, and opportunity. Of continuing concern to those persons is the future of education and how this particular moment in history provides a unique chance to reflect and imagine the possibilities for refocusing education for our nation's most vulnerable students. Planning for the future of public schools in New Orleans and other U.S. cities is daunted by dire indicators of financial viability, physical infrastructure, enrollment patterns, and leadership capacity (Hill & Hannaway, 2006). The pages that follow represent an effort to understand the contextual realities faced by some of the children Hurricane Katrina left behind. This analysis is also an overdue examination of the differences across, between, and among students at the intersections of power and advantage, race and class, and access and education.

Schooling in the United States: Context and History

The Sociology of Education: Past and Present

The sociohistorical basis of schooling in America is rooted in privilege and exclusion. As Collins (2004) asserts, schools usually are founded by powerful autonomous status groups to provide an exclusive education for their own children or to promulgate respect for their particular cultural values. In such bifurcated educational frameworks, differences between cultures typically emerge. Collins notes that most U.S. schools established throughout the 19th century were founded by religious groups, largely to oppose schools founded by rival religious groups. This conflict gave rise to the establishment of large numbers of colleges and the U.S. Catholic and Lutheran school systems. By contrast, the American public school system was founded mainly due to the impetus of WASP (White, Anglo-Saxon, and Protestant) elites for the purpose of teaching respect for Protestant, middle-class standards of cultural and religious propriety as a countermeasure to the massive influx of Catholic, working-class immigrants from Europe (Collins, 2004). Thus, Collins concludes, the content and context of public school education to this day reflect middle-class WASP culture.

Accordingly, Alexander (2004) asserts, the values of middle-class WASP students are more congruent with the values of the nation's schools, and students from such backgrounds respond more easily to the requirements of schooling than those who are not. As such, middle-class parents' social networks typically provide them with insights and information that help them manage their children's educational careers more successfully (Alexander, 2004; Lareau, 2000). Lareau (2000) and Useem (1992) further assert that middle-class parents have the cultural resources to navigate the complexities of educational opportunities more effectively than do working-class parents. Differential access to social networks that support educational success has been shown to contribute to inequality in educational outcomes (Coleman & Hoffer, 1987). Economic, social, and cultural resources therefore become a potent combination in privileged students' trajectory to educational attainment and achievement.

Given that schools are predisposed to middle-class values, differences in habits, tastes, attitudes, preferences, and linguistics are among the many cultural conditions that make it more difficult for students from disadvantaged families to succeed in school (Alexander, 2004; Bernstein, 1974). Cultural resources in the home also have been linked to educational success. Students whose families own more books, subscribe to newspapers and magazines, visit libraries, and engage in other compatible enrichment opportunities have been found to perform better on cognitive tests, receive higher grades, and stay in school longer than do students from families who lack these resources (Alexander, 2004; DiMaggio, 1982; DiMaggio & Mohr, 1985). Children whose parents have lower levels of education also find themselves at a disadvantage in the school system (Alexander, 2004; Bourdieu & Passeron, 1977).

The ideology that privileged students matter in school, and conversely that disadvantaged students do not, is consistent with reproduction theories which maintain that dominant social groups use educational credentials to preserve their positions of privilege (Alexander, 2004; Bourdieu & Passeron, 1977; Collins, 1971). Reproduction theorists recognize, however, that subordinate groups often strive for greater educational opportunities. In tandem, a society that expands its systems of mass education benefits concomitant groups by broadening the socialization of persons from lower-status origins into a common value system and thus preparing them for workforce roles (Alexander, 2004). By doing so, it also perpetuates what Raftery and Hout (1993, as cited in Alexander, 2004) refer to as maximally maintained inequality in schools—that is, a condition in which students from lower socioeconomic families are allowed to stay in school longer, but their relative position compared to their higher status peers remains constant despite improved educational opportunities for all members of society. For example, Alexander notes that only minimal social inequality is found in the rates of completion of lower secondary education in the United States, yet large disparities exist between U.S. racial and ethnic groups in terms of postsecondary enrollments and graduation rates. The inequality in this case, Alexander maintains, has merely shifted upward to preserve the relative differences between groups.

Unquestionably, racism and discrimination are endemic components within the institutionalized practices of America's public schools (Brown & Ratcliff, 1998). To eradicate these dual national vices, Gordon (1995) argues that a group-based model of distributive equity must be implemented. He offers support for a notion of group-based distribution in which equity not only "speaks to and references fairness and social justice" (p. 363) but "requires that the distribution of social resources be sufficient to the condition that is being treated" (p. 364). Stone (1997) also admonishes educators to pay greater attention to group-based equity, particularly for African Americans.

School is the great sorting device in America, and as Alexander (2004) asserts, American society is predisposed to privilege. The advantages of privilege in the United States are especially evident across school contexts. Resources available to children whose families have greater income and wealth—supplies, books, computers, places to study, tutors, and so on—contribute to their educational success (Alexander, 2004; Coleman et al., 1966). These economic, cultural, and social differences combine to preserve privilege across generations. Alexander posits that inequality in educational achievement and attainment by social background can be expected to persist throughout the 21st century. Moreover, persons in positions of power and advantage today will continue to use schooling to preserve the vantage points for themselves and their progeny, and privileged parents will continue to investigate ways to pass on their advantages to their children. Under this scenario, African American males have the least privilege and the worst access to quality schools and education in the United States (Brown & Davis, 2000; Polite & Davis, 1999).

The Impact of *Brown v. Board of Education* on the American Context of Schooling

In chronicling the beginnings of universal, state-supported public education in the United States, Anderson (1988) notes scholar W. E. B. Du Bois's assertion that "Public education for all at public expense was, in the South, an [African American] idea" (p. 6). Anderson contends that the former slaves sought to replace the negating ideology and system of education that had supported their oppression under slavery and lobbied for the support of Republican politicians, the Freedmen's Bureau, northern missionary societies, and the Union army in that quest. Until that time, privileged southern Whites tolerated the idea of public or "pauper" education as a charity to benefit poor White children only. This hegemonic social arrangement prevailed as the majority of Whites in the South maintained that state government intervention in the education of children was unlawful and would serve to disrupt the established social order.

As the watershed ruling regarding segregated public education, *Brown v. Board of Education* (1954) established the judicial and social standard for open access within school settings in the United States. More specifically, *Brown* had two primary planks: (1) a formal rebuke and condemnation of the American system of apartheid in public education, and (2) the issuance of a clarion call for the provision of educational opportunities for African American students (Carter, 1996; Lagemann & Miller, 1996; Wolters, 1984). Several policymakers hailed these two planks as the remedy for all of America's social ills, believing that 300 years of social, civic, and educational disparity could be resolved via a new initiative—school desegregation. However, despite the varied evidences of good faith toward achieving the goals of the *Brown* ruling, the formal structures of school desegregation did not eradicate the racial hierarchization that was by then virtually wedded to the national social structure, nor did they erase the damage done to the collective and individual consciousnesses of the nation's citizenry (Brown, 1999). Higginbotham (1996) elaborates on this point, positing the following:

> . . . [the] Brown v. Board of Education . . . decision merely struck down state-enforced segregation in public schools. It did not, however, convince a great many white parents in either the North or the South to send their children to school with black children. . . . Eventually the precept of black inferiority and white superiority worked itself into the fabric of the American legal process. The social and color ladder became a legal one as well. Looking for evidence of the precept of inferiority in the American legal process, however, is very much like looking for evidence of slavery in the United States Constitution as originally ratified. . . . Similarly the legal process institutionalized the premise of black inferiority without ever specifically delineating in any one case or statute the entire rationale for the precept of black inferiority. . . . But the legal process as a whole was more subtle in assimilating and perpetuating an ideology in which whiteness was the nimbus of superiority, and blackness the stigma of inferiority. (pp. 15–16)

Beyond the myriad faults, flaws, and failures of the public school (and later collegiate) desegregation case rulings, the general criticism remains the ineffectuality of legal precedent to resolve the systemic issue of African American student achievement, much less the prevailing psychological shackles of racial inferiority on America's public logic (Brown, 1999; Stefkovich & Leas, 1994). Even with nationwide good-faith efforts (and, on rare occasions, felicitous efforts) toward colorblindness in public education, Brown (1995) maintains that "the races [have] remained 'separate' and their education 'unequal'" (p. 34).

Post-Katrina Evidence of Persistent Inequality in the Battle for Dominance and Cultural Capital

This continuing inequality can be argued given recent national statistics, or better yet, statistics from the regions affected in 2005 by Hurricane Katrina. According to Steve Suitts of the Southern Education Foundation (personal communication, May 19, 2006), African Americans constitute the majority among public school students in both Mississippi and Louisiana, 66% and 48%, respectively. He further states:

- Only 13% of Mississippi and Louisiana ninth graders finished high school between 1990 and 2000.
- The high school dropout rate exceeds 40% for both states.
- Standardized test scores in both states are in the lowest quartile nationally.
- Mississippi and Louisiana rank 48th and 43rd in the national ranking of baccalaureate attainment, respectively.
- 21% of African American families in Mississippi, and 22% in Louisiana, earn less than $10,000 per year.

Dyson (2006) offers additional evidence of disparity in his conclusions about the educational status of Black children nationally and those in New Orleans specifically:

> . . . concentrated poverty stifles the academic success of black children. A child's socioe-conomic status, along with other influential factors like teacher/pupil ratio, teacher quality, curriculum materials, expenditures per student, and the age of the school building, greatly affects her academic success. Wealthier parents are able to send their children to better public schools and higher-quality private schools, which, in turn, clear the path for admission to prestigious colleges and universities. New Orleans has a 40 percent illiteracy rate; over 50 percent of black ninth graders won't graduate in four years. Louisiana expends an average of $4,724 per student and has the third-lowest rank for teacher salaries in the nation. The black dropout rates are high and nearly 50,000 students cut class every day. (p. 8)

The disparate social conditions of African American children in Mississippi and Louisiana give context to the disparate achievement rates of African American students within the nation's educational system as a whole. Consequently, the matter of African American students' failure to achieve widespread success in P-16 systems of public education is unlikely to pass soon, even though it is common parlance to assert that K-12 educational systems in the United States form the foundation of our democratic society.

Educators and policymakers often find themselves treading in unfamiliar water because public education historically has been provided broad discretion to establish the most effective means of realizing its professed goals, including goals related to its myriad functions.

The above observations are not new, however. In 1960, W. E. B. Du Bois spoke prophetically about post-segregated schooling in America. He warned educators that several ominous trends would result as American schools were transformed by the *Brown* ruling:

> [African American] teachers will become rarer and in many cases will disappear. [African American] children will be instructed in public schools and taught under unpleasant if not discouraging circumstances. Even more largely than today they will fall out of school, cease to enter high school, and fewer and fewer will go to college. (Aptheker, 1973, p. 151)

Du Bois's premonition has come true. Meaningful differences, and in some cases egregious ones, have come to pass in the school experiences of African American students in primary, secondary, and collegiate settings.

Notwithstanding, teachers continue to shape ideas in the classroom and provide value-added contributions to develop students into productive citizens. However, reports issued in the past half century suggest that American students are ill-equipped to meet the changes of an ever-evolving society. For example, the landmark 1966 Coleman Report was instrumental in promoting racial balance between schools and effecting change in government education policy. Key among the report's findings was evidence that poor African American students performed academically better in integrated, middle-class schools. The report concluded that non-White and White American schoolchildren performed at disparate levels and that this achievement gap only increased in high school.

The bifurcation of schooling in America is fundamentally rooted in the sociological need for domination. It is also rooted, as Collins (2004) contends, in the efforts of individuals to distinguish themselves from others in terms of various categories of moral evaluation such as honor, taste, breeding, respectability, propriety, cultivation, normalcy, and so forth. Collins draws this thesis from German-born sociologist Max Weber's (1978) outline of the three sources of status groups, namely:

- differences in life styles, based on economic situation (for example, social class);
- differences in life situations; and
- differences in life situations that derive directly from cultural conditions or institutions (i.e., geographic origin, ethnicity, religion, or education).

Collins (2004) defines status groups as persons "who share a sense of status equality based on participation in a common culture; styles of language, tastes in clothing and décor, manners and other ritual observances, conversational topics and styles, opinions and values, and preferences in sports, arts, and media" (p. 41). Similarly, contemporary conflict theory posits that educational expansion is best explained by status group struggle.

This discussion of status groups is useful for understanding the inherent need of groups to exclude others to achieve position and capitalist gains. Participation in such cultural groups, Collins asserts, has been shown to provide individuals with a fundamental sense of identity. Educational credentials such as diplomas thus are seen primarily as status symbols rather than indicators of actual achievement (Bourdieu & Passeron, 1977; Collins, 2004; Weber, 1978). The rise of what these scholars term "credentialism," however, does not indicate that society is becoming more expert; rather, it suggests that education increasingly is being used by dominant groups to secure more advantageous places in the occupational and social structure for themselves and their children.

The concept of cultural capital—that is, one's knowledge of particular forms of culture such as music, art, and literature—is also important to this critique because, as Bourdieu and Passeron (1977) assert, cultural capital is passed on primarily by families and schools. Moreover, the cultural characteristics of individuals and groups are significant indicators of their status and class position in society. A growing body of literature suggests that schools convey specific social identities to their students—identities that either enhance or hinder students' life chances (Brown, Dancy, & Norfles, 2006; Ferguson, 2000, in press; Garibaldi, 1992; Noguera, 2003). Thus, one might infer, for example, that graduates from elite prep schools have numerous educational and social advantages over public school graduates insofar as acceptance to elite colleges and occupational mobility are concerned. These advantages, however, are often unrelated to what the prep school graduates learned in school and typically have much more to do with the power of their schools' reputation for educating members of the upper class.

Bourdieu and Passeron's (1977) theories, combined with Collins's (2004) syntheses, provide a useful framework for understanding why education and schooling differences persist between status groups in America. Collins describes education as a mechanism of occupational placement whereby schools either provide students with training that enables them to enter the elite culture or to serve the elite culture. Accordingly, employers view better-educated job applicants as having been socialized more successfully into the dominant culture and as more likely to assume managerial-level positions or rise to the elite corporate ranks. Workers with less education are expected to demonstrate respect for the dominant culture, and for its elites, and are typically selected for lower-level positions.

Leaving Many Children Behind: Conditions and Challenges in Today's Urban Schools

Today's urban schools, in contrast to their suburban and rural counterparts, encounter many economic and demographic issues resulting from their higher concentrations of poor linguistic- and ethnic-minority students. Legters, Balfanz, Jordan, and McPartland (2004) provide keen insights into the myriad challenges facing urban school districts in the United States. As these researchers maintain, urban school districts enroll half of the nation's minority students and one-third of its poor students but only one-quarter of its total public school student population. Moreover, America's urban centers are charged to serve needy populations amid increasing poverty rates and eroding tax bases. Since 1940, Legters et al. contend, middle-class families have been attracted away from the nation's urban centers to suburban areas. Between 1940 and 1980, the proportion of residents living in central cities within a standard metropolitan statistical area (SMSA) dropped more than 22%, with the relocation of manufacturing plants from central-city locations to the suburbs exacerbating this trend. As a result, by the 1980s, urban students, unlike their non-urban counterparts, were more than twice as likely to attend high-poverty schools, or those schools in which more than half the students qualify for free or reduced-price lunches.

Legters et al. (2004) also point out that urban schools serve an educationally needier population of students and more often face the challenges of aging facilities that require expensive maintenance and renovation. Competition from wealthier suburban districts for teachers and dwindling tax bases arguably make urban education costlier than that in other, more advantaged settings. The resulting disparate spending for education virtually assures urban students' predisposition to academically deficient outcomes on most measures, including achievement and graduation rates. One-third to less than one-half of students in urban districts score at the basic level or higher in reading, mathematics, and science compared to over two-thirds of students in non-urban districts (Legters et al., 2004). Similarly, high concentrations of poverty among students in urban schools and their surrounding neighborhoods have implications for students' health, safety, and early transitions into adulthood as well as for the school's daily operations.

Further exacerbating these dilemmas, many students enter the nation's urban high schools with extremely poor prior preparation. According to national data obtained from various achievement tests, these students consistently score below their non-urban counterparts in mathematics, science, and reading (Legters et al., 2004). Students enrolled in urban high schools also are exposed to higher levels of academic, linguistic, and cultural diversity than those enrolled in non-urban high schools (Legters et al., 2004). This increased diversity is often attributed to the larger numbers of students in these schools who require special or individualized services. The predominance of students of color in urban high schools (in some cases reaching over 90%) has led some scholars to argue that increasing racial segregation has completely supplanted the democratizing ideal of comprehensive high schools (Orfield, Eaton, & The Harvard Project on School Desegregation, 1996).

Finally, many urban city school systems, as side effects to their large sizes, become susceptible to bureaucratic inertia, complicated and often contentious politics, and short-term leadership. According to Legters et al. (2004), the average urban school superintendent serves fewer than three years, and nearly a third of all urban school districts are led by superintendents who have served for one year or less.

Poverty has far-reaching ramifications not only for low-income urban neighborhoods but also for the outcomes of students who attend schools within those neighborhoods. Between 1970 and 1990, the population living in census tracts with poverty rates of 40% or greater increased from 5.2% to 10.7% in the country's 100 largest cities (Alexander, 2004). The experience has been even worse for African Americans and Hispanics. In 1990, one fourth of all African Americans (compared to 15.5% in 1970) and 41.6% of low-income African Americans (up from 28.1% in 1970) resided in extreme poverty tracts in these 100 cities; over 80% of low-income African Americans resided in high-poverty tracts (Alexander, 2004). The increasing concentration of poverty among African Americans in urban areas implies a simultaneous concentration of crime, violence, welfare, dependency, family disruption, and educational failure—trends that disadvantage African Americans' cultural and social environments and destabilize and reshape their well-being in society (Alexander, 2004). The considerations for impoverished African American and other students who attend schools under the conditions described above include:

- decreased number of years of schooling
- increased odds of school dropout;
- decreased childhood IQ; and
- increased likelihood of pregnancy and decreased age of first sexual intercourse among African American adolescent girls;
- increased joblessness among African American males
- increased single motherhood among African American females;

The Unique Educational Needs of African American Males

Perhaps the single most important challenge addressed in research reports, policy documents, and public commentary of recent years has been the alarming and increasing disparities found in the educational achievement of African American males vis-à-vis their peers. Indeed, achievement disparities and their consequences generally expose large urban school districts, such as that in New Orleans, and the national educational system as a whole as being in dire need of improvement and reform. Several researchers have reported that urban African American male students are victimized by chronic, systemic levels of poor performance, behavior problems, and disengagement in school (Ferguson, 2000; Noguera, 2003).

Historically, the function and "place" of African American males in American society has often been misunderstood, misinterpreted, and maligned. Current debates on this topic take on even more urgency given the positioning of African American male students relative to their school counterparts and the likely cost in human potential and productivity. Although the social constructions and plight of young African American males are definitely important issues to ponder, for men especially, the most important point of discussion is young African American males' connections to schooling (Brown & Davis, 2000). This issue is critical because of its broader implications for the future of education and for meeting the needs of students who have been estranged by schools. The fate of young, urban African American males from low-income families who are marginalized in the educational system keeps attracting the public's attention, but the public seems to lack the resolve and political will to intervene creatively. A large gap, both theoretical and practice-based, remains to be filled, both in how these young men are represented and constructed in academic and popular literature as well as in programs aimed at addressing their needs. This discontinuity, between what is known and what is actually going on in the lives of African American males in and out of school, begs to be addressed.

In a scathing report first issued in 1988, Garibaldi uncovered unconscionable disparities and experiences in educational and other areas for African American boys and young men in the city of New Orleans. In the wake of Hurricane Katrina, the moral and civic imperative for action for Black males in that region and others is arguably more urgent. While other issues, such as the need to develop and improve housing options, improve the city's damaged infrastructure and provide resources to meet increasing demand for employment opportunities and sustainable living wages are critically important, the implications for differential schooling experiences and outcomes for New Orleans's African American male students may be even more far-reaching. The negative consequences of the achievement disparities noted by Garibaldi (1988) are acute. The potential loss of resources—intellectual, cultural, and economic—resulting from the underachievement of that city's African American males reduces their capacity to be productive, integral and contributing members of society. For sure, the human resources of all New Orleanians will be needed to re-create and sustain the hurricane-wracked families, neighborhood, and communities in that region.

Balancing Agency and Strategy: Changing the Context of Schooling for African American Males in Urban Settings

The dominant perspective on the "African American male problem" calls for solutions that shed little attention on the active role African American males themselves play in creating their own school experience (Brown & Davis, 2000; Noguera, 2003; Polite & Davis, 1999). This is not to say that the ways in which schools, such as those in New Orleans, structure students' opportunities to learn is not salient; inequalities in schooling have lifelong consequences for educational attainment, employment, and family relations. Similarly, access to quality academic programs, curricula, and teacher quality are extremely important for students who bring to school backgrounds and behaviors that are at the margins of schools' expectations. To always suggest, however, that young African American males are victims negates for them any sense of agency in determining how they make meaning of who they are at school.

Very little is known about how school context affects African American male students' educational and social experiences, thus making the interaction of school context and masculine identity important to consider. With regard to masculine identity, an array of strategies has captured the attention of school administrators, local communities, and parents as possible solutions to the problems associated with African American males in public schools. These strategies are of two primary programmatic genres: assistive/supportive and reconstructive (Davis, 1999). Assistive/supportive programs aim to augment and support current school structures by providing African American male youth with the positive presence of adult Black men in school settings. Mentoring programs that assign African American male professionals as role models for young boys, typically in elementary and middle schools, have been established in many school districts, both urban and suburban. Similarly, Black men have been enlisted to serve as teacher's aids, tutors, and reading partners for African American boys needing academic support and guidance. The justification for these initiatives points to the need in educational settings for consistent and positive adult males who can provide role models for young African American males to emulate (Canada, 1998). These programs attempt to counter the negative gender-role socialization of African American males that is peer-inspired and that too often leads to maladaptive masculine identity (Winbush, 2001). Their objective is to develop conceptions and expressions of masculinity that are not antithetical to high-achievement behaviors and attitudes.

Reconstructive programs attempt to counter the negative gender-role socialization of African American males that is peer-inspired and that too often leads to maladaptive masculine identity (Winbush, 2001). The objective of reconstructive programs is to develop conceptions and expressions of masculinity that are not antithetical to high-achievement behaviors and attitudes. Reconstructive programs focus intensely on self-esteem and ethnic identity and include initiatives such as masculine identity development programs (i.e., pathways to manhood, rites-of-passage, etc.).

Economic success is closely linked to success in school, and school failure contributes to limited economic opportunities for African American boys as adults. Schools do not always offer a level playing field for these youth. Rather than fostering positive and productive social environments, schools far too often reduce or minimize their spirit and potential. Much evidence exists to support the claim that schools not only neglect the social, emotive, and developmental needs of African American males but also abuse them emotionally (Brown & Davis, 2000). Whereas African Americans traditionally have placed much faith in public schools, regardless of outcomes and deliverables, the current schooling experiences of many African American males remain yet another disappointment. For many of these young men, school is a place that ignores their aspirations, disrespects their ability to learn, fails to access and cultivate their hidden talents, and restricts their identity options. Unfortunately, too many of these students simply give up and give into low expectations and misguided notions of "authentic" self-definition. In this regard, however, African American males are no different from other students in schools across the nation.

Stone (1997) defines security as "protecting people's identities as well as their existence" (p. 90). Although often disregarded, needs are critical components of security. In order to substantiate or establish some sense of academic authority, schools must first ensure that all reasonable student needs are met or accommodated. Hence, any examination of student achievement must necessarily include an investigation of student needs. This line of reasoning begs the question: Do African American students, especially males but indeed all students, have access to meaningful networks, adequate resources, and enriching opportunities—their most basic academic needs?

The motivation behind the desegregation of schooling in the American South in the 1950s was originally the provision of a better education for African American students (Halpern, 1995; Kluger, 1975). The original logic posited that desegregated education would grant African American students access to resources, networks, and opportunities unavailable in their segregated schools. However, this thinking did not include any alteration in the culture, climate, or constitution of the existing instructional setting—which, though segregated, embodied for Whites equity, efficiency, community, security, and liberty. Even though the segregated school systems provided a uniquely affirming educational environment for African American students, proponents argued that desegregated schools would provide Black youth with new intellectual outlets and serve as catalysts for universal social mobility. What appears to have gone unexplored since desegregated schooling became the law of the land is the significant role of education as a source of empowerment.

Empowerment only occurs when educational settings provide students with a sense of ownership and belonging. However, as Kunjufu (1988) and other researchers assert, African American students generally do not feel a sense of ownership and/or belonging in desegregated school settings. To counter this, Delpit (as cited in Halsey, Lauder, Brown, & Wells, 1997) argues that African American students must be granted participation in the "culture of power" that exists within schools and in broader social contexts. Delpit asserts that five aspects of this culture of power should be considered insofar as the matriculation of African American students in P-16 public education is concerned. They include the following:

- Issues of power are enacted in classrooms;
- There are codes or rules for participating in the structures of power;
- The rules of the culture of power are a reflection of the rules of the culture of those who have the power;
- If you are not already a participant in the culture of power, being told explicitly the rules of that culture makes acquiring power easier;
- Those with power are frequently least aware of—or at least not willing to acknowledge—its existence, while those with less power are often most aware of its existence. (p. 583)

Delpit maintains that educational settings must engage in mutually respectful relationships with their primary constituents—students. To the extent that this goal can be accomplished, many of the P-16 pipeline issues involving African American students, particularly African American males, in primary, secondary, and higher education must be addressed.

Conclusion

> Race and class are two of the most salient social issues that the [nation] has failed to come to grips with. Katrina blew their cover—and if we are honest, it blew our cover, too. We will remain imperiled if we postpone grappling with the lethal effects of race and class in our society. (Dyson, 2006, p. 138)

Despite the best efforts of a broad range of stakeholders, many of our nation's children are still being left behind. Nowhere across the country is this more evident than in the data and phenomena washed ashore by the floodwaters of Hurricane Katrina. Media pundits have scurried to conceptualize the interim and long-term implications of a hurricane whose damaging consequences were as meaningful and far-reaching as its tempest. Hurricane Katrina did not simply tear the roofs from homes. It also tore the roof off the American educational system to reveal glaring differences between school types, cultures, successes, failures, and national responses—before a worldwide audience.

In the aftermath of the Katrina disaster, the federal government continues to send out a loud and clear message of hypocrisy that commands American children to endure the woes of disparate public education. The national conglomeration of educational associations and affiliations has by and large conjoined in silence with the amorphous conclave of "privileged" parents whose children attend "good" schools. The goal of providing quality schooling for all children—without respect to advantage or privilege—has been spitefully disengaged with all the concern of a drearily cloaked mistress peering sternly down her nose and over the edge of her spectacles at a disappointing child. However, this lack of regard should not be allowed to become the status quo. Education in the United States must be redefined and revamped to accommodate diverse student populations. Radical systemic change is required in order to move from the equality of educational opportunity offered by *Brown v. Board of Education* to the equity of educational outcomes demanded by the global economy. As novelist and social activist James Baldwin (1962/1993) opined in an essay titled "My Dungeon Shook: Letter to My Nephew on the One-Hundredth Anniversary of Emancipation":

> I know what the world has done to my brother and how narrowly he has survived it. And I know, which is much worse, and this is the crime of which I accuse my country and my countrymen, and for which neither I nor time nor history will ever forgive them, that they have destroyed and are destroying hundreds of thousands of lives and do not know it and do not want to know it. . . . But it is not permissible that the authors of devastation should also be innocent. It is the innocence which constitutes the crime. (pp. 5–6)

Now, in the early years of the 21st century, African American students and other similarly situated groups must be sufficiently prepared to meet the challenges of an ever-evolving global society. Acknowledging and embracing the full ambitions of education on a massive and broad scale will enable educators to formulate a systemic remedy to the problems that hinder student success. If all students succeed, the world will prosper and benefit. Should our best efforts to improve the quality of schooling for all students fail, the words of the African American spiritual might be found true—"God gave Noah the rainbow sign. No more water, the fire next time!"

REFERENCES

Alexander, K. L. (2004). Public schools and the public good. In J. H. Ballantine & J. Z. Spade (Eds.), *Schools and society: A sociological approach to education* (2nd ed., pp. 234–49). Belmont, CA: Thomson Wadsworth.

Anderson, J. D. (1988). *The education of Blacks in the south, 1860–1935.* Chapel Hill: The University of North Carolina Press.

Aptheker, H. (Ed.). (1973). *The education of Black people: Ten critiques, 1906–1960.* Amherst: University of Massachusetts Press.

Baldwin, J. (1993). *The fire next time.* New York: Vintage International. (Original work published 1962)

Bernstein, B. (1974). *Class, codes, and control.* London: Routledge & Kegan Paul.

Bourdieu, P., & Passeron, J. C. (1977). *Reproduction in education, society and culture.* London: Sage.

Brown v. Board of Education of Topeka. 347 U.S. 483 (1954).

Brown, M. C. (1999). *The quest to define collegiate desegregation: Black colleges, title VI compliance, and post-Adams litigation.* Westport, CT: Bergin & Garvey.

Brown, M. C. (1995). In defense of the public historically Black college and its mission. *The National Honors Report, 16,* 34–40.

Brown, M. C., Dancy, T. E., & Norfles, N. (2006). A nation still at risk: No child left behind and the salvation of disadvantaged students. In F. Brown (Ed.), *No child left behind and other special programs and urban districts* (pp. 341–64). Oxford: Elsevier.

Brown, M. C., & Davis, J. E. (2000). *Black sons to mothers: Compliments, critiques, and challenges for cultural workers in education.* New York: Peter Lang.

Brown, M. C., & Ratcliff, J. L. (1998). Multiculturalism and multicultural curriculum in the USA. *Higher Education in Europe, 23,* 11–21.

Canada, G. (1998). *Reaching up for manhood: Transforming the lives of boys in America.* Boston: Beacon Press.

Carbonaro, W. J. (1998, October). A little help from my friends' parents: Intergenerational closure and educational outcomes. *Sociology of Education,* 71, 295–313.

Carter, R. (1996). The unending struggle for equal educational opportunity. In E. Lagemann & L. Miller (Eds.), Brown v. Board of Education: *The challenge for today's schools* (pp. 19–26). New York: Teachers College Press.

Coleman, J. S., Campbell, E. Q., Hobson, C. F., McPartland, J. M., Mood, A. M., Weinfeld, F. D., & York, R. L. (1966). *Equality of educational opportunity.* Washington, DC: U.S. Government Printing Office.

Coleman, J. S., & Hoffer, T. (1987). *Public and private high school: The impact of communities.* New York: Basic Books.

Collins, R. (2004). Conflict theory of educational stratification. In J. H. Ballantine & J. Z. Spade (Eds.), *Schools and society: A sociological approach to education* (pp. 41–49). Belmont, CA: Thomson Wadsworth.

Collins, R. (1971). Functional and conflict theories of educational stratification. *American Sociological Review, 36,* 1000–1019.

Davis, J. E. (1999). Forbidden fruit: Black males' constructions of transgressive sexualities in middle school. In W. J. Letts & J. T. Sears (Eds.), *Queering elementary education: Advancing the dialogue about sexualities and schooling* (pp. 49–59). Lanham, MD: Rowman & Littlefield.

DiMaggio, P. (1982). Cultural capital and school success: The impact of status culture participation on the grades of United States high school students. *American Sociological Review, 47,* 189–201.

DiMaggio, P. & Mohr, J. (1985). Cultural capital, educational attainment, and marital selection. *American Journal of Sociology, 90,* 1231–61.

Dyson, M. E. (2006). *Come hell or high water: Hurricane Katrina and the color of disaster.* New York: Basic Civitas.

Ferguson, A. A. (in press). Making a name for yourself: Transgressive acts and gender performance. In M. Kimmel & M. Messner (Eds.), *Men's lives* (7th ed.). Boston: Allyn & Beacon.

Ferguson, A. A. (2000). *Bad boys: Public schools and the making of Black masculinity.* Ann Arbor: University of Michigan Press.

Gamoran, A. (2004). American schooling and educational inequality: A forecast for the 21st century. In J. H. Ballantine, & J. Z. Spade (Eds.), *Schools and society: A sociological approach to education* (2nd ed., pp. 249–65). Belmont, CA: Thomson Wadsworth.

Garibaldi, A. (1992). Educating and motivating African American males to succeed. *Journal of Negro Education, 61*(1), 4–11.

Garibaldi, A. M. (1988). *Educating Black male youth: A moral and civic imperative.* New Orleans, LA: Committee to Study the Status of Black Males in the New Orleans Public Schools.

Gordon, E. (1995). Toward an equitable system of educational assessment. *Journal of Negro Education, 64*(3), 360–72.

Halpern, S. C. (1995). On the limits of the law: The ironic legacy of Title VI of the 1964 Civil Rights Act. Baltimore: The Johns Hopkins University.

Halsey, A. H., Lauder, H., Brown, P., & Wells, A. S. (Eds.). (1997). *Education: Culture, economy, and society.* Oxford: Oxford University Press.

Hess, F. M., & Petrilli, M. J. (2006). *No child left behind: A Primer.* New York: Peter Lang.

Higginbotham, A. L. (1996). Shades of freedom: Racial politics and presumptions of the American legal process. New York: Oxford University Press.

Hill, P. T., & Hannaway, J. (2006). *The future of public education in New Orleans* [Online]. Available: http://www.urban.org/publications/900913.html

Kluger, R. (1975). Simple justice: The history of *Brown v. Board of Education* and Black America's struggle for equality. New York: Knopf.

Kunjufu, J. (1988). *To be popular or smart: The Black peer group.* Chicago: African-American Images.

Lagemann, E., & Miller, L. P. (Eds.). (1996). Brown v. Board of Education: *The challenge for today's schools.* New York: Columbia University.

Lareau, A. (2000). *Home advantage* (2nd ed.). Lanham, MD: Rowman & Littlefield.

Legters, N. E., Balfanz, R., Jordan, W. J., & McPartland, J. M. (2004). Comprehensive reform for urban high schools. In J. H. Ballantine & J. Z. Spade (Eds.), *Schools and society: A sociological approach to education* (2nd. ed., pp. 220–27). Belmont, CA: Thomson Wadsworth.

Moore, D. M. (1999). *National experts judge Chicago's program of retaining students a failure* [Online]. Available: http://www.dfc1.0rg

National Commission on Excellence in Education. (1983). *A nation at risk* [Online]. Retrieved February 1, 2006, from http://www.ed.gov/pubs/NatAtRisk/index.html.

Noguera, P. (2003). The trouble with Black boys: The role and influence of environment and cultural status on the academic performance of African American males. *Urban Education, 38,* 431–459.

Orfield, G., Eaton S., & The Harvard Project on School Desegregation. (1996). *Dismantling desegregation.* New York: The New Press.

Polite, V., & Davis, J. E. (1999). African American males in school and society: Practices and policies for effective education. New York: Teachers College Press.

Raftery, A. E., & Hout, M. (1993). Maximally maintained inequality: Expansion, reform, and opportunity in Irish education, 1921–1975. *Sociology of Education, 66,* 22–39.

Stefkovich, J., & Leas, T. (1994, Summer). A legal history of desegregation in higher education. *Journal of Negro Education, 63*(3), 406–20.

Steinberg, J. (2000, December 22). Student failure causes states to retool programs. *New York Times,* A1, A19.

Stone, D. (1997). *Policy paradox: The art of political decision making.* New York: W. W. Norton.

Useem, E. L. (1992). Middle schools and math groups: Parents' involvement in children's placement. *Sociology of Education, 65,* 263–279.

Weber, M. (1978). *Economy and society,* Vols. 1 & 2 (G. Roth & C. Wittich, Eds. & Trans.) Berkeley: University of California Press.

Winbush, R. A. (2001*). The warrior method: A program for rearing healthy Black boys.* New York: Amistad.

Wolters, R. (1984). *The burden of* Brown: *Thirty years of school desegregation.* Knoxville: University of Tennessee Press.

■|■|■

CHAPTER 7

Reflections on Educational Equity in Post-Katrina New Orleans

VIVIAN L. GADSDEN & SUSAN FUHRMAN

Although some time has passed since Hurricane Katrina, the future of the schools in New Orleans, the future of the city's education system, and that of its children and families are uncertain. For those who follow schooling and school reform efforts in urban centers, and for us as researchers committed to improving urban schools, New Orleans offers a particularly compelling context to discuss the issues of equity and promise. The past problems of the city and the school district mirror those of many other urban school districts; however, focusing on its future has the potential to be instructive for observers of urban schooling and policy. In the process of rebuilding, educators, politicians, policymakers, and residents have unprecedented opportunities to rethink issues of educational equity and to reform the educational system for the better. Unfortunately, the actions taken by the state and federal government since the hurricane have failed to allay fears that long-standing problems affecting the most vulnerable will not be addressed. A future-oriented effort toward educational change and equity for New Orleans and other areas in the region must redress past failures to ensure equity while committing to the elimination of potential inequities of quality and access to resources and opportunity.

In this chapter, we are interested in examining the problems and promise for equity and quality schooling in New Orleans, sensitive to and concerned about the limitations of both concepts in reaching those in greatest need. We believe that a focus on these issues, accompanied by an emphasis on excellence (addressed by scholars in a recently published issue of *Voices in Urban Education,* 2006) is necessary—not simply to change the circumstances of children and families but specifically to improve them. At the same time, we acknowledge the inequities and the intricacies of race and poverty that existed prior to the hurricane and that will persist into post-hurricane planning in the absence of dedicated, strategic goals and efforts.

In the remainder of this essay, we focus briefly on three areas: educational equity and the attendant problems of racial and economic disparities; the implications of displacement and relocation on children; and redress of past problems and viable alternatives to shape the future.

(In)Equity as a Context in New Orleans

The devastation of Hurricane Katrina brought to the surface a range of educational problems—i.e., poor schooling, inequity, and low academic achievement—that have long plagued New Orleans and the Gulf Coast region and that have been at the center of debates among policy analysts, researchers, and practitioners. Before the hurricane, the Louisiana Department of Education, itself challenged by problems of uneven resources for urban and rural parishes in the state, had determined that New Orleans was in academic crisis (Center for American Progress, 2005). The hurricane destroyed most of the public education system in New Orleans (i.e., its physical school structures) with fewer than 20 of the 120 school buildings being usable (Hill & Hannaway, 2006). Concurrently, it destroyed local and state tax bases, the district's primary source of revenues. Among the children and families who left the city after the hurricane were teachers and administrators, many of whom relocated to other communities in and out of the state. The superintendent and other top administrators reportedly had returned to the city by early 2006, but the actual number of teachers who have returned since is unclear; recent accounts suggest that many children and their parents will not return either.

Similar to many other urban school districts, the students who attended the public schools in New Orleans prior to the hurricane were disproportionately poor and minority, mostly African American. High school dropout rates were high, and achievement scores were low. Educational and social inequities were evident in low teacher salaries, high unemployment and underemployment among the parents of children in the school system, and single-mother births accounted for more than half of the births in poor families. A culture also existed among whites and blacks in which few questions were asked, and traditions that reinforced race and class barriers were rarely challenged.

Hence, even before the hurricane, New Orleans was positioned as a site requiring critical examination of educational equity and student achievement. Interpretations of educational equity often focus on the ways that issues of racial and social equality, equal access, and distribution of funding and revenue are inextricably linked (Koski & Levin, 2000; Orfield & Lee, 2005). New Orleans was a prime site in which to examine these issues and their relationship to funding disparities. School funding discrepancies are both derived from and affect the economic disparities in neighborhoods, with poor neighborhoods comprised of primarily African Americans and other minorities who shoulder the burdens of the inequities. In 2004, African Americans constituted 68 percent of the population of New Orleans, and the median earnings of those 16 years and older were $18,939 (Center for American Progress, 2005). In the Katrina-affected areas, 90,000 people had incomes of less than $10,000; New Orleans, which is located in the second poorest state in the United States, had a poverty rate 76 percent higher than the national average in 2004 (Center for American Progress, 2005).

The issues of quality, equity, structure, and operational competence have challenged almost all school districts (Koski, 2003). The disparity results not from a failure of poor communities to participate in self-taxing; in fact, poor communities often over-tax themselves (Hoff, 1997). When these poor communities over-tax themselves, the funding disparities decrease, but only slightly and only over the short term. Communities with low property values have low per-student funding levels, and the communities with high property values have high per-student spending levels, despite low property tax rates. With existing formulas, poor districts can never catch up or achieve comparable funding to wealthier districts. In addition, wealthier districts have other financial and human resources that are not factored in state funding formulas.

Funding disparities, and the reduced resources, affect poor children and poor minority children in the quality of resources available to ensure their achievement. Students in under-funded school districts such as New Orleans typically score lower on standardized measures than do students in well-funded districts, regardless of family income. These achievement patterns reflect the same problems as the national picture. However, on some indices of children's well being (e.g., outcomes for young children), the local and state picture in New Orleans and Louisiana is worse than the national picture (Golden, 2006; *Kids Count,* Annie E. Casey Foundation, 2005). Hill and Hannaway (2006), drawing upon data from the Louisiana Department of Education, indicate that in the 2004–2005 academic year, only 44 percent of fourth graders in Orleans Parish were proficient in reading and only 26 percent in math. Eighth graders performed even worse: 26 percent were proficient in reading and 15 percent were proficient in math. Almost 75 percent of the schools in the district had received an academic warning or were rated "academically unacceptable" in the 2003–2004 academic year. Moreover, the school district faced a $25 to 30 million deficit for 2005–2006 (Hill & Hannaway, 2006).

The slow rebuilding over the past year makes it difficult to imagine the former Orleans Parish emerging again any time soon or at all. The district will not know for some time how many students it will serve. Like other urban school districts, the New Orleans school district was neither designed for nor prepared to handle the kinds of traumas created by the hurricane; it was prepared to think about the future only in the context of past student populations, amount and distribution of resources, and dilemmas around poor student achievement (Hill & Hannaway, 2006). The questions that persist are: Will these children return to a system that is prepared to provide quality schooling? Will they be able to face the dilemmas created over time by segregation and the accompanying issues of race and class disparities that influence how, when, how well, and with what commitment those in power take up the responsibility of educational equity?

Issues around equity cannot be solved by the New Orleans school district without external urging and support—from state sources and expertise available from other states and localities, educational specialists in and outside of institutions of higher education, institutions of higher education outside the region, and from a compassionate public willing to provide personal and professional resources. The federal government must contribute increased and strategic assistance to equalize school funding through programs that it supports as well. Lastly, the city and nation must commit themselves to change. Interventions that might have alleviated the problems prior to the hurricane were not implemented.

Although their implementation would not have forestalled the hurricane, they would have provided the fundamental infrastructure and safety net to address much needed policy and on-the-ground efforts of the present. Turner (2006) reports that only half of the 500,000 pre-Katrina residents of New Orleans expect to return by 2008. However, it is likely that this number may be dramatically higher, depending on the experiences of the displaced in their new homes; the degree to which kin and other social networks are created; and the availability of employment, housing, and schools for their children.

The Faces of the Children of New Orleans

Issues of educational equity and social equality often take on a different appearance when they are associated with individual faces of children and families. In the early aftermath of the hurricane, *NBC News* interviewed and presented the striking commentary of Charles Evans, a nine-year-old boy from New Orleans who summed up poignantly the frustration, despair, desperation, and fledgling hope of the displaced. He became the voice of the displaced and in a series of targeted statements captured the incredulity of both the disaster and the government's response. Since the interview, Charles and many other school-age children have been attending schools in other parts of Louisiana, Mississippi, and cities throughout the United States. While news reports highlight the conditions of these displaced children and families and, more recently, of the increased crime waves in cities such as Atlanta and Houston (described as a by-product of the relocation), fewer reports have addressed issues of education and schooling—either the efforts of the schools and school districts that now house the Gulf Coast region's displaced or the plans of local agencies in the Gulf Coast region to address the needs of displaced/returning students and their families. One can imagine that an assumption guiding current efforts is that once housing and other basic needs are addressed adequately, the reorganization of the schools and educational systems will follow. This assumption is problematic.

Should the relocated children return to New Orleans, they will be different from when they left. They will have experienced school districts and settings that, in September, were unfamiliar to them; some will have had many positive experiences while others will have had a preponderance of negative experiences. They will return with memories of their past, both fond and painful. However, they will not change their ethnic and racial identities, and they probably will not be better off economically. During the year and upon the children's return, there well may be talk about their resilience, but not enough talk about the personal, familial, and school storms they have weathered.

The impact of experiencing poverty and observing trauma and undue stress of the magnitude and duration experienced by the children and families of New Orleans may be massively underestimated. There is a curious pattern of unstated expectation by adults of children placed at risk and in vulnerable circumstances: That the children have at their disposal a package of strategies that they can access readily to rise above any adverse circumstance. This view does not lead to the creation or implementation of needed support for children. In other words, children are revered for their persistence and resilience—to get along with so little and to be able to withstand hardship—but this admiration does not necessarily relieve them of the weighty responsibilities for self-care and survival (Burton, 2001; Rutter, 1986; Spencer, 2006).

The children may well be resilient, but they are also vulnerable—not only to typical developmental transitions and the effects of their Hurricane Katrina experiences but also to the ambivalence of a society that continues to wrestle with issues of access and opportunity for the poor and minorities. The thousands of displaced children of New Orleans and their families who have relocated in other cities are predisposed to a range of residual effects of their displacement, the trauma of the disaster, and the apparently indeterminable response to their plight. Children such as Georgnell Addison and Nicholas Wright, who were featured in the press, were forcefully wrenched from known, cherished possessions, familiar locales, and family and friends and relocated to places that are different along multiple dimensions (Gordon, 2005). Many other children have been accepted in districts as a function of legal mandates as well as human generosity. Not surprisingly, many of the relocated children have experienced difficulties. The trauma of the disaster coupled with the uncertainty and temporal nature of their resettlement disrupted the developmental transitions of childhood and adolescence.

Research on the well-being and welfare of children in developmental psychology, psychiatry, medicine, social work, and other disciplines highlights the real and potential impact of trauma for children in different parts of the world. In the United States, this work has addressed the experiences of children and families affected by natural disasters, e.g., Hurricane Andrew and Hurricane Hugo (Krueger & Stretch, 2003). It shows "varying and divergent estimates" of a causal link between disaster and psychopathological consequences, among them, affective disorders, post-traumatic stress disorder (PSTD), behavioral difficulties, or general emotional distress (Krueger & Stretch, 2000).

These effects differ by race and gender, with race being dominant. For example, March, Amaya-Jackson, Terry, and Constanzo (1998) demonstrated that race as well as gender led to differential outcomes following a disaster. After both Hurricane Andrew and Hurricane Hugo, African Americans (both male and female) were more likely to exhibit PTSD than Whites, White women exhibited it more than White men, and African American youths reported PTSD symptoms more frequently than either White or other minority youths (Lonigan, Shannon, Finch, Daugherty, & Taylor, 1991; March et al., 1998). Lonigan and his colleagues' (1991) study of children three months after Hurricanes Andrew and Hugo found a correlation between increased disaster exposure and increased anxiety among females. Riad and Norris (1996) found high levels of stress in children six months following a disaster, while Prinstein and his colleagues (1996) found that for the 606 elementary school-age children in their study a considerable amount of PTSD persisted ten months after Hurricane Andrew. Researchers are typically cautious in generalizing findings from studies focused on brief disasters to longer-term trauma. However, in the case of Hurricane

Katrina, the failure of the government's response shifted the disaster from a short-term incident with serious implications to a protracted experience of uncertainty and anxiety that is unlikely to disappear soon.

In comparison to the schools that the displaced students left, the new schools exhibit little difference in terms of student achievement data, particularly for poor African American children. Most of the relocated African American children attend schools where the demographics of the student body are similar to those of the schools they left. Of the 11 cities with the highest numbers of displaced families, half are predominantly black, and the poverty rates among blacks is two to four times higher than the percentage rates of poor whites.

In Houston, many displaced African American students attend Scarborough High School where most of the 950 students are from poor African American and Latino families (Herrick, 2005). In 2004–2005, the school failed to meet federal guidelines for progress in math and language arts, encountered low graduation rates, and had few of its graduates attending college. One social worker from Scarborough reported that Black students entering the system "were threatening to the black kids" already in the district while another suggested that the students from New Orleans moved quickly into a "survival mode," attempting to maintain a little semblance of self and dignity (Herrick, 2005). Bereft of other resources, the children relied on elements they could control—their personal and physical strengths. This often created confrontational situations that exacerbated rather than reduced their problems (Herrick, 2005).

All evacuees, regardless of age, social position, or responsibility, face uncertainty about the future, their perceived status in new communities, and perceptions of those in the receiving communities. Displaced children were often separated from their families for extended periods of time which compounded their trauma. Parents who were able to find their children early faced questions of where to turn and how they and their children would fare in new settings. Children relocated to new dwellings and new schools have had to adapt to new situations, new students, new ways of working in school, and new expectations. If and when they return to New Orleans, they will need to return to a system of promise as well.

Supporting Children to Achieve Their Promise

The work toward rebuilding the educational system in New Orleans is on its way as is evidenced by the report of the New Orleans post-disaster Education Commission that was released on January 17, 2006. Providing an administrative framework including leaner district offices, charter schools, and partnerships with parents and communities, its 33 recommendations also include new goals, approaches, and services[S1] (The Education Commission Final report, 2005). However, the future of the schools and the children of New Orleans is also uncertain, particularly with regard to the reforms needed to make sure that their education will prepare them to assume critical roles in society. Rebuilding will require both vision and considerable investment of time, energy, and work. Because of the magnitude of the devastation and the complexity of the relationships between the state and the local school district, no single or strategic plan has emerged. However, several promising ideas have been suggested—from creative instructional ideas to innovative ways of using technology. The efficacy of these ideas may vary, depending on how many children and families return and over what time frame. Whatever the plan, it must situate the most vulnerable children and families to achieve their goals, making the circumstances of their birth secondary to their potential. As discussions about schools occur efforts must be undertaken to secure employment, housing, training, and support for the parents and other caregivers of the children who currently attend the schools and of those who will return to ensure that all have the chance to be better off when they return than when they left. In recent monographs by the Urban Institute as well as short commentaries in other printed venues, different models have been presented. For example Hill and Hannaway (2006) suggest that "demography will be destiny," referring to the reality that the New Orleans of the future may have a dramatically different population from the New Orleans of the past. However, it is unlikely that the city will be constituted with upper middle-income families only. Indeed, the poor and minorities, whether African American or not, not will be there, and the demographic shifts may dictate increases in different kinds of services, e.g., bilingual educational and resettlement programs.

There are multiple concerns that will require different levels of government to address collaboratively. These should be the concerns of educational institutions (in other school districts and in colleges and universities) that have the capacity and expertise to contribute. Hill and Hannaway propose four factors that New Orleans and Louisiana should consider in creating and enacting next steps:

- the provision of quality schooling for children who return to New Orleans, as soon as they arrive and whenever they arrive;
- matching the needs of the student population and the diversity of schools and instructional programs;
- the provision of the most qualified, competent, and committed teachers, prepared to take on the uncertainties and the certain difficulties of rebuilding;
- investment in buildings, instructional programs, and people who meet the needs of the district in the present, with an eye toward the future but without promises in an uncertain future.

In addition, if New Orleans is going to move forward successfully, the city and the state must develop a plan to decomplicate the mission of systems that undermine the development of effective and positive change and to increase the likelihood that children will succeed. Because the state cannot assume oversight for all of the city's schools, the charter schools and externally contracted schools have received considerable attention, although the potential for either to address the problems of equity and access cannot be assured if past successes are to be used. Moreover, the significant support for charter schools is both a plus and a minus if there is concern about equity and quality teaching. Charter schools vary vastly in quality and are not on their own a single response to a multi-tiered complex problem. In much the same way that wealth influenced the funding levels of districts in old formulas, charter schools located in more affluent areas will likely have access to more resources, higher expectations of children, and quality experiences. Grappling with the demographic shifts, linguistic differences, and cultural, racial, familial, and poverty problems in most urban school systems such as New Orleans requires a level and type of knowledge, preparation, and commitment unprecedented in the past. In both charter schools and externally contracted schools, local, state, and federal governments will need to be determined, demanding, and vigilant. Furthermore, all levels of government need to build on the compassion, commitment, and support of the public and construct appropriate systems to bring about positive change.

Systems change has at least two faces that should be considered in the effort to align local and state goals in the rebuilding. The first highlights the historically adversarial relationships that exist between large urban centers (and their school systems) and state education departments. Urban centers are seen by both state government officials and by residents in small towns and rural areas as liabilities. In other words, there is a shared perception that cities are a drain on the resources of the state, fed by a variety of negative images of cities and portrayals of the people in them, because large urban school districts often differ dramatically in demography from other areas throughout a state. Second, politics—and resources—tend to favor the communities that occupy the majority of the state rather than the urban centers.

Many researchers suggest that in asserting such change urban school leaders should not attempt to transform every part of a district's program at the same time. Rather, they should conduct a careful survey of the field of issues, past and present programs, and the people within the systems to determine where the potential points of convergence, possibility, and opportunity lie—i.e., between identifiable and emerging problems and possible or proven remedies. Determining what constitutes a problem may depend on the degree to which the problem debilitates students, families, and teachers or the likelihood that solutions will provide results, be replicable, and increase learning for students, administrators, and teachers. Strong programs need to be implemented not only in response to the emergency triggered by Katrina but also over the long term.

In addition, any effort intended to identify the needs of children and families returning should bring together the multiple agencies focused on children and families within and outside of schools—social services and health systems—as well as the court and corrections systems that have traditionally not focused on the children of their constituency. If the system is decentralized, organized team school and municipal leaders, teachers, and parents might serve to enhance the development and implementation and review the processes of implementation.

Lastly, a primary ingredient for children's achievement and educational success is teachers' commitment to high quality teaching, administrators' support of teachers and students, and teachers' and administrators' commitment to engaging students through interesting curricula. Teachers are essential to the rebuilding of the system—teachers who place appropriate and necessary importance on building reciprocal relationships of trust and respect within classroom settings and with parents and community members, the expectation of excellence, motivating students, and investing in tasks that will help students achieve their learning potential. The planners and implementers must be sure that the ceiling for achievement is raised. Schools must not become stuck at getting children to grade level, reveling in the short-term gains instead of using these gains as a mechanism to spur the development of sound pedagogy and high-quality schools with quality teaching.

Closing Considerations

Two themes ground our discussion and our assumptions about what can constitute promise for the children of New Orleans—those who will return and those who never left. The first is that the individual and systemic educational problems facing displaced children and families are not situated in schools and school systems alone. The second is that a focus on educational systems and schooling will not happen naturally—that, in fact, such a focus at the outset of any effort is perhaps an unnatural act, given the range and severity of needs of families and the comparably limited resources. Any consideration of the past must include redress of the past. Any consideration for the future must accept the challenges of the present facing schools and of the transitions that children and families are now forced to make. Any effort for the future must construct an image of promise in which the multiplicity of needs and prospects and of problems and possibilities for children and families are imagined, wrestled with, and addressed.

The problems of New Orleans are the problems of the nation, and effort to improve will require the investment of the nation. There is little doubt that urban school districts such as New Orleans and the poor children and families in them are increasingly isolated and vulnerable, not simply by the day-to-day complexities of urban life but also by the intergenerational legacies of unemployment, hardship, inadequate resources, crime, strained family and community life, and a range of other circumstances. Despite the problems created by the hurricane and the ensuing distress and anger, children and families who return to New Orleans will, as they have in the past, depend on the system for help and will expect their confidence in the system to be merited, unlike their experiences in the past. On the one hand, schools can be seen often (or remembered by parents) in uncomplimentary ways: e.g., as unfriendly buildings, spaces of discontent, sources of cultural discontinuity, or places for failure. On the other hand, schools and other educational resources can be seen as sites for and of learning, places of safety and engagement, community resources, gathering spaces, or sources of caring.

REFERENCES

Burton, L. M. (2001). One step forward and two steps back: Neighborhoods, adolescent development, and unmeasured variable. In A. Booth & A. C. Crouter (Eds.), *Does it take a village? Community effects on children, adolescents, and families* (pp. 149–159). Mahwah, NJ: Lawrence Erlbaum. .

Center for American Progress. (2005, September 2). *Who are Katrina's victims?* Retrieved September 3, 2005, from http://www.americanprogress.org/site/pp.asp?c=biJRJ80VF&b=1023681

The Education Commission Final Report. (2006, January 17). www.bringneworleansback.org

Fuhrman, Gadsden, V. L. (1995). *The absence of father: Effects on children's development and family functioning.* Philadelphia, PA: University of Pennsylvania, National Center on Fathers and Families.

Golden, O., & Turner, M. A. (2005, November 29). *Resiliency is not enough: Young children and the rebuilding of New Orleans.* Retrieved November 30, 2005, from http://www.urban.org/publications/900900.html.

Gordon, J. (2005, September 18). A golden rule: Enrollment for all; Schools around the state are opening their doors to children displaced by Hurricane Katrina. *New York Times,* p. 1.

Herrick, T. (2005, December 2). Teen tension trails hurricane evacuees into Houston school. *Wall Street Journal,* p. A.1.

Hill, J., & Johnson, F. (2005). *Revenues and expenditures by public school districts: School 2002–03.* Retrieved November 30, 2005, from http://nces.ed.gov/pubs2006/2006312.pdf

Hill, P. T., & J. Hannaway, J. (2006, January 30). *The future of public education in New Orleans.* Retrieved February 1, 2006, from http://www.urban.org/publications/900913.html.

Hoff, D. J. (1997a, April 16). Chapter 1 study documents impact of poverty. *Education Week,* p. 22.

Hoff, D. J. (1997b, April 2). Chapter 1 aid failed to close learning gap. *Education Week,* p. 1.

Johnston, R. C. (1998, June 24). Report finds no easy solutions for disparities in school funding. *Education Week,* p. 41.

Koski, W. S. (2003). Of fuzzy standards and institutional constraints: A re-examination of the jurisprudential history of education finance reform litigation. *Santa Clara Law Review, 43,* 1185–1298.

Koski, W. S., & Levin. H. (2000). Twenty-five years after Rodriguez: What have we learned?" *Teachers College Record, 102*(3), 480–513.

Krueger, L., & Stretch, J. (2003). Identifying and helping long term child and adolescent disaster victims: Model and method. *Journal of Social Service Research, 300*(2), 93–108 .

Krueger, L., & Stretch, J. (2003). Long term PTSD among adolescent disaster victims: An empirical assessment. In M. Zakoure (Ed.), *Disaster and traumatic stress research: Tulane studies in social welfare* (pp. 151–173). New Orleans: Tulane University Press.

LaRock, J. D., & Rodriguez-Farrar, H. (2005). Katrina and Rita: What can the United States learn from international experiences with education in displacement? *Harvard Educational Review, 75,* 357–363.

Lonigan, C. Y., Shannon, M. P., Finch, A. J., Daugherty, T. K., & Taylor, C. M. (1991). Children's reactions to a natural disaster: Symptom severity and degree of exposure. *Advances in Behaviorial Research and Therapy, 13,* 135–154.

March, J., Amaya-Jackson, L., Murray, L., & Schule, A. (1998). Cognitive-Behavioral psychotherapy for children and adolescents with PTSD after a single-incident stressor. *Journal of the Academy of Child and Adolescent Psychiatry, 37,* 585–593.

Orfield, G., & Lee, C. (2005, January). Why segregation matters: Poverty and educational inequality. Retrieved March 1, 2005, from http://www.civilrightsproject.harvard.edu/research/deseg/Why_Segreg_Matters.pdf.

Prinstein, M., LaGreca, A., Vernbery, E., & Silverman, W. (1996). Children's coping assistance: How parents, teachers, and friends help children cope after a natural disaster. *Journal of Child Psychiatry, 25,* 463–475.

Riad, J., & Norris, F. (1996). The influence of relocation on environmental, social, and psychological stress experienced by disaster victims. *Environment and Behavior, 28,* 163–182.

Rosenberg, M. (2005, December 18). Displaced by Katrina, coping in a new school. *New York Times,* p. 2.

Rutter, M. (1987). Psychosocial resilience and protective mechanisms. *American Journal of Orthopsychiatry, 57,* 316–331.

Spencer, M. B. (2006). Phenomenology and ecological systems theory: Development of diverse groups. In W. Damon (Series Ed.) & R. Lerner (Series Ed; Vol. Ed.), *Handbook of child psychology: Vol. 1. Theoretical models of human development* (6th ed., pp. 829–893). New York: Wiley.

Turner, M. A. (2006, February 17). Building opportunity and equity into the New New Orleans: A framework for policy and action. Retrieved February 19, 2006, from http://www.urban.org/publications/900930.html.

Wells, A. S. (Ed.). (2002). *Where charter school policy fails: The problems of accountability and equity.* New York: Teachers College Press.

■|■|■

PART TWO

Preparing Professionals
for the Possible

■|■|■

CHAPTER 8

Disastrous Opportunity

IRA LIT & JON SNYDER

There arrives a time following a disaster, inevitably, when a sense of the promise of rebirth returns, when thoughts turn from destruction to opportunity. Hurricane Katrina, an event of nearly unparalleled catastrophic magnitude, left in its wake multiple voids. Well before the destruction had abated, people from all walks of life began to consider the possibilities of healing and rebuilding from the devastation to families, communities, buildings, schools, businesses, landmarks, and cultural centers caused by Katrina and the aftermath of our human response.

In this chapter we explore one approach to revitalizing the shattered educational system left behind in New Orleans. We focus on education because education is our chosen profession, and learning, teaching, and schools are what we know by preparation, experience, and scholarship. We chose to focus on New Orleans, not because the children of New Orleans were the only ones to have their education affected by Katrina, but because New Orleans is the largest urban area affected by this calamity and thus allows us to tap into the more general challenge of education in urban settings. We do not offer the single right answer, as none exists. Anyone who has ever raised children, been a teacher, and/or studied teaching and learning knows that children, by nature and nurture, grow and learn differently and respond differently to their environments. Instead, we propose a framework for thinking about and acting upon the issues embedded in this challenge.

Across the political spectrum, simplistic ideological responses to the complex human endeavor that is public education abound (e.g., free market capitalism, scientism, laissez-faire, command and control, and so on). However, political and philosophical ideologies do not translate directly into a consistent and universally successful "on the ground" method of educating children. We try to move beyond this traditional failure of educational debate by providing specific, concrete examples of some, but certainly not all, of the structures and processes possible within the framework we elucidate below.

Assumptions

People or organizations proposing solutions for reform bring with them a set of assumptions about what matters and what works. Especially in education, these assumptions derive simultaneously from interwoven webs of values, experiences, and knowledge. Judging solutions, whether ours or others, requires a clear understanding of those webs and their influence on designs and outcomes. Therefore, we begin with a description of a framework for educational renewal that includes an expression of our own assumptions, beliefs, and understandings, and we urge others to do the same.

Societal Goals of Public Education

Education clearly has benefits for the individual being educated, but the impetus for free, public education in this country was not individual advancement but rather the public good. The goals of public education, while applying to the individual, must add up to the public good.

At an abstract level, our own assumptions about education are embedded in a particular expression of its goals:

- an engaged and informed citizenry to support and strengthen the American experiment in democracy;
- macro-economic stability for the country;
- active participants in enriching the quality of our American civilization;
- economic security and personal growth and expression for the individual.

These are not "either/or" goals, but rather "both/and." In fact, they are mutually interdependent. At times, however, they can seem to be in conflict with each other. For instance, what is best for the economic security of a particular individual may not simultaneously be in the best interest of the stability of the existing macro-economic system. Democracy and capitalism, though often conflated, are not the same, and, indeed, they contain an inherent and inevitable tension.

Goals for Our Children

Moving to the level of what we want for children as we strive toward these larger social goals of public education, we assume all children, regardless of their economic status, are blessed at birth with an innate desire and capacity to make sense of their world. All children, as Barbara Biber said, have "a healthy fund of curiosity and a drive to produce an effect on the environment" (in Fisher, 2005). The will to learn is the lynchpin of all learning.

Closely allied to the will to learn is engagement with learning. This requires a pro-active approach to children's learning that has definite standards of achievement and rests on an understanding that engaging the child is a prerequisite for ensuring that she will meet or exceed those standards.

We want children equipped to make sense of the world, the ultimate and unending human task. People make sense of the world all their lives, yet how well they do so depends on how well equipped they are by knowledge, skills, and experience, all of which are supported in our public school systems.

We want to foster in children both competence and a sense of competence. We want children to be willing to take risks, to explore, to experiment, and to test their burgeoning ideas.

We want children to develop a sense of community, an awareness of others, and a capacity for building constructive relationships. Such an awareness of and commitment to community entails respect for others, for their rights, their beliefs, and their culture. It entails sensitivity to the needs and wants of others. It entails gentleness in judging and the ability to resolve conflicts constructively.

Closely allied to a sense of community, we want children to value and to practice the principles of democracy, in and out of school. We want them to be fair, just, and humane, and to take us a little further on the way to a better world (Fisher, 2005).

Designing Education in the Public Sphere

Because public education is about the public good, it is inherently political, and, in a democracy, inherently contentious. In a successful experiment in democracy and for public education to more closely approximate its potential, conflict is not only good, it is essential. Unchecked partisanship, however, is not the politics of a successful democracy. As opposed to harnessing the constructive energy of conflict, partisanship focuses on winning and losing, rather than a solution, and thus the public, and democracy itself, suffer as a result.

Because conflict is both appropriate and inevitable in the public sphere, conflicts about public education cannot, and should not, be avoided, but rather resolved constructively. This goal requires all responsible parties to fulfill their rights and responsibilities to shape and support public education. This is not some pie-in-the-sky radical notion. It is already embedded financially in the fabric of each and every state in the form of public tax dollars supporting public education. Thus, with the exception of the rare few who believe education is solely an individual and not a public good, the question is not whether we all have to play together, but rather, put prosaically, how can we all play together for the benefit of both the individual and the collective?

Recently it seems that "special interests" have taken on a negative connotation. This, like attempting to avoid inevitable conflict, is unfortunate. Individuals and groups do indeed have special needs and interests. It is not the having of special interests that is of concern, but rather how we pursue them that is at issue. In order for public education to meet its goals, all individuals and groups, with the full complement of their intra- and inter-group conflicts among their special needs and interests, must find ways to agree, to work together, and to continue relationships through disagreements. The end of the public good requires open, healthy, and constructive conflict resolution among competing interests and needs.

Growing from Strengths

We make no claims to expertise regarding the specific historical or current state of the educational infrastructure of New Orleans, and no brief recitation of the "basic facts" of the situation would do justice to any educational context, let alone one devastated by catastrophe. In fact, one of our assumptions is that external expertise, no matter how sage, will cause more harm than good without the collaboration and insights of local, "on the ground" expertise.

We do assume, from what we have read and what we know of other urban areas, that the public schools in New Orleans were not consistently meeting their goals for students prior to Katrina. As elsewhere, we assume that those goals were more likely to be met the greater the income level of the families and that poor children and children of color were less likely to have quality teachers or to attend schools that supported teacher and student learning.

We also assume that many hard-working and well-intentioned educators (and other community members from all walks of life) were at work in the New Orleans schools and committed to the success of its students. Surely there were success stories; yet in all probability, they were produced despite contextual conditions rather than because of them. Hence, as we conceive of a reorganized and revitalized educational system for the children of New Orleans, we must take advantage of the "disastrous opportunity" of Katrina. We must think boldly and creatively, moving beyond the failed systems and structures Katrina has washed away. We must overcome entrenched forces and accreted mistakes from the past, to learn from history rather than repeat it. This will require locating the strengths, the human resources, and relationships that did, and in some cases still do, exist and invent processes for coalescing them into constructive action, and the sooner the better.

Envisioning a "Quality Schools Collaborative" for New Orleans

In the following pages we will apply these assumptions through a thought experiment to show ways how they might be enacted in New Orleans. As stated before, the specifics of the plan laid out below are not meant to encapsulate the one best way to create educational excellence for all. Rather, our hope is that the particulars elucidated here may provide a starting point for imagining and enacting a system of public schools in New Orleans that can better meet the strengths, interests, and needs of its children and communities.

Scope and Scale

In imagining a better system of schooling for the children of New Orleans, one could tackle the question at many levels: Policy makers might be inclined to envision system-wide structures and regulations; others might start with the design of a model school or even the description of one successful classroom. Our own experience and knowledge base suggests that we begin with what we would call a "manageable association of mutually supportive schools." We are envisioning a collection of schools within a particular community in the rebuilt city of New Orleans. This system would need to be large enough to take advantage of some economies of scale and to encapsulate the full pre-K-12 experience. For example, the system should have sufficient numbers of elementary students and schools to feed into at least one or two small high schools. However, we would also suggest that the system remain small enough to be nimble and flexible, particularly since a capacity for ongoing assessment and renewal is a key feature of our initiative. This collection of schools and communities must be committed to a set of core goals and be willing to collaborate, share, and be open to the critical support of the larger association. The group of schools would fit together under a loose umbrella that we will call the "Quality Schools Collaborative" (QSC).

This system would not be a school district per se. We would prefer not to be tied to prior formulations, frameworks, or expectations. The association would need to provide some centralized services to take advantage of economies of scale (e.g., payroll, building maintenance, and transportation). Core cross-school decisions would reside at the nexus of the QSC and the schools, while the vast majority of the personnel and other resources would reside at the school level and be targeted at the strengths, interests, and needs of children. In our mind's eye, the QSC is set in a rebuilt neighborhood in New Orleans, one primarily populated by the children of the laboring forces amassed to rebuild this great American city.

Outcomes for Students

We would begin the process of school restructuring in the same places we suggest that teachers begin their curriculum planning: first, with a focus on children, their families, and communities; second, with the formulation of concrete goals and objectives.

A deep understanding of children—how they grow, develop, and learn—is essential for teachers to be successful. In addition, educators must account for the specific strengths, interests, and needs of the particular children, families and communities they serve.

As for goals and objectives, we would begin by building agreement with key stakeholders who hold an investment in the question: What is it that we want our schools to accomplish? While we would suggest directly engaging community stakeholders in just such a discussion in the development of any educational system, we provide a framework for what such a list might look like. First, to summarize the discussion above, one essential outcome for schools is the development of an engaged and productive citizenry, one that can support and strengthen our pluralistic, democratic society. Next, what concrete knowledge, skills, and dispositions must schools provide to students in order to meet this aim? Here is a possible starting point:

(A) *Basic Literacy:* Core competencies, including a capacity for reading, comprehension, writing, computation, and mathematical understanding are essential to a productive life. In and of themselves, though, these basic skills are also insufficient to the achievement of our aims.

(B) *Knowledge Base in the Disciplines:* A knowledge base and understanding of the ways of thinking and organizing knowledge in other disciplines including the sciences, literature, history/social sciences, and the arts are also indispensable. One might also include language, engineering, and other areas as well.

(C) *Attention to the Whole Child:* Physical health, social and emotional growth, and moral development are also areas in which schools can and should play a critical (but not solitary) role.

(D) *Preparation for an Information-Based Economy:* Functional competencies including critical thinking, a capacity for learning, perspective taking, and collaboration are also important for success in the work force and in the public arena of a thriving democracy; and

(E) *Real-World Applicability:* Making connections from school-based learning to the real world of commerce, community, and citizenry is also indispensable.

As a fundamental principle of effective schools, we would also add that this educational system must foster a commitment to the achievement of these basic goals for all students. Given the previous experience in New Orleans and this country's broader history of public education, a keen and explicit focus on issues of race, class, and equity must be made a priority for any system of schools.

We would hope that a set of priorities, such as the one above exemplifies, would excite and unite stakeholders, make sense to families and teachers, and serve the needs and interests of children. While the specific elements included or excluded from such a list will vary, building stakeholder agreement on a core set of outcomes is an indispensable step in developing a successful system of schools.

Focusing on Teaching Quality

To achieve these aims, the QSC would focus its efforts on what we currently know about what works best for children. Over the past several decades, parents, policy makers, educators, and researchers have moved toward a consensus that of all that is within the control of the educational "system," the quality of teaching is what matters most for children's learning, growth, and development. Because we know that high quality teaching is central to achieving our educational aims, schools and school systems should be designed to produce and nourish quality teaching from preparation, to induction, through retirement. As a consequence, serious attention must be paid to the structures and process of classrooms, schools, and systems of schools to foster and promote high quality teaching. Moreover, we would design the system to contribute directly to enhancing our understanding of what works for which children, how and why.

High-quality outcomes for children require cohesive responses to the following questions about teaching (NCTAF, 1996):

- What is it that matters most about teaching?
- How can we recruit and retain talented people into the profession who are capable of doing what matters most?
- How do we successfully prepare and support teachers to do what matters most?
- How should we organize schools so that teachers can do what matters most?
- How do we productively encourage and reward teachers for doing what matters most?

As one practical example that integrates responses to several of those questions, the QSC might partner with a local college or university working to prepare new teachers. Following sufficient initial preparation (which would be directly supported by the QSC), novice teachers might take up a true residency in one of the local schools. Rather than placing beginning teachers, no matter their route to entry, as isolated, full-time instructors of record, the QSC would provide a sheltered and supported entry into the profession. For instance, at the secondary level, a novice teacher could co-teach several class periods with an experienced teacher, then be responsible for a class period or two under the direction and support of an experienced faculty member. This kind of apprenticeship or teacher residency would support the development of the skills of the novice, create time and opportunity for a leadership role for the experienced teacher, and provide administrative flexibility in scheduling and teaching assignments. As the novice teachers gain experience, they would also gain additional responsibility, eventually leading their own classes, and, down the road, if they demonstrate the capacity and the interest, working to support novice teachers themselves.

With the time provided by the sheltered entry residents, more expert teachers could take up important leadership roles—not leaving instruction to work in a district office, but providing essential services aimed at the core functions of the school. These might include mentoring for novice teachers; providing roving instructional support to other teachers; demonstrating innovative lessons; assisting with assessments, data collection and analysis, and the like.

While experience is important, age and seniority alone, of course, do not equate with expert practice. Interests and expertise vary among teachers too. Some faculty may excel in the teaching of science while others may have a talent for building strong classroom communities. Schools should be organized to take advantage of both in the collective service of the ongoing development of the entire staff in order to better meet the strengths, interests, and needs of all children. Assignments in leadership roles should be based on demonstrated expertise, fulfill identifiable goals, and be assessable and improvable. Similarly, teachers who take on additional roles and responsibilities must be adequately compensated. Variation of professional roles as well as differentiation of pay based on responsibilities would help make the field a more exciting and viable one for many talented individuals to enter and remain.

Quality instruction is extraordinarily difficult to accomplish. Across contexts, it requires a set of core commitments; an array of knowledge, skills, and dispositions; and systemic supports. Quality instruction for all our children requires that teachers, as a collective, share and enact four commitments:

- an inviolable, fundamental commitment to children and their families;
- a commitment to use the best of existing knowledge to support the growth and development of their students;
- a commitment to create new knowledge and develop new practices;
- a commitment to share knowledge, wisdom, and experience with others toward an ever-increasing understanding of what it is that matters most about teaching.

Quality instruction also requires a specific set of knowledge and skills related to children (including their families and communities); subject matter; and pedagogy (a large repertoire of how to solutions). Most difficult, quality instruction requires the ability to integrate knowledge and skills in those three areas—the ability, in real time, with real kids and with substantive content, to match the strengths, interests, and needs of children, with deep and appropriate understanding of the content, and with the right pedagogical strategies (which vary depending upon the demands of the subject to be learned and the children who are doing the learning) to support student growth and development. All three are essential; any one or two is insufficient; all are mutually interdependent. To argue for one area over another, for subject matter knowledge over knowledge of teaching or over knowledge of children, their families, and communities is to miss the point and guarantee failure.

Of course, the supports available in the instructional context are also essential to a teacher's capacity to enact quality instruction. A teacher who works with 180 students a day, is less likely to be able to know them well than one who works with 25 students a day. A teacher is more likely to employ a wide repertoire of instructional strategies if she has a well-provisioned classroom. A teacher is more likely to know the subject matter deeply if she has a solid grounding in the subject matter, as well as continuing opportunities to study subject matter in the contexts in which she uses that knowledge—that is, in the context of children and teaching.

We also know that our current school systems tend to distribute quality teaching ineffectively and inequitably. Thus we also need to focus attention on the placement and retention of quality teachers that will help to promote the success of all students. We must develop a culture and a system of incentives where expertise flows to where it is most needed, not where it is least taxed.

Furthermore, we are keenly aware that there is much we still do not yet know about what works, for whom, how, and why, in terms of preparing and supporting high quality instruction and the processes by which quality instruction impacts student growth and development. Hence, a sustainable and improvable system of schools must also be embedded with systems of inquiry, assessment, and ongoing renewal so that knowledge creation and dissemination are built directly into the foundation of the endeavor. Knowledge about teaching and learning must be visible, sharable, and improvable.

Stakeholders and Partnerships

Bringing together constituencies with an interest in sustainable, strong outcomes for all students is essential in building a successful system of schools. Consider your own local states and communities. The schools that work are supported by a coalition of stakeholders, including some if not all of the following: parents, community advocates, non-profits, community volunteers, local businesses, institutions of higher education, museums, and more. Community engagement is essential. Teachers and schools cannot do this work alone, nor should they. As we work to rebuild the schools in New Orleans, a cornerstone of the effort should be to foster broad-based community partnerships to support the students in the schools.

As one concrete measure, each school in the QSC would have at least one active and committed external partner, bringing its unique expertise, knowledge, and resources to bear. Imagine in our collective of local schools if one were partnered with the local arts museum, another with a biotechnical firm, a third with a local institute of jazz, a fourth with a county hospital, a fifth with a local community college, and so on. The opportunities for sharing knowledge, providing real-world experience and exposure, and the possibilities for sharing resources and expertise are immense. In addition, the school system should develop public spaces, opportunities, and an expectation to share what they are doing, why and how it is working, and how they plan to improve. Engaging the community in this way would help to develop a deeper understanding of a common set of goals for schools, and, in turn, greater community engagement in the form of public policy, taxation, volunteerism, and the like.

Facilities

Successful schools require well-designed spaces for growth and learning, for both students and teachers. The issues in New Orleans are particularly acute in this regard as much of the educational infrastructure was literally destroyed by Katrina. Again, we would suggest that the QSC take advantage of this disastrous opportunity to re-conceptualize the kinds of spaces that might best help our schools achieve their aims.

Close your eyes. Imagine a classroom. Envision a school. Likely, each one of us can readily visualize these ubiquitous spaces. These pictures will vary, but they would have far too many features in common, and many of those are not ideally suited to supporting our aims for children. Most of our classrooms are designed as single, enclosed, unconnected spaces. Teachers and students are isolated. Architecturally speaking, sharing, learning, and collaboration across spaces are prohibited.

The most prevalent model of schools remains based on a system developed at the turn of the century, when we moved from the model of a one-room school house to one of the large, comprehensive school system. Schools of the twentieth century were designed to house and sort large numbers of children and in the process to prepare only a small percentage of them for higher education. The remainder were either trained for manufacturing or other blue-collar professions or destined for other positions requiring minimal knowledge and skills. We can argue about the merits of that educational system for the economy of the last century, but there is no denying that it is a system totally unsuited for the current context. Nearly all members of an information economy must be prepared for some form of postsecondary education. Moreover, the basic elementary and secondary education must achieve much more robust objectives to meet the needs of our current political economy. In order to do so, we need to build spaces, structures, and processes designed with these goals in mind.

We make no claims to knowledge or skill in architecture, design, or contracting, and so we dare not propose a specific kind of structure for QSC schools. Even so, a functioning school building in this system would be a place designed with the essential aims of the endeavor foremost in mind, rather than the parochial issues of housing children and books (which should be secondary issues). For example, since sharing knowledge and resources is an essential element in improving instruction, schools would be designed to comfortably facilitate interactions and observations between and among teachers and classroom spaces, while avoiding the lack of pragmatism of an earlier open era of school design. Common resources might be centralized and shared, increasing contact and communication among faculty and students. These might also be built with the larger community in mind: a central technology center, a community library, and spaces for the arts and for physical recreation.

QSC schools would be laboratories of learning, both for students and teachers, and about learning, teaching, and schooling. We need to know more about what successful teachers are doing. Hence our school buildings require a capacity for easy observation and fluidity of space to facilitate the movement of faculty and students.

For some students, perhaps, education as such may exist beyond the walls of a particular building site we call a school. When they best meet the strengths, interests, and needs of children and work to support our long-term educational goals, opportunities such as distance learning, internships or trade apprenticeships, community college courses, Outward Bound programs, and other non-traditional forms of learning should be explored.

The absolute nature of the problems in New Orleans offers the opportunity to reshape and restructure schools from the inside out. We should not squander such an opportunity by rebuilding the kinds of structures we already know impede the aims of our efforts.

Structures and Processes for Student Success

Within these buildings, how should we organize the faculty and students to best serve the needs of the children and meet the goals of the QSC? Again, the principle in play here remains a focus on decisions in service of children and their growth and development. When thinking about how to assign personnel, for example, we know that teachers need to know students and their families well in order to serve them well. Consequently, we must organize students, teachers, and schedules to help ensure the building of strong relationships between students and faculty. As just one example of a way to support this effort at the elementary school level is to utilize the full faculty at a school site (including any specialists) in order to provide a small, cross-age group advisory assignment for each student. Advisory groups might meet once a month, and students' advisors would meet with individual students and the families several times a year. Students and their families would be paired with a particular faculty member for their entire school career, providing a knowledgeable advocate for each student and his family, as well as cross-age peers for students at the school site.

At a different level, schools must be cautious about prioritizing efficiency over educational outcomes. For example, designing effective school schedules is a complicated endeavor, one that truly takes talent and creativity. However, we are all too familiar with stories of students eating lunch at ten o'clock in the morning to support the efficient running of the cafeteria, or high schoolers with a first period gym class (and no showers), making focusing on learning for the remainder of the day a challenge. In the same vein, many school districts build school schedules and bus routes around what is most efficient from the perspective of the routing of vehicles. This approach can lead to odd and deleterious consequences for children such as an hour-long bus ride to a school location fifteen minutes from one's home or a school day that begins promptly at 7:58 A.M.

Creative ideas for the organization of students, faculty, schools and school systems abound. The key here is that to the degree possible, personnel should be focused on instructional services rather than bureaucratic systems. Teachers need time and opportunities to get to know students and to learn and share information about and in service of students, instruction, and learning. Schedules and classroom and teaching assignments need to attend first to the educational aims of the system and only secondarily to the facilitation of an efficient bureaucracy.

Structures and Systems for Improvement

Assessment is essential for learning about what is working and what is not for individual children, for teachers, for schools, and for systems of schools. Any educational enterprise truly committed to long-term success will pay careful attention to developing systems of assessment, data collection and display, and opportunities for inquiry and renewal around the use of these data. The appropriate use of the right kind of data for the various decision makers is also important. The kinds of data and analyses a teacher needs are different from what a principal, a superintendent, a school board member, or a governor might need. For an assessment system to serve its purposes, it is essential to understand these differences and not foist the wrong types of data and analyses on any of the nested levels of the public educational system. We must make certain, however, that the growth and development of children, rather than the collection of data, remain the focus of our efforts.

The QSC will develop robust systems for collecting and utilizing data on students, teachers, instructional methods, and schools. Of course it is essential that assessment and analysis encompass dynamic, varied, and integrated systems. Furthermore, no single outcome measure can provide all of the information necessary for assessing and revitalizing instruction. Consequently, the QSC would need to rely on a host of assessment instruments to help achieve its aims.

For example, in our own work at Bank Street (supported by the Carnegie Corporation of New York's Teachers for a New Era initiative), we are using a host of assessment tools to assess the impact of our programs on our candidates, graduates, and the learning of their pupils. These measures include not only ongoing surveys of candidates and graduates and an analysis of the student achievement test scores of the pupils of our graduates in New York City's public schools but also more contextually refined measures of teaching practice. These include follow-up studies of graduates based on classroom observations and interviews, and a curriculum-embedded assessment measure of the cognitive complexity of the assignments our graduates provide to students in the context of a real curriculum and the sophistication of the response of pupils based on actual work samples. Similarly, schools must contemplate the kinds of assessment tools that will best help them gauge how well they are meeting their own aims and then use those measures to enhance practices and outcomes.

Beyond the necessity for local assessment, analysis, and renewal, schools and systems of schools need to cultivate a culture of learning and sharing. We must become comfortable, confident, and committed to sharing what works and what does not; for whom, how, and why; in order to serve the needs of our own students, to further develop the knowledge base for the field, and to enhance opportunities for others. Such a system is a hallmark of professionalism and a goal toward which our school systems should strive.

Conclusion

We conclude this thought experiment with the Quality Schools Collaborative of New Orleans with the development of a cycle for success:

- focusing on knowledge about children, families, and communities;
- designing structures and processes with a keen attention to the principal aims of schooling;
- utilizing ongoing, multi-faceted assessment to illuminate what's working, for whom, how, and why;
- creating opportunities to engage in cycles of renewal that allow for the use of assessments to sharpen practice; and,
- committing to the dissemination of learning to strengthen the profession and to build community engagement and support.

Ideally, this cycle will continue in an ever-improving system of schools for our children.

School reform at any level is an intricately complicated enterprise. Tackling the range of issues and the level of destruction now faced by the communities of the Gulf Coast may seem nigh insurmountable. However, the need for our commitment of energy, creativity, and resources has rarely been greater, and, in fact, circumstances may currently work in favor of bold and radical reform. Something extraordinary is surely worth pursuing, and the children of Katrina deserve nothing less. Let us hope that the lessons we will uncover from their experience will be ones that help to spur a national renewal in urban education.

Note: While original in its formulation, this chapter is built upon the significant scholarship of numerous others. The wells from which we draw are deep and vast, but in particular we are indebted to the following: Barbara Biber, Linda Darling-Hammond, Mort Deutsch, Elliot Eisner, Phillip Jackson, Robert Kunzman, Ann Leiberman, Edna Shapiro, Lucy Sprague Mitchell, and David Tyack.

REFERENCES

Fisher, P. (2005). Passionate intelligence. Unpublished manuscript.

National Commission on Teaching and America's Future. (1996). *What matters most: Teaching for America's future.* Washington, CDC NCTAF.

CHAPTER 9

Post-Katrina Educational Contexts

Breaking the Rules

M. JAYNE FLEENER, JERRY WILLIS,
SISTER JUDITH BRUN & KRISTY HEBERT

Colleges and schools of education located in the urban centers of America often live there uncomfortably, and with mixed feelings about their close proximity to schools that are struggling to meet the needs of some of the nation's most disadvantaged children. That discomfort is most acute in major research universities, where an important goal is often to produce "scientifically based" research that can guide policy makers and educators around the world as they create better educational opportunities for children. In the unwritten rulebooks that define appropriate activity for research universities, the clean work of writing papers and conducting tightly controlled research or abstract theoretical studies has generally been accorded a much higher status than the dirty-hands work of helping improve local schools in messy, complex, and dynamic environments.

Third World Backyards

Often, while those of us in research university colleges of education are searching for the answers, we keep our heads down and try not to look out our windows because the view often spotlights the problems and needs of children, schools, and parents right down the street. Charles Underwood, an anthropologist in UC Berkeley's Graduate School of Education has commented (personal communication, May 2006) that "Every once in a while, someone will hear about my fieldwork in South America and ask, 'How can I do something to help in a Third World situation?'" Underwood, Director of University Community Links (UC Links), a program funded by the state of California to support service learning, commented that "If they're here at Berkeley, they do not have to buy a plane ticket. I can take them to *Third World* situations three miles from the campus." He was talking about neighborhoods in Oakland where children have trouble sleeping some nights because of the gunfire, and where those same children and their parents struggle to rise above poor housing, poor wages, and schools that have not yet found the answer to helping them achieve.

Some may be offended by the application of a term like *Third World* to any part of America. The Icons Project at the University of Maryland (www.icons.umd.edu/pls/reslib/display_glossary) defines Third World this way:

> The poorest nations of the world. Most third world nations are in debt to Western banks and governments or international lending organizations. Many depend on international aid to meet the basic needs of their population. . . . This term has fallen into disfavor in recent years, replaced by terms such as Less-Developed Country (LDC), developing nations, and the Global South.

There may be something comforting about exporting the problems of poverty, poor health care, poor educational opportunities, and limited job possibilities to a group of countries we can call Third World. If we look out our windows, however, we can often find all the characteristics of the Third World right here at home. Hurricane Katrina forced colleges of education in Louisiana, Mississippi, and Alabama to look out their windows and confront the realities of persistent, generational, isolating poverty experienced by a significant percentage of the population in the Gulf Coast region of the United States. The public education children of persistent poverty receive in this region has not been a major force in helping generations break the grip of limited learning and employment opportunities and move up from jobs that pay sub-subsistence wages to jobs that offer health benefits, vacations, and salaries that are the ticket to an "American" lifestyle.

While the 2005 hurricanes did cause major devastation to the region, including the schools, they did not drag the region into Third World conditions. We were already there. The *Kids Count* database maintained by the Annie E. Casey Foundation (2006) tracks many statistics about the lives of children, and the data document the Third World living conditions of many children in Louisiana, Mississippi, and Alabama.

It begins even before birth. Louisiana ranks 49th in the percentage of low birth weight babies (trailed only by Mississippi), and ranks 48th in the percentage of babies born prematurely (only Alabama and Mississippi rank lower). Then, of Louisiana's more than one million children, one in every four (26%) lives in poverty, which puts Louisiana in the bottom 10% of the states in America (U.S. Census Bureau, 2004). Only the District of Columbia and Mississippi have higher percentages of children living in poverty. In Louisiana (and Mississippi, and the District of Columbia) poverty also tends to be clustered in ghettos. In New Hampshire, only 1% of poor children live in poor neighborhoods—that is, in ghettos of poverty. The percentage in Louisiana is a startling 44%. In addition, these ghettos are often racially segregated as well, in part because of the history of segregation in the South and in part because the poverty level among minority citizens of Louisiana is much higher than among the White population. It has now been over 50 years since the Supreme Court, on May 17, 1954, issued the *Brown vs. Board of Education* decision that outlawed racial segregation of schools in America. For many, it even feels odd that there was ever a time when children were sent to this or that school based on their race. However, we can take you to school after school within 10 miles of the LSU campus where the student population is 92%, 94%, and 97% African American. In America, neighborhoods are segregated by income level, and where large percentages of the African American population are poor, the neighborhood schools will reflect the concentration of poor, African-American families in the area. Busing and other strategies to negate the de facto segregation by income levels of neighborhood schools does not work in states like Louisiana where we have the largest per capita percentage of students in private schools and a long tradition of parochial/private education for those who can afford it.

Such depressing statistics can be enumerated for pages, but they are only an abstract, objective, and sanitized way of telling a story that is concrete, personal, and deeply emotional for those who live those statistics. For example, a surprising 55% of grandparents in Louisiana have responsibility for caring for at least one of their grandchildren. One of the authors saw a child who represented that statistic at a shelter for Hurricane Katrina victims. He was quiet, shy, and withdrawn. He was living with his grandfather in a temporary FEMA trailer because he had been separated from his mother while they were trying to escape the rising floodwaters in New Orleans. He did not know where his mother was and he did not know what the future held for him. He was dealing with that uncertainty while also dealing with his feelings about having been abandoned by his mother so she could escape the black, oily floodwaters that were quickly rising around them.

However, in spite of billions of dollars spent, by federal and state governments as well as foundations and community groups on schools serving ghettos of persistent poverty, we have not found the silver bullet that solves the problem of adequately educating poor minority students. In fact, some scholars believe schools for poor African American students have been, and continue to be, part of the problem rather than part of the solution:

> African Americans have endured and continue to encounter systematic discrimination in all spheres of society. . . . Possibly the most debilitating of those are barriers that exist in the economic and educational realms. The twin evils of educational and occupational inequity have conspired to limit the upward mobility of generations of African Americans. Far from being the 'great equalizer,' schools have served to maintain and entrench socioeconomic disparities. . . . The education procured by the African American population has, for the most part, been separate from and unequal to that made available to the dominant cultural group. The hidden curriculum in the form of low teacher expectations of Black students, a Eurocentric curriculum, and streaming into non-college preparatory or special education programs . . . has undermined the educational and, consequently, the occupational potential of Black students. African American students frequently leave school without the academic skills necessary for securing even entry-level positions in the job market. (Smith & Lalonde, 2003, pp. 142–143)

We do not have to completely agree with Smith and Lalonde to share with them a concern that many school systems have not been able to address the persistent problem of providing an adequate education to some of the nation's most vulnerable and needy children. In the case of the Orleans Parish School District where many hurricane evacuee children attended school, performance matches the criticisms made by Smith and Lalonde. The President of Tulane University, Scott Cowen (2006), is chair of a Mayor's subcommittee charged with making recommendations about what to do with the district. He noted that "New Orleans had one of the worse-performing public school districts in the country, pre-Katrina." The Louisiana Department of Education also expressed its lack of faith in the local school board when, in November of 2005, it took direct control of 90% of the schools in the district. Such a move is made only as a last resort after other options have failed. Cowen and his group have made a number of recommendations about how to fix the mess that was the Orleans Parish School District, but it is too early to know whether the recommendations will be implemented and whether the results are positive. While there is hope that smaller school districts, and a growing number of charter schools, will successfully replace the district Hurricane Katrina virtually destroyed, there is not much in the research literature to undergird that hope.

Adaptive Responses to Unusual Circumstances

The disaster of Hurricane Katrina created unprecedented needs for immediate, life-saving services in the Gulf Coast region. At Louisiana State University, for example, a triage hospital was set up for injured and ill evacuees in the Pete Maravitch center where basketball was replaced by emergency surgery and miles of IV tubing. For weeks the thump-thump of rotors on heavily laden helicopters was the background music on campus as they landed on the track field and delivered the sick, injured, and dying. At the same time, hundreds of ambulances snaked through the campus, where traffic often moves slowly anyway as students and faculty hunt for that most elusive quarry—a convenient parking space.

Moreover, while medical volunteers from LSU and all over the world were doing triage and operating a huge critical care hospital, many other activities were also underway—from helping parents move into their children's dorm rooms because they had no other place to live, to creating a complete emergency registration system so that students from flooded and damaged universities in New Orleans could enroll at LSU and avoid missing an entire semester of study. Ultimately, LSU's campus in Baton Rouge enrolled over 3,000 students who were forced from their home campuses in New Orleans.

No one would pretend that everything went fine or that there were no problems with the university's response to Katrina. There were many problems, issues, and difficulties that had to be addressed, and there were many lessons learned about how to do it "the next time" and "how not to do it the next time!" However, one guiding principle in the university's response to the immediate needs of Katrina victims was validated over and over. It was that the rules are for ordinary times and that these are not ordinary times. People were empowered to solve problems without following all the rules that might make sense under ordinary circumstances but did not in extraordinary situations. In the book, *LSU in the Eye of the Storm* (Bacher & Devlin, 2005) there is a section titled "Rules Were Made to Be Broken" and it describes how LSU officials "bent" and "broke" rules in order to meet the needs of evacuees. At least some of LSU's success in responding to immediate needs is due directly to this guiding principle. Indeed, we all read and saw on television the stories of failures that could be attributed directly to the opposite guidelines—sticking to rules made for different times and circumstances. One of the saddest and most upsetting examples of this was what happened at the New Orleans airport after the hurricane. The story, as reported by Laurie Anderson (2005), a local reporter for the Baton Rouge newspaper *The Advocate,* is a sad one.

Dr. Mark Perlmutter, an orthopedic surgeon in Pennsylvania, realized that people were dying in New Orleans for lack of medical care. He borrowed the jet of a businessman and flew to Baton Rouge with a load of much needed medical supplies, another physician, and a medical student. He convinced the pilot of a Blackhawk helicopter to take him to New Orleans. The helicopter was transporting patients from New Orleans to Baton Rouge and was thus often flying empty on the return trip. Dr. Perlmutter arrived on the tarmac at the Louis Armstrong New Orleans International

Airport, where hundreds of patients were waiting to be airlifted to hospitals in Baton Rouge and elsewhere. He said "scores of non-responsive patients lay on stretchers. Two patients died in front of me." At first FEMA staff at the airport welcomed the help of Dr. Perlmutter and another physician, Dr. Clark Gerhart. Gerhart began working inside the terminal and Perlmutter attended to patients outside on the tarmac. Then, a problem developed. The official running the operation told them they would have to leave because they did not have the official FEMA authorization to be there. Dr. Perlmutter showed the person in charge his identification and explained why he did not have a card from FEMA designating him an "approved" physician. "I showed him my medical credentials. I had tried to get through to FEMA for 12 hours the day before and finally gave up. I asked him to let me stay until I was replaced by another doctor, but he refused. He said he was afraid of being sued. I informed him about the Good Samaritan laws and asked him if he was willing to let people die so the government wouldn't be sued, but he would not back down. I had to leave."

After being told that liability lawsuits were a prime concern and that the only two physicians were at the airport where people were dying for lack of medical care, Dr. Gerhart said, "That shocked me, that those would be his concerns in a time of emergency." Forced to return to Baton Rouge, the two doctors finally found the office where they could be "certified" to work as volunteer physicians. It was a formality that took only a few seconds.

One of Dr. Perlmutter's comments is particularly relevant to this discussion. He noted that "I have been going to Ecuador and Mexico on medical missions for 14 years. I was at ground zero. I've seen hundreds of people die. This was different because we knew the hurricane was coming. FEMA showed up late and then rejected help for the sake of organization. They put form before function, and people died" (quoted in Anderson, 2005).

Dr. Perlmutter's story is about how bureaucracy and the rules for normal situations can get in the way of providing much needed, even life-saving, services in an emergency. We are justifiably outraged that people died on the tarmac at New Orleans airport because bureaucracy triumphed over the greater goal of helping people in need. However,, that same veneration of bureaucracy and rules can also become a barrier to adequate, or even inadequate, education. It can also stifle creative responses to what often become opportunities resulting from crisis situations.

Renaissance Village is the name FEMA gave to the trailer park built in Baker, Louisiana to house 1,900 evacuees from New Orleans. It comprises row after row of small RV trailers with names such as Wanderer, Nomad, and Wildwood emblazoned on the sides, surrounded by a high fence and guarded by a black-shirted private security force. The residents are mostly Black, and there are around 600 children living there. The FEMA village sits on the boundary between two school districts, Baker and East Baton Rouge, and school buses arrive each morning to pick up children and transport them to various schools in the two districts, two of which were schools that were not scheduled for use this year but were re-opened for the displaced children.

A number of parents in the dusty, shadeless trailer park were optimistic when they learned that buses would be taking their children to school. However, having heard that some of the schools in the districts were rough, that their children might be harassed and even attacked by other children, and that a number of the area schools were "low performing," some parents wanted to visit the school, talk to the teachers and administrators, and ease their minds about the unknown school they were being asked to entrust to their children. On the first day of school, they waited patiently with their children to board the various buses. When they came, the parents were not allowed to board as the rules did not allow for parents to ride the bus. One mother, who had had to push floating bodies out of the way to get her three children to the safety of boats that rescued them from their home in New Orleans, pulled her children off the bus and waited for the city bus that also served the isolated trailer park. She would use the only other transportation option she had to get herself and her children to school. When the city bus came, she learned that she could get to Wal-Mart but not to her children's schools (or to many other services the residents would need).

Rules, routines, and regulations created for life-as-usual situations again kept someone in need from receiving services that were available but beyond reach. If there is one lesson Katrina has taught us in countless stories like these is that we need to be able to respond to the unusual in creative and adaptive ways. But what, in these times of rapid change, is the usual and what—the unusual?

Revisioning Roles and Responsibilities: Getting Dirty

Colleges of education have historically, at least for the past 100 years, played an important role in meeting the needs of society through the preparation of teachers, through in-service professional development and leadership programs for practicing teachers, and through research on teaching, learning, curriculum, and other factors impacting the success of schools and children. For most of the twentieth century, research in education has been dominated by the paradigms and research methods of psychology emphasizing controlled experimental design studies.

In *The New Scholarship Requires a New Epistemology*, Donald Schon (1995) expanded on the ideas that Ernest Boyer (1990) proposed in *Scholarship Reconsidered*. Boyer argued that the traditional definition of scholarship in American universities must be expanded. In addition to the scholarship of discovery Boyer proposed three other types of scholarship: *Scholarship of Integration, Scholarship of Application,* and

Scholarship of Teaching. Schon argued that for these three "new forms" of scholarship to be meaningful and accepted as "real" research, the universities must develop ways of justifying "claims to validity, and criteria of appropriate rigor" (p. 27). Further, he proposed that the ways of establishing validity and rigor for new scholarship are not necessarily the same as the ways of the "old scholarship of discovery." Schon concluded that these new forms of scholarship require us to abandon the foundations, rules, and assumptions of old scholarship and embrace a different approach to research. "If the new scholarship is to mean anything, it must imply a kind of action research with norms of its own, which will conflict with the norms of technical rationality—the prevailing epistemology built into the research universities" (p. 27).

As colleges of education are no longer the sole providers of preparation and development of teachers, and as social complexity mandates convergence of social support structures in meeting the needs of schools and children, the roles of colleges of education, in terms of teaching, research and service missions, need to be re-examined. The lessons of Katrina and the emergence of significant partnerships in response to the crisis in public education caused by and ultimately revealed as a result of the hurricanes in the fall of 2005 suggest the need for us all to "get dirty"— to engage in the hard, hands-on work of making a difference in kids and families' lives. In the social science of economics there is a debate about "clean models" versus "dirty hands" models when discussing the processes of economic strategy. Wayne Baker (2006) summarized the differences in these two approaches this way,

> Fundamental differences in style, method, and assumption divide sociology on the "clean models" of economics versus the "dirty hands" of sociology. Sociologists favor inductive, data-driven, many-variable, messy but realistic explanations of the world, while economists prize deductive, abstract, elegant, parsimonious models that predict but do not describe or explain. These central tendencies are not always true, of course, but they are powerful tendencies in the disciplines. (p. 1)

"Dirty hands" approaches involve working in messy, real world environments and developing ideas about the way the world works *from practice* rather than imposing those ideas *on practice.*

The dirty hands approach has much in common with a model for research often referred to as *bricolage* (Denzin & Lincoln, 2000, p. 3). The French word *bricoleur* means "a handyman or handywoman who makes use of the tools available to complete a task" (Kincheloe, 2001, p. 680). Denzin and Lincoln built on the ideas of Claude Levi-Strauss (1966) to develop a concept of scholarship in education and the social sciences that is similar to a tinkerer, handywoman, or bricoleur. In education research the bricoleur works in the real world of learning, uses a variety of research tools and methods in creative, adaptive ways; draws from many rather than one discipline, and focuses on solving a problem rather than testing a theory. Research methods are thus not passively accepted as givens. Instead "we actively construct our research methods from the tools at hand rather than passively receiving the 'correct,' universally applicable methodologies" (Kincheloe, 2005, p. 324). The goal is often the solution to a local problem rather than the discovery of universal truths. "The researcher-as-bricoleur abandons the quest for some naïve concept of realism, focusing instead on the clarification of his or her position in the web of reality and the social locations of other researchers and the ways they shape the production and interpretation of knowledge" (Kincheloe, 2005, p. 324). That means "community-based participatory processes for developing the tools that solve problems are another of the key characteristics of the bricoleur" (Coleman, Bartolo, & Jones, 2004, p. 377).

Stepping outside our safe campus structures, we have engaged a bricolage of method and connectiveness to work within our community to help meet the needs of students in our local post-Katrina context. While this chapter is an appeal to value the work of "messy" collaboration and "dirty" research, it is also a recognition that what used to be "normal" is no longer. The crisis of public education in the South, our "dirty little secret" of forgotten masses and institutionalized inequities, requires rethinking education, educational partnerships, and the roles colleges of education can play in re-creating public education.

A Dirty, Practical Framework to Support University Engagement

If we will look out our windows, many colleges of education will see Third World conditions in our own backyards and we will see social, economic, political, and educational conditions that at best do not help, and at worst, are part of the problem. If we are to become vital in our own communities, we must recognize those conditions and acknowledge that our traditional methods of research and scholarship are failing us. There is an old joke about the man who has lost a contact lens and is searching for it in the light of a streetlamp. When a passerby asks him where he thinks he lost the lens, the man says he lost it in the alley. After the obvious question about why search for it under the street lamp, he replies that "The light is better here." Much of the research in education today seems to be conducted "where the light is better" rather than in the complex and confusing settings where the problems are. Looking in the right places for answers may involve following Ernest Boyer's (1990) advice and elevating new forms of scholarship to honored and respected positions in colleges of education. (It may also involve teaching the rest of the university about their value.) Furthermore, it will certainly involve following Schon's (1995) advice to create new epistemological superstructures that can serve as foundations for new scholarship. In essence, we have to get our hands dirty in the real world, and we have to do it in ways that, *à là a bricoleur,* do not involve attempts to find simple, one-note answers. We have to be creative bricoleurs who help build solutions from the tools and resources at hand, solutions that are likely to be multifaceted, complex, and compound, even theoretically contradictory! There are, fortunately, some examples of colleges of education, and universities that are already exploring these possibilities.

There is also an element of "on the fly," non-linear decision making in the work of the bricoleur that goes against the orderly, standardized, preplanned nature of research and partnerships. In their book, *Creating a New Kind of University,* Stephen Percy, Nancy Zimpher, and Mary Jane Brukardt (2006) tell the story of how the University of Wisconsin, Milwaukee developed a comprehensive approach to engaging the university with the surrounding community. At the time Nancy Zimpher was Chancellor of UW-M. Before becoming Chancellor, she had been Dean of the College of Education at Ohio State University, and she is now President of the University of Cincinnati. The book describes *The Milwaukee Idea* which is an application of the concept that universities have a responsibility to become engaged with the surrounding community. In the case of UW-M the engagement is broad, and it includes a great deal of work to support the transformation of Milwaukee schools. What is perhaps just as important, however, is what is reflected in the title of the book. Sustained, encouraged, and supported community engagement led to a "new kind of university" that took responsibility for making a difference in the community. This new kind of university values what Percy, Zimper, and Brukardt call the *scholarship of engagement.* It is an example of bricolage, of dirty hands scholarship that combines the search for knowledge and understanding with the search for local solutions to local problems. It is a necessary combination because colleges in research universities cannot, and should not, abandon their traditional roles as producers of scholarship. The scholarship of engagement is a way to accomplish our traditional role in a new way and to engage in the effort to solve the serious and pressing problems of education in our local communities.

Bricolage Partnerships

As we reflect on the roles our college has played in the traditional areas of teaching, scholarship, and service, we have come to recognize the need for, and value of, multiple and dynamic ways of putting into practice the concepts we have discussed thus far—dirty hands, that is bricolage research that can be summed up as the *scholarship of engagement.* Hurricanes Katrina and Rita have flooded us with opportunities for such partnerships. The following examples hold promise for ensuring that our "getting dirty" could help us bridge the gap between our ivory tower isolation and community engagement.

Example One—Delta Express: Since about 1994, the University of California system has supported service learning through a grant program funded by the state legislature (see http://www.uclinks.org). Most of the programs on campuses of the University of California system involve after school educational activities for at-risk children. The children work with UC students on everything from "city archaeology digs" to "digital storytelling" projects. The projects are led by UC faculty and graduate students. Typically, undergraduate students who work with the children do it as part of an academic course in disciplines like education, anthropology, archaeology, mathematics, or some other field. The LSU College of Education is the anchor institution for the Delta Express Project which is based on UC Links. With support and participation from the Baton Rouge Area Foundation, Advance Baton Rouge, national foundations, and Charles Underwood and his staff, we have developed an after school program for children living in the largest FEMA trailer park for children who were evacuated from New Orleans after Hurricane Katrina. This project began oddly. David Obst, a Hollywood screenwriter and producer who is perhaps best known for writing the screenplays for *Revenge of the Nerds* and *Johnny Be Good,* became interested in organizing a project to deliver education programs to children evacuated from New Orleans. Through his efforts, LSU and the UC Berkeley group began collaborating on an after-school project in the Baker FEMA trailer park. Partners include the parents of children in the trailer park, the Louisiana Department of Education, and Advance Baton. The name, Delta Express Project, comes from a passenger train named Delta Express that connected Louisiana to California. The program began with a short two-month trial project to "figure out how to do it right." It was funded by David Obst and the Access2 Foundation. We learned a great deal from that trial run and are now moving into a second phase that is based on what we learned from the trial project. Once a robust and localized model is working well, we will try to expand and "institutionalize" the Delta Express Project by linking it to courses students take at LSU and offering the program to cooperating area schools. The scholarly output from the project will include papers about starting and building after-school support programs, and an edited book on university-based service learning programs that includes chapters on work in the UC Links and Delta Express programs. Currently, we are working on creating an online video conferencing system to link college students in California and Louisiana with children who need help in specific academic areas.

Example Two—Charter Schools: In the Orleans Parish School System, the windows were painted shut several decades ago as the air conditioning was installed. Not only was the air "conditioned," but so were the generations of lives filtered through the system, incubating the bacteria of poverty. Though the mildewing milieu took the breath away from many passionate communities, poverty didn't prevent them from feeling, thinking, and acting. One result of their action has been the formation of charter schools.

Colleges of education need to evolve to teach the leadership skills necessary for those who design, create, build, and instruct in charter schools. No longer can "supervision" and "evaluation" remain synonymous in creating effective professional growth models for implementation in charter schools. One course in traditional school finance will not suffice. (It never has.) Charter schools call for colleges of education to transform their educational administrative programs into educational programs that promote entrepreneurial education.

What LSU has learned is that if our efforts to use charter schools as a change agent are to be successful, a rigorous program that prepares multi-faceted leadership has to be developed and implemented. Our sister institution, the University of New Orleans, has already chartered (pun intended) new territories by establishing two charters in New Orleans before Katrina. With the devastation of the aftermath of the hurricanes, these schools were temporarily closed, as were all schools in the New Orleans area. One of the charter schools has since re-opened and several of the communities within the now defunct Orleans Parish Schools are working with UNO to develop new charters to help their communities come back. These schools will serve a vital function within their neighborhoods not only as an educational institution but as a barometer of health of these communities struggling to re-build.

Example Three—Autonomous Schools: A hybrid of charter schools is emerging. Autonomous schools are schools that are not ruled separately by a board of trustees as are most charter schools but belong to a network of district schools still under the governance and jurisdiction of the local public school board. An autonomous school zone or network is to serve as a spade for planting within the system a seed of differentiation that may grow to transform other public schools. Essentially the goal of this effort is to have an existing traditional school in the district become a part of the autonomous school network—doing precisely what its name implies—making autonomous decisions for the good of the children who attend, yet networking with all so that systemic change can be realized.

Immediately following Katrina, the Gates Foundation became involved in assessing educational needs and responding to the recovery. In Baton Rouge, the immediate new home for approximately 200,000 displaced neighbors from New Orleans, Gates partnered with the Baton Rouge Area Foundation and its educational reform organization, Advance Baton Rouge, to provide opportunities to meet immediate needs of children as well as to help create educational structures that are designed to be more focused and flexible. This initiative resulted in the creation of an Autonomous School Network.

The model in Baton Rouge is based on a partnership facilitated by the Baton Rouge Area Foundation among the Gates Foundation, Advance Baton Rouge, and the East Baton Rouge Parish School System, which registered almost 6,000 displaced students after Katrina. The first set of Autonomous Schools in Baton Rouge is challenged to deliver high performing schools for students whose success in school has been limited. The autonomous nature of the schools allows them to be more responsive as they are not bound by the district bureaucracy; the network dimension creates a system that develops and grows through collaboration and support.

Example Four—Incubator Schools: Charter schools, and to a lesser extent, even autonomous schools, emerged as a national response to an emerging consensus among some critics of education that some public school systems are broken and may not be fixable. Based on that assessment of the situation, some have proposed charter and autonomous schools as a way of bypassing the bureaucracies and established structures of public schools on the assumption that charter or autonomous schools can do better with the same children.

One alternative to both charter and autonomous schools and reform projects in failing schools is the idea of incubator schools. These are schools that have strong links to other public schools in the area but which have funding and staff to experiment with and adapt to local conditions, and to develop innovative ways to meet the needs of children within that community. The idea of incubator schools comes from the Business Incubator Center and Research Park concepts that are popular in business. Several hundred business incubators and research parks are currently operating in the United States, usually in close proximity to at least one research university.

The LSU College of Education is currently working with the East Baton Rouge School District and Advance Baton Rouge to explore the possibility of opening an incubator community school in the district. Such a school would be run collaboratively by LSU, parents and community participants, and the school district. It would be equipped, funded, and staffed as an experimental school in which potential innovations—at all levels from classroom practice to leadership and organizational structure—could be tried out, adapted, and developed. Through active participation on the part of LSU faculty in the College of Education and many disciplines, we would bring expertise to a table where other experts also sit—including parents, community partners, and administrators/teachers from the district. Those at that table would decide what innovations to try, how to evaluate them, and how to adapt them to the local context.

In addition to the "test bed" function, the incubator community school would also plan strategies for the dissemination and adoption process. For example, a school interested in adopting a group of innovations might transfer several teachers to the incubator school for one or two years to study and use the innovations. At the same time, they would be working with colleagues at their home school. After their year (or two) at the incubator school they would return to their home school and continue to work on the innovations there. This process represents our most ambitious effort and the most tentative one. Unlike "clean" research, the effort to create and operate an incubator community school involves many levels and many groups. There are political issues to be considered, histories that must be kept in mind, and many groups that will have to work together collaboratively.

Beyond Opening Windows

These bricolage partnerships are important considerations as we address the crisis that is the educational context of South Louisiana post-Katrina. We can no longer reside in the sanctuary of a university that allows us to keep our heads down. Not only must we look out our windows, but we must push open doors and connect our colleges of education with the face of poverty and the burden of a poor education we have seen up close and personal in the aftermath of Katrina.

One final example is offered, as a parable, to explain what we understand our challenges to be. Lenora, a 5-year-old girl who lives in the FEMA trailer park near Baton Rouge, was having great difficulty doing her school work, struggling even to write her letters and numbers. She consistently chose darker colors—black and brown—making circles and figure eights, going over them again and again, creating circular motions upon circular motions. When asked about her drawings, Lenora shared that the circles were the water surrounding her family as they waited to be rescued. The particularly over-circled section in the left-hand corner was her Auntie who drowned and whose body remained close by as the family waited. Working in the make-shift school, an open tent at the trailer park, being there and being a part of the dusty, windy warmth of the school-sanctuary, Lenora's teacher guided her in finding a way to help Auntie out of the putrid waters. Lenora can now concentrate on writing her letters and numbers. She still draws Auntie sometimes but always with wings.

The wounds are many, the scars are deep. Ours is not to take over or to solve the ills that have been created both over a long period of time and as an immediate aftermath to tragedy but to redraw the educational landscape whereby colleges of education have a role, in partnership, with providing wings for flight.

REFERENCES

Anderson, L. S. (2005). Doctor says FEMA ordered him to stop treating hurricane victims. *The Advocate,* Sept. 16, p. 1A.

Annie E. Casey Foundation. (2006). Kids Count State Level Data Online. Available: http://www.aecf.org/kidscount/sld/index.jsp

Bacher, R., & Devlin, T. (2005). *LSU in the eye of the storm: A university model for disaster response.* Baton Rouge: Louisiana State University.

Baker, W. (2006). Bridging the philosophical divide between sociology and economics: The risk and challenge of economic sociology. *American Sociological Association's Economic Sociology Section-in-Formation Web site* Available: http://www.gsm.uci.edu/econsoc/Baker.html [accessed 5–31–06]

Boyer, E. (1990). *Scholarship reconsidered.* San Francisco: Jossey-Bass/Carnegie Foundation for the Advancement of Teaching.

Coleman, A., Bartolo, L., & Jones, C. (2004). Bricoleurs: Exploring digital library evaluation as participant interactions, research, and processes. *Proceedings of the Joint ACM/IEEE Conference on Digital Libraries.* Available: http://portal.acm.org/citation.cfm?id=996443&dl=GUIDE&coll=GUIDE

Cowan, S. (April, 2006). Quoted in K. Vail, Rebuilding New Orleans schools. *American School Board Journal, 193*(4). Available: http://www.asbj.com/current/coverstory2.html

Denzin, N., & Lincoln, Y. (Eds.) (2000). *Sage handbook of qualitative research, 2nd edition.* Thousand Oaks, CA: Sage.

Kincheloe, J. (2001). Describing the bricolage: Conceptualizing a new rigor in qualitative research. *Qualitative Inquiry, 7*(6), 679–692.

Kincheloe, J. (2005). On to the next level: Continuing the conceptualization of the bricolage. *Qualitative Inquiry, 11*(3), 323–350.

Levi-Straus, C. (1966). *The savage mind.* Chicago: University of Chicago Press.

Percy, S., Zimpher, N., & Brukardt, M. (2006). *Creating a New Kind of University: Institutionalizing Community-University Engagement.* Bolton, MA: Anker Publishing Company.

Schon, D. (1995, November/December). The new scholarship requires a new epistemology. *Change,* 27–34.

Smith, A., & LaLonde, R. (2003). "Racelessness" in a Canadian Context? Exploring the link between Black students' identify, achievement, and mental health. *Journal of Black Psychology, 29*(2), 142–164.

U.S. Census Bureau. *Current Population Survey 2004 Annual Social and Economic Supplement,* July 2004. Available: http://pubdb3.census.gov/macro/032004/pov/new46_100125_03.htm

■|■|■

CHAPTER 10

Leadership for the New Normal

LINDA SCHAAK DISTAD

If the misery of the poor be caused not by the laws of nature, but by our institutions, great is our sin.

Charles Darwin

When the levees broke and the floodwaters rushed over New Orleans Parish, stranding thousands upon thousands of poor and mostly Black Americans, it was not the first time. In 1965 Hurricane Betsy had done something similar. Back then, eighty percent of the Lower 9th had been covered by water from ten-foot waves that had overwhelmed the levees, leaving 81 people dead and hundreds more homeless. For years, the Army Corps of Engineers had known that the levee system was inadequate. They had also known that it was only a matter of time before a catastrophic event would overtake the levees and devastate the surrounding areas.

The damage caused by Hurricane Katrina came in two forms. First, there was the event itself—the mass and scale of the devastation left by the hurricane was unprecedented in U.S. history. Second, there was the mass and scale of the emotional and spiritual devastation caused by what Michael Dyson (2006) calls our deliberate naiveté. In his recently published book, *Come Hell or High Water: Hurricane Katrina and the Color of Disaster,* he writes about how much easier it is to feign ignorance. Not knowing rationalizes inaction. Our surprise and dismay about the poverty exposed in the aftermath of the hurricane is a way to remain deliberately naïve and by doing so, avoid the responsibility that comes with understanding, but Katrina changed all that. It's hard to erase the televised images of people stranded for days on rooftops, crying out for help, stunned that none was arriving.

Now it has been several months since the hurricane hit and life in the Gulf Coast is characterized by a new normal. While many stores, restaurants, churches, and schools have re-opened, the impact of the storm remains. By October 2005, two months after Katrina, Baton Rouge Superintendent of Education Cecil Picard estimated that 20,000 to 50,000 students had not yet returned to school. For children living in poverty, school often represents access to resources that may not be available at home. The loss of this key stabilizing factor is devastating for families and the community. After six months, many families in Bay St. Louis, Mississippi still traveled 30 minutes to reach a grocery store, child care was at a minimum, unemployment escalated to 21 percent, and every student in the district had missed at least 47 days of school. It is difficult to comprehend this happening in the United States. However, 13 million American children live in poverty. In addition, some families in "extreme poverty" live on only twenty dollars a day (Children's Defense Fund, 2005). After Hurricane Katrina, Mississippi Assistant Superintendent Debbie Cox said, "Nothing is the same. It's just a whole new normal for us" (Richard, 2006).

In the introduction to Paulo Freire's *Pedagogy of the Oppressed* (1992), Richard Shaull writes,

> There is no such thing as a *neutral* educational process. Education either functions as an instrument which is used to facilitate the integrations of the younger generation into the logic of the present system and bring about conformity to it, *or* it becomes "the practice of freedom," the means by which men and women deal critically and creatively with reality and discover how to participate in the transformation of their world. (p. 15)

As a teacher for over thirty years and as someone who has been closely involved with teacher preparation for over twenty years, I have struggled with how those of us in teacher preparation best respond to the demands of a post-Katrina world. Certainly our conscience cannot allow us to continue "business as usual." The challenge before us is to determine how to transform our teacher preparation programs in light of our understandings of the "new normal," a normal in which being neutral or deliberately naïve is not tolerated. To accomplish this, strong leadership is essential in all aspects of teacher preparation—from program development to program expectations. We certainly need program administrators to be effective leaders, but, we also need to elicit leadership from others in our departments, colleges, and from our prospective teachers. Teacher preparation programs that emphasize focused, personal leadership position their graduates to take on the courageous work of teaching for the new normal.

In the mid-1980s, the College of St. Catherine adopted a leadership statement that is particularly meaningful for teacher education today. The eight characteristics of a St. Catherine's leader draw from an extensive research base related to transformative education, critical pedagogy, feminist theory, and ethics. The eight characteristics of a teacher-leader are as follows:

1. A teacher leader lives a commitment to the values of justice and caring. High-quality teacher preparation is dedicated to modeling practices that ensure that all students' needs are met. Maxine Greene (Ayers, Hunt, & Quinn, 1998) reminds us that "teaching for social justice is teaching what we believe ought to be—not merely in terms of moral frameworks, but in material arrangements for people in all spheres of society. Moreover, teaching for social justice is teaching for the sake of arousing the kinds of vivid, reflective, experiential responses that might move students to come together in serious efforts to understand what social justice actually means and what it might demand" (p. xxix). It is teacher preparation's responsibility to model teaching practices in which "intellectual opportunities are accessible to all on equable and easy terms" (Dewey, 1916/1968, p. 88).

2. A teacher leader acts from a strong self-concept. Culturally relevant and transformative teachers need a clear sense of who they are and what they represent. Sometimes it takes courage. Brian Sevier (2005) lists four themes that guide culturally relevant/transformative teachers. First, "allow students' cultural/historical experiences entry into the classroom." Second, "focus content and practices on educational/social inequities." Third, "create opportunities for students to critically examine knowledge and normalized beliefs." Fourth, "encourage students to use their knowledge to connect with the community beyond the classroom" (p. 352). Using culturally relevant and transformative teaching practices, teachers "work *with* diverse student populations and *for* social justice" (p. 351).

Questioning the structures of power and dominance is an essential element of culturally relevant teaching, a practice that may be uncomfortable in the beginning. It requires constant attention to the "taken for granteds" in curriculum content and the messages embedded in the hidden curriculum. The *Teach for Diversity* model (Ladson-Billings, 2001) uses a theoretical framework of culturally relevant pedagogy that is comprised of three propositions: academic achievement, cultural competence, and sociopolitical consciousness. Culturally relevant pedagogy instills a value for empowering students to critically examine society's power structures and to work for social justice. Prospective teachers need opportunities to see culturally relevant/transformative teaching in action through carefully planned coursework linked to structured field experiences and student teaching.

3. A teacher leader thinks critically and creatively. Within the course of a day, a teacher makes thousands of decisions—Are the students ready? Am I clear? Should I intervene? Should I ignore? Should I move on? Should I slow down? A teacher also must be able to think creatively about how to meet each student's needs and then encourage creativity in her students. Extensive experience in the field is a key component of a teacher preparation program that emphasizes critical and creative thinking based on relevant coursework and authentic experiences.

Starting in the 1980s, fieldwork came to be an expected component of most teacher preparation programs. Over the years, the requirements increased with most programs expecting their students to engage in several fieldwork experiences as an extension of foundations and methods courses.

Early fieldwork experiences help students to reinforce, apply, and synthesize concepts that they learn in their methods courses (Darling-Hammond & Bransford, 2005). This process is complex and involves carefully chosen field settings, consistent interactions between college faculty and their prospective teachers, and debriefing about fieldwork experiences.

Carefully choosing field sites is the first step in designing strong fieldwork experiences. Fieldwork that reinforces the philosophy and practices of the teacher preparation program is effective and fieldwork that does not do so is problematic. Placements that do not align with learned philosophies and practices are confusing to the developing teacher. LaBoskey and Richert (2002) found that "even when students who already have experience, who are well grounded in their disciplines, who are generally reflective, and who have already embraced the goal of social justice have difficulty in discrepant placements" (p. 30).

There is no question that prospective teachers need experience with children in classrooms. However, there is also a clear directive—the experiences must link to and support those methods and philosophies that are taught in the college classroom. There also must be ample and consistent opportunity to de-construct the fieldwork experience with the careful guidance of college faculty. Without guided reflection, there is a risk that negative stereotypes about students and misconceptions about practice can occur (Ladson-Billings, 2001). In addition to learning about teaching as a profession, the purpose of fieldwork is to learn about the students. Because most programs require that prospective teachers spend time in culturally/ethnically diverse classroom settings, the imperative to combine carefully chosen field sites with structured opportunities for reflection becomes even more critical. Several authors (Ladson-Billings, 2001 in Darling-Hammond & Bransford, 2005) suggest that prospective teachers must have opportunities to debrief their experiences, especially when they are in settings different from their own experiential background. If teacher preparation programs are going to participate in the "practice of freedom," then fieldwork must be structured so that prospective teachers "deal critically and creatively with reality and discover how to participate in the transformation of their world" (Shaull, 1992).

4. A teacher-leader communicates and interacts effectively within groups. A teacher communicates in multiple ways throughout the school day. Sometimes she or he communicates in written form, sometimes orally, sometimes through body language, and sometimes with technology. A teacher also communicates with multiple audiences—students, parents, colleagues. A leader can discern the appropriate style and format to use with each group.

Participation in Reflective Practice Groups (Cady, Distad, & Germundsen, 1998; Distad, Chase, Germundsen, & Brownstein, 2000) is an extremely effective process for professional dialogue that includes deconstructing teaching events. Using a structured reflection process and the guidance of an experienced faculty member, prospective teachers share their experiences with other prospective teachers; expand their experiential background, and "try out" strategies for managing instruction, resources and materials, and behavior.

The eight-step reflective practice process allows each prospective teacher an opportunity to engage in problem-solving techniques that link theory with practice. Modeling the habit of reflective practice increases prospective teachers' efficacy, making them feel more confident, affirmed, and validated by their experiences in the classroom. Weekly seminars in which field experiences are discussed promote integration of theory with practice and group problem solving. Authentic experiences coupled with reflection establish habits and patterns of inquiry in which prospective teachers examine the agreement between the realities of the classroom and idealized images (Cole & Knowles, 1993). This then, leads to a more realistic impression of what the teaching profession actually entails.

5. A teacher-leader takes risks willingly. Culturally relevant pedagogy involves risk, the kind of risk that defines leaders. In *Reframing Organizations: Artistry, Choice, and Leadership* (1991), Lee Bolman and Terrence Deal describe three types of leadership. First, they discuss leadership and context. When the context affects not only what leaders must do but also what they can do, then contextual leadership is required. Circumstances frame and clarify the kind of leadership that is critical to a particular situation or context. Jaime Escalante challenged the system by insisting that his Latino students were capable of passing the advanced placement calculus test; he was a contextual leader. He knew the capabilities of his students and he led them to believe in themselves. Then, when their passing scores were disputed by the Educational Testing Service, while certainly unfair, he encouraged them to re-sit for the exam. Throughout this ordeal, Escalante took risks—he risked his reputation as a teacher; he risked losing his job; and most importantly, he risked adding to his students' lack of hope and trust. With Escalante's contextual leadership, there is a new normal for a group of students in East Los Angeles.

The second type of leadership is relational leadership. This is particularly relevant for teacher preparation. The reciprocal relationship between the teacher (leader) and his or her students (constituents) causes the actions of the teacher to be shaped and re-shaped by the students' needs, actions, and reactions. Critical examinations of curriculum, modeling of differentiated teaching strategies, and carefully structured fieldwork prepare prospective teachers to understand the relational nature of leading in a classroom.

The third form of leadership is positional leadership. In most school settings, the principal is the person in obvious authority or with perceived power, even though she or he may not be a leader. On the other hand, a teacher can be an excellent leader without holding a position of formal authority. Deborah Meier used her position as a teacher and then as a principal to test her theories about school effectiveness. Working in East Harlem's Central Park Elementary School, Meier experimented with the concepts of greater teacher autonomy, more parent involvement, active learning, and democratic community-based schooling. The school went from the lowest performing in the district to a highly successful alternative program with a 90 percent graduation rate and 90 percent of its graduates going on to college. Meier used her position to challenge a system that was not working for most of its students. Like Escalante, she took both personal and professional risks because she believed that she was in a position to take action.

All three forms of leadership—contextual, relational, and positional, demand a willingness to take risks. Teacher preparation programs that provide prospective teachers with opportunities to discuss "risky" situations will better equip them for the challenges ahead.

6. A teacher leader exercises power appropriately. It is important for teacher preparation programs to help prospective teachers understand the extent of their influence over their young learners. In *Preparing Teachers for a Changing World: What Teachers Should Learn and Be Able to Do,* the authors state that "teaching is a profession with certain moral as well as technical expectations and, second, . . . in the United States, education must serve the purposes of a democracy." This latter condition suggests that "schools have a responsibility to prepare young people to participate fully in political, civic, and economic life in our society. In addition, education, and teaching is intended to support equitable access to what that society has to offer" (Darling-Hammond & Bransford, 2005, p. 10).

The challenge to non-Gulf Coast residents is to recognize that the issues that Hurricane Katrina exposed are not just a localized problem. Children are being left behind in communities across the nation, not just in the Gulf Coast. Jonathan Kozol continues his crusade to expose educational injustices in *The Shame of the Nation: The Restoration of Apartheid Schooling in America* (2005). He provides a detailed explanation of how federal educational funding legislation has created chasms of inequity among poor and minority students across the nation, dating as far back as the 1970s. Some might say that Kozol presents a skewed picture of America or that he ignores the headway that individual programs are making and that may be true. However, it is hard to refute the fact that a childhood spent in poverty has a lifelong impact, and it is even harder to deny the link between poverty and educational attainment. According to the Children's Defense Fund, "poor children consistently achieve at lower levels than their more affluent peers. Only 15 percent of fourth graders eligible for free and reduced-price lunch could write at grade level compared to 42 percent of those who are not eligible. In math, only 46 percent of eligible fourth graders performed at grade level compared to 79 percent of those who are not eligible" (2005, p. 91). Not only do children living in poverty come to school with differences in knowledge, skills, and experiences, the schools they come to are quite different from those more affluent children attend. One of the most significant differences is the quality and experience of the educators teaching in many depressed socioeconomic areas.

- Schools with the highest percentage of minority, limited English proficient, and low-income students are more likely to employ beginning teachers than those with the lowest percentage of minority, limited English proficient and low-income students.
- Classes in high-poverty schools are 77 percent more likely to be assigned to teachers who did not major in the field in which they are teaching than are classes in low poverty schools. Classes in majority non-White schools are over 40 percent more likely to be assigned to an out-of-field teacher than those in mostly White schools.
- Teachers with master's degrees are less likely to teach in high-minority, low-income schools than they are to teach in high-income, low-minority schools.
- Teachers are significantly more likely to leave a school because of poor working conditions. Teachers in high-minority, low-income schools report significantly worse working conditions, including inadequate facilities, fewer textbooks and supplies, less administrative support, and larger class sizes. As a result, the turnover rate for teachers in high-poverty schools is almost

one-third higher than the rate for all teachers in all schools. (Children's Defense Fund, 2005, p. 95)

Over time, these accumulated deficits have an irreversible impact on students' achievement. It is the responsibility of teacher preparation programs to advocate for high, consistent standards for all teachers, regardless of their route to the classroom. Teacher preparation programs must also be vocal about the need to establish structured induction programs for all teachers new to the profession, with additional support provided for those who teach in high poverty schools.

7. A teacher leader articulates a positive disposition. Many years ago, a cooperating teacher told a group of our prospective teachers that she had a policy in her classroom. When one of her students did not know an answer to a problem, she insisted that the student say "I don't know the answer *yet.*" The simple word "yet" conveyed to the students that learning is a process and that she had complete confidence that they would eventually be successful.

The children of Hurricane Katrina, and other children who are living in chaos, need teachers who "allow students' experiences entry into the classroom." In *STAR Teachers of Children in Poverty* (1995), Martin Haberman describes what "star" teachers consistently do and conversely what they never do. For example, star teachers are persistent. They understand that learning is a developmental process that sometimes requires that they use many different strategies before students are successful. They accept that problem-solving is an inherent part of their job. They derive great satisfaction from facilitating students' learning, particularly when learning has been difficult for the students. Conversely, star teachers do not worry about discipline. They accept that children living in poverty sometimes act out. So they focus on creating a learning environment that is caring, supportive, and reflects the needs and interests of its students. Most children living in poverty have highly developed problem-solving skills—they know how to read their environment for signs of danger, and they know how to straddle the cultures in their schools with that in their neighborhoods. Prospective teachers in a new normal know how to build on their students' assets while diminishing their deficits. The new normal model in teacher preparation includes a shift from a deficit model of teaching to an asset model.

8. A teacher leader evokes hope. Hope is at the heart of the educational experience. It is through education that we envision an optimistic future for our students, even when they do not see it for themselves. It is comforting to know that the leadership that is needed is within all of us. It is a myth that leadership is only at the top of an organization; inspiring leaders can be found everywhere. "There's a generation of leaders searching for the opportunities to make a difference. [There's] hope, because right down the block or right down the hall there are people who will seize the opportunity to lead you to greatness. They're your neighbors, friends, and colleagues. And you are one of them, too" (Kouzes & Posner, 2002, p. 20).

On August 29, 2005, a terrible hurricane hit the Gulf Coast area of the United States. When the water receded, the country was left with a whole new normal. This new normal demands that teacher preparation programs help prospective teachers become leaders who have the courage and confidence to teach for social justice; leaders who teach what they believe ; leaders who participate in the transformation of a world that can no longer be naive.

REFERENCES

Ayers, W., Hunt, J. A., & Quinn, T. (1998). *Teaching for social justice: A democracy and education reader.* New York: New Press and Teachers College Press.

Bolman, L. G., & Deal, T. E. (1991). *Reframing organizations: Artistry, choice, and leadership.* San Francisco: Jossey-Bass.

Cady, J., Distad, L. S., & Germundsen, R. (1998). Reflective practice groups in teacher induction: Building professional community via experiential knowledge. *Education,* Spring, 459–470.

Children's Defense Fund. (2005). *State of America's children 2005.* Washington, DC:

Cole, A. L., & Knowles, J. G. (1993). Shattered images: Understanding expectations and realities of field experiences. *Teaching and Teacher Education, 9*(5/6), 457–471.

Collins, J. C. (2001). *Good to great.* New York: HarperBusiness.

Darling-Hammond, L., & Bransford, J. (2005). *Preparing teachers for a changing world: What teachers should learn and be able to do.* San Francisco: Jossey-Bass.

Dewey, J. (1916/1968). *Democracy and education: An introduction to the philosophy of education.* New York: Free Press.

Distad, L. S., Chase, B., Germundsen, R. A., & Cady Brownstein, J. M. (2000). Putting their heads together. *Journal of Staff Development,* Fall.

Dyson, M. E. (2006). *Come hell or high water: Hurricane Katrina and the color of disaster.* New York: Basic Civitas.

Freire, P. (1992). *Pedagogy of the oppressed.* New York: Continuum.

Haberman, M. (1995). *STAR teachers of children in poverty.* West Lafayette, IN: Kappa Delta Pi, an International Honor Society in Education.

Kouzes, J. M., & Posner, B. Z. (2002). *The leadership challenge.* San Francisco: Jossey-Bass.

Kozol, J. (2005). *The shame of the nation: The restoration of apartheid schooling in America.* New York: Crown.

LaBoskey, V. K., & Richert, A. E. (2002). Identifying good student teaching placements: A programmatic perspective. *Teacher Education Quarterly, 29*(2), 7–34.

Ladson-Billings, G. (2001). *Crossing over to Canaan: The journey of new teachers in diverse classrooms.* San Francisco: Jossey-Bass.

Richard, A. (2006), The 'new normal.' *Education Week.* http:www.edweek.org/ew/articles/2006/02/15/23waveland.h25html?querystring=hurricankatrina (retrieved 4.10.06).

Samuels, C. A. (2005). Educators discover that tracking displaced students is a challenge. *Education Week.* http://www.edweek.org/ew/articles/2005/10/26/09katenroll.h25.html?querystring=hurricanekatrina (retrieved 4.10.06).

Sevier, B. (2005). "What does this have to do with us?" Pursuing transformative possibilities and cultural relevancy in a social foundations teacher education course. *Theory and Research in Social Education, 33*(3), 347–375.

Shaull, R. (1992). Introduction. In P. Freire, *Pedagogy of the oppressed.* New York: Continuum.

CHAPTER II

Benign Neglect
or Deliberate Exclusion?

Lessons Learned from Hurricane Katrina

P. RUDY MATTAI & JACQUELINE M. WILLIAMS

The aftermath of Hurricane Katrina has produced many analyses. To be sure many of these analyses are undergirded by the writers' ideological orientation primarily because it was not merely a natural disaster in and of itself, but it also manifested deep ideological issues that have gone unaddressed in any degree of genuine concern. However, the sociological and political commentaries on the effects of Katrina particularly for issues of race and class are not new in the discourses of social justice within the American society and more so for schooling contexts, professional preparation, and community politics. David Levering Lewis, noted author of W. E. B. Du Bois's biography and the Julius Silver University Professor and professor of history at New York University, reminds us even more poignantly that not only is this discourse around race and class not new but the nuances of partisan racial travesty in a natural disaster of such an ilk as Hurricane Katrina while seemingly déjà vu, are more than merely a reoccurrence. What Lewis is referring to is what is now euphemistically referred to as the 1927 Great Mississippi Flood that led W. E. B. DuBois to encourage Black folks in Mississippi, "Let them ride, run and crawl out of this hell. There is no hope for the black man there today . . . Mr. Hoover is too busy having his picture taken and Mr. Coolidge . . . tells the world of the privileges of American civilization" (Lewis, 2005, p. 17).

Lewis's (2005) article, *Unchanged Melody: The Negro and the Flood,* goes even further to draw the parallels between the 1927 Great Mississippi Flood and Hurricane Katrina and the implications for the issues of race and class in the American society and concludes that

> [i]n the wake of Katrina, White America rediscovered these poor Blacks overnight, 78 years after the Great Mississippi Flood.
>
> There they were, unsheltered, uninsured, unpossessed even of the getaway car (every American talisman), yet still enduring and striving like all poor people anywhere. But, unlike their poor White analogs, vilified, ridiculed and demonized by the national media as being almost congenitally depraved because they "took" whatever they could to feed, warm and solace their families. Meanwhile, assistance was almost completely absent from either municipal and state authorities or the Bush administration's version of the Special Mississippi Flood Committee—FEMA. (p. 19)

Lewis's conclusion is that "Fifty-one years beyond legal segregation . . . a natural disaster out of the Gulf of Mexico has forced Americans to profess astonishment that race remains the great unresolved perennial of the national experience" (2005, p. 19).

Lewis's (2005) comparative analysis raises two important points for schooling contexts, professional preparation, and community politics. More specifically, the issues of race matter for schooling and, as such, the professional preparation of teachers who are either oblivious to the relevance of issues of race in the process of schooling or prone to using a surrogate—social and economic class to address issues of race and schooling and who may yet "rediscover these poor Blacks overnight," albeit within the context of partisan racial travesty.

Race and Schooling

The notion, if not temptation, to use socioeconomic class as a surrogate for race within the context of schooling as well as in everyday living, particularly for Blacks in American society is well documented within the literature. Foremost among scholars who use socioeconomic class as a surrogate for race are John Ogbu (1978, 1999, 2000, 2002, 2003, 2004); Shelby Steele (1988, 1989, 1990a, 1990b, 1990c); and William Julius Wilson (1980, 1987, 1991a, 1991b, 2003). To a large extent, the argument is that while race and socioeconomic class may be seen as both contributing to the disproportion of educational achievement and poverty among Blacks in the

United States, greater emphasis ought to be placed on socioeconomic class. Wilson (2003) makes such a point when he suggests that "Race continues to be a factor that aggravates inner-city black unemployment problems. But the tendency to overemphasize the racial factors obscures other more fundamental forces that have sharply increased black joblessness" (p. 1104, emphasis added). He is willing to admit that while economic factors have adversely and disproportionately affected Blacks within the United States, there is substantial evidence that what Levy (1998) refers to as "equalizing institutions" such as public schooling have also wreaked havoc on this segment of the population. Indeed, Wilson (2003) goes so far as to admit that race, as an exogenous factor, does matter but concludes that greater emphasis should be placed on endogenous factors which obscure the importance of race.

> The endogenous factors also include social isolation, which is a characteristic feature of the social environment of the ghetto poor. Social isolation deprives inner-city ghetto residents not only of limited access to institutions in the broader society and to economic and social resources, including conventional role models whose presence buffers the impact of neighborhood joblessness, but also curtails their contact with mainstream social networks that facilitate economic and social mobility in modern society. The limited access to societal institutions; lack of neighborhood, economic and social resources; declining presence of conventional role models; and circumscribed cultural learning produce outcomes that restrict social advancement. Some of theses outcomes are structural (weal labor-force attachment and lack of access to informal job networks) and some are social-psychological (limited aspirations and negative social dispositions). (p. 1102)

Much of the discourse that treats socioeconomic class as a surrogate for race also implicitly usurps the notion of deficit thinking in their analysis, and this is rather evident in Wilson's reference to "exogenous factors," Steele's reference to the "content of our character," and Ogbu's inadequate (if not apologetic) theoretical treatise on "voluntary vs. involuntary immigrants." In essence they all beg the question as to the historical antecedents if not primordial conditions that created the manifested behaviors that such proponents use in making their assumptions/presumptions.

There is a seeming willingness of those who attribute the plight confronting racial and ethnic minorities within the United States and particularly those who are Black to be the end result of learned helplessness and what Wilson (2003) defines as "limited aspirations and negative social dispositions." In fact, this explanation, particularly with regard to schooling, is a more desirable explanation rather than the seemingly more "racist" explanations advanced by Herrnstein and Murray (1994) and popularized as the "Bell Curve Theory." Noguera and Wing (2006), looking at the apathy that surrounds the low levels of academic achievement among racial and ethnic minorities in the Berkeley, California, area have a rather interesting take on such avoidance and offer a rather plausible explanation that sheds light on why the children Katrina left behind were almost invisible before and after the deluge:

Those who wish to avoid the thorny issue of race and racism can find solace in knowing that there is no proof that racism of the old type is the cause of the achievement gap in Berkeley, certainly not the racism of bigots wearing sheets. That perception makes it possible for earnest liberals to shake their heads in disappointment when they hear statistics about the large numbers of black and Latino students who fail. If they care enough, they can call for something to be done—more tutoring perhaps—without having to incur any sense of guilt or culpability for the problem.

For this reason, Berkeleyans, like many other Americans, prefer to attribute the causes of the achievement gap to the effects of poverty and the unfortunate influences of family background—that is, parents who are presumed to have less education and know-how when it comes to raising their children. (p. 6)

Figueroa (1991), writing on similar situations in the United Kingdom is even more pellucid in his contentions:

I do not accept that racism or ethnicism can be reduced to social class or adequately accounted for simply by a class analysis, even though there are parallels, commonalities and interaction between these phenomena. A class-structured society is not necessarily racist or ethnicist (while a classless society may be), and racism and ethnicism operate across social classes. (p. 53)

The upshot is that this kind of analysis fosters among those who are architects and guardians of such thoughts feelings of resignation and unwillingness to address the root causes for such pathology. Indeed, they seem justified in apathetic behaviors, which they feel are buttressed by the mantra that "the poor will always be among us" and because of that inevitability there is a seeming meaninglessness (albeit a rationalization), to any action that may be suggested. Alternatively, could it be that such a rationalization is really a manifestation of the dictum made popular by famous sociological theorist W. I. Thomas (1928), "If men believe their situations to be real, they are real in their consequences"? (Thomas and Thomas p. 572). Indeed, one may argue that what may appear as benign neglect is really a manifestation of a perception developed over time and buttressed by an underlying deficit model theoretical disposition that those who are not successful in academic pursuits or upward social mobility (doomed to a lower socioeconomic position) are products of "limited aspirations and negative social dispositions." Consequently, their inevitable demise will in due season occur. Unfortunately, the nexus between race and socio-economic class within the United States is rather strong, and the players in this self-fulfilling prophesy are more often than not characterized by such variables with racial and ethnic minorities at the lower and lowest levels of the proverbial totem pole. Interestingly, those who harbor such perceptions often feel vindicated in their dispositions when racial and ethnic minorities fail to match the achievements of seemingly similar groups and as Noguera and Wing (2006) so aptly observe:

... Many observers of academic trends have argued that the achievement gap in communities like Berkeley is less about race than class ... After all, the vast majority of those who fail, are suspended or expelled, or labeled educationally deficient and siphoned off into remedial courses are poor and often come from families headed by parents or guardians who lack a college education. In contrast, the vast majority of academically successful white students come from affluent families, and they generally have parents with high levels of education. ... Although their families may be technically middle or even lower middle income, these students nevertheless possess the valued "cultural capital" inherited from their typically well-educated parents (Bourdieu & Passeron, 1977). They also benefit from prevailing *assumptions [perceptions?] about the relationship between race and academic ability.* (pp. 4–5; emphasis added)

The observations made by Noguera and Wing (2006) and Bourdieu and Passeron (1977) were echoed in the pre- and post-Katrina fiasco especially with respect to students of color and, more particularly, Black children. One may argue that such children, as were their parents and guardians, "tracked" into a pathway of failure and the devastation brought on by Hurricane Katrina merely reified the thoughts of those who possessed such perceptions.

Gloria Ladson-Billings, the Kellner Family Professor of Urban Education in the Department of Curriculum & Instruction at the University of Wisconsin-Madison and one of the foremost scholars on Black children and schooling in the United States, provides a rather interesting perspective as to why, despite the preponderance of existing pathological analyses regarding Black children's academic status, there appears to be a paucity or almost non-existent body of literature addressing prescriptive ameliorative situations.

One reason is a stubborn refusal in American education to recognize African Americans as a distinct cultural group. While it is recognized that African Americans make up a distinct *racial* group, the acknowledgement that this racial group has a distinct *culture* is still not recognized. It is presumed that African American children are exactly like white children but just need a little extra help. Rarely investigated are the possibilities of distinct cultural characteristics (requiring some specific attention) or the detrimental impact of systemic racism. Thus the reasons for their academic failure continue to be seen as wholly environmental and social. Poverty and lack of opportunity often are presented as the only plausible reasons for poor performance. And the kinds of intervention and remedies proposed attempt to compensate for these deficiencies. (1994, p. 9)

Ladson-Billings (1994) hits an important note in what is required to turn around the prevalent current analysis and certainly what is to a large extent responsible for the children Katrina left behind. Ladson-Billings calls for " ... the possibilities of distinct cultural characteristics (requiring some specific attention) or the detrimental impact of systemic racism. ... " while not being a panacea would undoubtedly provide the kind of analysis that gets to the root of the problem and thereby provide the proverbial remedy. However, the tendency is to further obfuscate " ... the possibilities of distinct cultural characteristics (requiring some specific attention) or the detrimental impact of systemic racism. . . ." One such effort within the academy that has been popularized is the resort to multiculturalism.

The multiculturalism movement may be dated back to an original statement issued in 1972 by the American Association of Colleges for Teacher Education (AACTE) euphemistically titled, *No One Model American*. Ostensibly, the statement was intended to draw attention to "the possibilities of distinct cultural characteristics (requiring some specific attention)" but certainly not to its complementary piece, i.e., bring attention to " . . . the detrimental impact of systemic racism." That statement contended that "[m]ulticultural education is education which values cultural pluralism. Multicultural education rejects the view that schools should seek to melt away cultural differences or the view that schools should merely tolerate cultural pluralism. . . . It affirms that major education institutions should strive to preserve and enhance cultural pluralism. To endorse cultural pluralism is to endorse the principle that there is no one model American." (AACTE, 1973, p. 264)

Subtly underscored in this pronouncement is that there is a level playing field among the various racial and ethnic groups within the American society or another way of making manifest Ladson-Billings's (1994) erudite observation that "[i]t is presumed that African American children are exactly like white children but just need a little extra help" (p. 9). However, such an opposition is fraught with contradictions as is so evidently portrayed in James Banks's attempt to reconcile multiculturalism with a pursuit of ethnic studies within the curriculum. This is particularly evident in some of his earliest writings (Banks, 1981, 1983, 1986, 1987, 1988) when he contends that while multiculturalism framed itself as a comprehensive treatment of the diversity that exists within the American society, it lacked the depth to incorporate the needs of certain racial and ethnic groups in particular and thereby rendered itself as an inadequate concept. However, by 1997, in a sixth edition of his, *Teaching Strategies for Ethnic Studies,* there appears to have been a recanting of such a position albeit covertly. Indeed in the preface to the sixth edition, he juxtaposes multiculturalism for ethnic studies and the once-held inadequacy of the former concept to address " . . . the possibilities of distinct cultural characteristics (requiring some specific attention) or the detrimental impact of systemic racism" is not only blurred but appears nonexistent:

> The accelerating demographic and economic changes within our society, the deepening racial divide and the elusive quest for equality and justice make *multicultural education* imperative as we enter the twenty-first century. Since the fifth edition of *Teaching Strategies for Ethnic Studies* was published, the gap between the rich and the poor has widened, visible signs of the racial crisis have become stark, and the rate of increase of low-income youth and youth of color within the nation's schools and universities has continued to outpace the growth rate of Whites. . . .

> The sixth edition of *Teaching Strategies for Ethnic Studies* is designed to help teachers to conceptualize, design, and implement a democratic, thoughtful, and just curriculum that honors and reflects the experiences, hopes, and dreams of all Americans. (p. xv)

The recognition of the inadequacy of multicultural education to address "the possibilities of distinct cultural characteristics (requiring some specific attention) or the detrimental impact of systemic racism" is indeed rather astute. In fact, Mattai (1992) joining the voices of a plethora of proponents of antiracist education (Carby, 1982; Dhondy, 1978; Figueroa, 1991; JanMohamed, 1987; JanMohamed & Lloyd, 1987; McCarthy, 1990; Modgil, Verma, Mallick, & Modgil, 1986; Mullard, 1981, 1982, 1983, 1985; Stone, 1981; Troyna & Williams, 1986; Verma, 1984.) argues:

> [there is a] seeming inability of multicultural education to address the issues of race despite the contention that race is an important variable in the consideration of the disenfranchisement, largely attributable to the educational system, that minorities experience. [He further] argues that multicultural curricula do not directly address eliminating racism and its vestiges nor do they provide strategies for empowering minorities to effectively counteract such phenomena. . . . the present manifestations of multicultural education in higher education lack institutional commitment and are thus palliative in nature. Consequently, attempts to introduce multiculturalism to the curricula are suspect in most cases and seem to be political responses to relatively powerful interest groups . . . (pp. 66–67)

In essence, one of the lessons learnt from the children Katrina left behind is that there must be a genuine emphasis that recognizes that Black children in schools exhibit according to Mattai (1992) "the possibilities of distinct cultural characteristics (requiring some specific attention)" and are more often than not the recipients of " . . . the detrimental impact of systemic racism." Indeed, such an analysis compels us to re-examine the modus operandi as well as the content of the curricula and, by all available evidence, revisit the popularized effectiveness of the multicultural curriculum. This introspection raises quite naturally the professional preparation of teachers who are either oblivious to the virility of issues of race in the process of schooling or prone to using a surrogate—social and economic class—to address issues of race and schooling and who may yet "rediscover these poor Blacks overnight" albeit within the context of partisan racial travesty.

Teacher Preparation and Race and Schooling

There is an evident recognition by certification and accreditation agencies that the classroom demographics are undergoing rapid transformation. The National Center for Educational Statistics (NCES) in a 2005 report, *The Condition of Education*, indicated:

The percentage of public school students who are racial/ethnic minorities increased from 22 percent in 1972 to 42 percent in 2003, primarily due to growth in Hispanic enrollments. In 2003, minority public school enrollment (54 percent) exceeded White enrollment (46 percent) in the West. (p. 5)

The sharp increase in enrollments among minorities was accompanied by an inverse relationship in academic performance and interestingly, a similar situation regarding the presence of teachers of color in the classroom. According to Darling-Hammond and Baratz-Snowden (2005),

In today's schools, teachers must be prepared to teach a diverse student population. Students of color now comprise 40 percent of elementary and secondary students . . . To teach all children well, teachers must know how to tailor their curriculum and instruction so that their students will be engaged in meaningful work. A basic principle of learning is that people need to begin with what they already know and have experienced and connect it to new information or ideas they are trying to learn. Thus, beginning teachers need to know how to learn about their students' experiences in order to construct curriculum and teaching that build on these experiences and students' prior knowledge. (p. 21)

However, the research on teachers' proficiency in doing what is suggested by Darling-Hammond and Baratz-Snowden (2005), particularly with respect to their dexterity in adopting culturally responsive pedagogy, is not very encouraging. Ansalone (2003), Antiles, Trent, & Hoffman-Kipp (2000), Ford (1995a, 1995b, 1998, 1999, 2003), Grinberg and Goldfarb (1998), Hyun and Marshall (1997), Irvine (1990), Ladson-Billings (1994), Milner and Ford (2005), Monroe & Obidah (2004), Pigot and Cohen (2000), Webb-Johnson, Antiles, Trent (1998), Zeichner, Grant, and Gay (1998) have all commented on the high probability of a mismatch between teachers' knowledge of their students' experiences and their classroom placement.

Grant and Gillette (2006) reinforce those findings by reminding us that the need to understand each student as an individual whose cultural identity is shaped by a plethora of factors including "[racial]/ethnic group, social class, gender, language, sexual orientation, and religious affiliation" (p. 295) is equally important and that those factors are relevant in the learning process. However, understanding those factors presumes that there is both openness to changing one's prior knowledge and that professional preparation takes an active role in causing such changes to occur particularly for those teachers whose cultural repertoire is almost devoid of experiences with the "Other"—not let them as was the case in *the* children Katrina left behind, "rediscover these poor Blacks overnight." This is precisely why teacher preparation programs must resist the temptation to water down the real issues confronting our society especially with regard to the inequities of schooling and engage teachers during their professional preparation in the discourses of racism. Futhermore, as Kailin (1999), challenges us:

because teachers play a pivotal role in the sum total of race relations in education, being the professional group that has the most ongoing contact with our children, it is imperative to consider how they perceive the problem of racism in their classrooms and schools so that they may develop effective strategies to counteract their impaired consciousness. . . . Because of the subtleties of White privilege and relative entitlement of members of the dominant group, many White teachers reveal a confused or contradictory consciousness about racism and its manifestations. Racism must be understood and measured, not only by its intent, but by its effects. (p. 746)

Conclusion

The lesson learned from the children Katrina left behind is , we hope, not contained in W. E. B. Du Bois's exhortation to Black "folks" caught in the 1927 Great Mississippi Flood, "Let them ride, run and crawl out of this hell. There is no hope for the black man there today" (Lewis, 2005, p. 17). Furthermore, we hope that the issues of race and schooling that have become so apparent since the aftermath of Hurricane Katrina will ensure that we will not only in times of distress "rediscover these poor Blacks overnight," albeit within the context of partisan racial travesty. Rather, the important lessons for schooling contexts, professional preparation, and community politics, will be that we deliberately address the issues of race that matter for schooling and, as such, cause the professional preparation of teachers who are either oblivious to the virility of issues of race in the process of schooling or prone to using a surrogate—social and economic class—to address issues of race and schooling to see racism not only by its intent, but by its effects.

REFERENCES

American Association of Colleges for Teacher Education. (AACTE), Commission on Multicultural Education. (1973). No One Model American. *Journal of Teacher Education, 49*(3), 361–386.

Ansalone, G. (2003). Poverty, tracking, and the social construction of failure: International perspectives. (1), 3–20.

Antiles, A. J., Trent, S. C., & Hoffman-Kipp, P. (2000). From individual acquisition to cultural-historical practices in multicultural teacher education. *Remedial and Special Education*, 21, 79–89.

Banks, J. A. (1981). *Multiethnic education: Theory and practice.* Boston: Allyn & Bacon.

Banks, J. A. (1983). Multiethnic education at the crossroads. *Phi Delta Kappan, 64*(8), 559–569.

Banks, J. A. (1986). Multiethnic education and its critics: Britain and the United States. In S. Modgil, G. K. Verma, K., Mallik, & C. Modgil (Eds.), *Multicultural education: The interminable debate.* London: Falmer Press.

Banks, J. A. (1987). *Teaching strategies for ethnic studies.* Boston: Allyn & Bacon.

Banks, J. A. (1988). *A multicultural education: theory and practice* (2nd ed.). Boston: Allyn & Bacon.

Banks, J. A. (1997). *Teaching strategies for ethnic studies.* (6th ed.). Boston: Allyn & Bacon.

Bourdieu, P., & Passeron, P. (1977). *Reproduction in education, society, and culture.* Thousand Oaks, CA: Sage.

Carby, H. (1982). Schooling in Babylon. In Center for Contemporary Cultural Studies. *The empire strikes back: Race and racism in the 70's* (pp. 182–311). London: Hutchinson.

Darling-Hammond, L., & Baratz-Snowden, J. (2005) *A good teacher in every classroom: Preparing the highly qualified teachers our children deserve.* San Francisco: Jossey-Bass.

Dhondy, F. (May 1978). The Black explosion in schools. *Race Today,* 80–85.

Figueroa, P. (1991). *Education and the social construction of "race."* London: Routledge.

Ford, D. Y. (1995a). *A study of underachievement among gifted, potentially gifted, and general\education students.* Storrs, CT: University of Connecticut, National Research Center on the Gifted and Talented.

Ford, D. Y. (1995b). *Correlates of underachievement among gifted and nongifted Black students.* Storrs, CT: National Research Center on the Gifted and Talented, The University of Connecticut.

Ford, D. Y. (1996). *Reversing underachievement among gifted Black students: Promising practices and programs.* New York: Teachers College Press.

Ford, D. Y. (1998). The underrepresentation of minority students in gifted education: Problems and promises in recruitment and retention. *The Journal of Special Education, 32,* 4–14.

Ford, D. Y. (1999.). *Factors affecting the career decision making of minority teachers in gifted education.* Storrs, CT: The University of Connecticut, National Research Center on the Gifted and Talented.

Ford, D. Y. (2003, Summer). Two other wrongs don't make a right: Sacrificing the needs of diverse students does not solve the gifted education unresolved problems. *Journal for the Education of the Gifted,* 26(4), 283–291.

Grant, C. A., & Gillette, M. (2006, May/June). A candid talk to teacher educators about effectively preparing teachers who can teach everyone's children. *Journal of Teacher Education,* 57(3), 292–299.

Grinberg, J., & Goldfarb, K. P. (1998). Moving teacher education into the community. *Theory into Practice,* 37(2), 131–139.

Herrnstein, R. J., & Murray, C. (1994). *The bell curve.* New York: Free Press.

Hyun, E., & Marshall, J. D. (1997). Theory of multicultural/multiethnic perspective-taking ability for teachers' developmentally and culturally appropriate practice. *Journal of Research in Childhood Education,* 11, 188–198.

Irvine, J. J. (1990). *Black students and school failure.* Westport, CT: Greenwood Press.

JanMohamed, A. (1987). Introduction: Toward a theory of minority discourse. *Cultural Critique.* 6, 5–11.

JanMohamed, A., & Lloyd, D. (9187). Introduction: Minority discourse—What is to be done? *Critique.* 7, 5–17.

Kailin, J. (1999, Summer). How white teachers perceive the problems of racism in their schools: A case study in "liberal" Lakeview. *Teachers College Record, 100*(4), 724–750.

Ladson-Billings, G. (1994). *The dreamkeepers: Successful teachers for African American teachers.* San Francisco, CA: Jossey-Bass.

Levy, F. (1998). *New dollars and dreams: American incomes and economic change.* New York: Russell Sage Foundations.

Lewis, D. L. (2005, November/December). Unchanged melody: The Negro and the flood. *The Crisis,* 17–19.

Mattai, P. R. (1992). Rethinking the nature of multicultural education: Has it lost its focus or is it being misused? *Journal of Negro Education, 61*(1), 65–77.

McCarthy, C. (1990). *Race and curriculum: Social inequity and the theories and politics of difference in contemporary research on schooling.* New York: Falmer Press.

Milner, H. R., & Ford, D. Y. (2005, Fall). Racial experiences influence us as teachers: Implications for gifted education curriculum development and implementation. *Roeper Review, 28*(1), 30–36.

Modgil, S., Verma, G. K., Mallick, K., & Modgil, C. (1986). *Multicultural education: The interminable debate.* London: Falmer Press.

Monroe, C. R., & Obidah, J. E. (2004, May/June). The influence of cultural synchronization on teachers' perceptions of disruption. *Journal of Teacher Education, 55*(3), 256–268.

Mullard, C. (1981). Black kids in White schools: Multiracial education in Britain. *Plural Societies, 12,* 1–12.

Mullard, C. (1982). Multiracial education in Britain: From assimilation to cultural pluralism. In Tierney, J. (Ed.). *Race, class and education* (pp. 15–27). London: Holt, Rinehart & Winston.

Mullard, C. (1985). Racism in society and school: History, policy and practice. In F. Rizvi (Ed.), *Multiculturalism as educational policy* (pp. 64–81). Victoria, Australia: Deakin University Press.

Noguera, P. A., & Wing, J. Y. (2006). *Unfinished business: Closing the achievement gap in our schools.* San Francisco: Jossey-Bass.

Ogbu, J. (1978). *Minority education and caste: The American system in cross-cultural perspective.* New York: Academic Press.

Ogbu, J. (Summer 1999). Beyond language: Ebonics, proper English, and identity in a Black-American speech community. *American Educational Research Journal, 36*(2), 147–184.

Ogbu, J. (2000). Collective identity and schooling. In H. Fugita & K. Shimizu, (Eds.), *Education, knowledge and power.* Tokyo: Shinyosha Ltd.

Ogbu, J. (2002). Black-American students and the academic achievement gap: What else you need to know. *Journal of Thought, 37*(4), 9–33.

Ogbu, J. (2003). *Black students in an affluent suburb: A study of academic disengagement.* Hillsdale, NJ: Lawrence Erlbaum.

Ogbu, J. (2004). Collective identity and the burden of "acting white" in Black history, community, and education. *The Urban Review, 36*(1), 1–35.

Pigott, R. L., & Cohen, E. L. (2000). Teacher race, child race, racial congruence, and teacher ratings of children's school adjustment. *Journal of School Psychology, 38*(2), 177–196.

Steele, S. (1988). I'm Black, you're White, who's innocent? Race and power in an era of blame. *Harper's, 276*(1657), 45–53.

Steele, S. (1989). The recoloring of campus life: Student racism, academic pluralism, and the end of a dream. *Harper's, 278*(1665), 47–55.

Steele, S. (1990a). Ghettoized by Black unity. *Harper's, 280*(1680), 20–23.

Steele, S. (1990b, May 13). A negative vote on Affirmative Action. *The Sunday New York Times Magazine,* 46–49, 73.

Steele, S. (1990c). *The content of our character: A new vision of race in America.* New York: St. Martin's.

Stone, M. (1981). *The education of the Black child in Britain: The myth of multicultural education.* Glasgow, Scotland: Fontana.

Thomas, W. I., & Thomas, D. S. (1928). *The child in America: Behavior problems and programs.* New York: Knopf.

Troyna, B., & Williams, J. (1986). *Racism, education, and the state.* London: Croom Helm.

U.S. Department of Education, National Center for Education Statistics. (2005). *The Condition of Education 2005* (NCES 2005–094). Washington, DC: U.S. Government Printing Office.

Verma, G. K. (1984). Multiculturalism and education: Prelude to practice. In G. K. Verma, & C. Bagley (Eds.). *Race relations and cultural differences.* London: Croom Helm.

Webb-Johnson, G., Antiles, A. J., & Trent, S. C. (1998). The status of research on multicultural education in teacher education and special education: Problems, pitfalls, and promises. *Remedial and Special Education,* 19, 7–15.

Wilson, W. J. (1980). *The declining significance of race.* (2nd ed.). Chicago: University of Chicago Press.

Wilson, W. J. (1987). *The truly disadvantaged.* Chicago: University of Chicago Press.

Wilson, W. J. (1991a). Public policy research and the truly disadvantaged. In C. Jenks & P. Peterson, (Eds.), *The urban underclass.* Washington, DC: The Brookings Institute.

Wilson, W. J. (1991b). Studying inner-city social dislocations. *American Sociological Review, 56,* 1–14.

Wilson, W. J. (Nov 2003). Race, class and urban poverty: A rejoinder. *Ethnic and Racial Studies,* 26(6), 1096–1114.

Zeichner, K., Grant, C. A., & Gay, G. (1998). A research informed vision of good practice in multicultural teacher education: Study principles. *Theory into Practice, 37,* 163–171.

CHAPTER 12

For They Are Us

"Tools" for Post-Katrina Curriculum and Community

PAMELA K. SMITH & PAT WILLIAMS-BOYD

> *United States citizens tend to believe that tragedy will happen, but it will occur outside this nation's boundaries. We are accustomed to seeing marginalized countries in other parts of the world struggling with natural and human destruction. With many of our citizens having grown up in an atmosphere where dinners were eaten while the U.S. body count in Vietnam blared from the television, we are used to the media panopticon that provides us with our opinions, our ideas of reality, and our notions of truth.*
>
> (Foucault, 1975)

When Hurricane Katrina approached the Gulf Coast heading for New Orleans, this nation reacted with the same degree of complacency and self-assuredness that was evident in the days prior to September 11, 2001. The hurricane would not hit. It would not happen here. It would miss one of this country's most prominent recreational areas and strike some nondescript area in Texas that no one would remember even after a few trailer parks had been swept away.

However, Hurricane Katrina struck with all of her fury, and despite all government agencies' promises to the contrary, the levees did not hold, sending cascades of flood water into the city's poorest districts. The unthinkable had happened, and cable news showed us the graphic images of devastation 24 hours a day. Some of us were unable to turn away from the television, remembering our own visits to New Orleans where we watched tap-dancing boys on street corners gathering our change while we laughed without question. As the extent of Katrina's devastation unfolded, we watched in despair. As the storm's victims were herded into ill-equipped football stadiums, we watched with disbelief and guilt. We struggled to find a way to offer our own reparations to a part of our country that still remained enslaved by poverty, with little awareness of a world that lay beyond their boundaries.

We watched because we knew that what previously had been kept hidden in the shadows of the backstreets, backwoods, and bayous lay now in the glaring lights of television cameras sending signals that would be viewed by the world. That global community would soon judge us all, and we knew that we would fail the test of our own morality's judgment. We sat helpless after 9/11. Perhaps this time, we could do something. Katrina struck our people in our country, and suddenly checkbooks came out and the Red Cross saw one of its biggest paydays.

While respecting the actions of faith-based groups, community agencies, and individuals who simply wished to give, members of the College of Education at Eastern Michigan University put on the mantle of Katrina as a felt experience. We could not simply gather donations and send them down, and we could not simply conduct our newly begun classes, discuss social agency and remain safely apart. Talk became a call to action, and Project Backpack was born. Two weeks after watching the Saturday-night cable news special, four professors and a Dyer, Indiana, law enforcement officer climbed into a van loaded with backpacks and headed for Baton Rouge, Louisiana, a city swollen beyond all proportions with the influx of evacuees. We went into a storm of our own, not certain of what we would find, not knowing if we had the tools needed for the work which lay ahead.

Our team chose to work with two previously condemned schools that had been reopened for evacuated teachers and students, living now in a nearby shelter. It took little time for us to begin to see the damage wrought not only by Katrina but even more by a society that disenfranchises those who are not privileged. A father of an elementary school student spoke with the sort of candor that is born from watching an entire life's work blown apart.

> Aaron and his wife stood in the circular driveway of the East Baton Rouge school that had just accepted another 325 Children of the Storm. Their daughter was one of them. Our team approached him as he and his wife turned to get back into their truck, a testament

to another time. Pretentiously, we asked if there were anything we could do to help. "I need a job," was his unhesitating response. "I don't want any handouts or charity. I need tools. I'm a carpenter. The storm took everything I need to do my work. I've tried the local home centers and hardware stores. As soon as they find out I'm from New Orleans, they won't trust me with credit to simply buy some basic tools. I don't know what I'm going to do."

What do you say to someone whose life has been swept away in a moment, to someone who has lost loved ones, property, the self-dignity that comes with work? They are proud, dignified, courageous people. (Williams-Boyd, Journal sent to College of Education, Eastern Michigan University, September 22, 2005)

At that moment, our journey's direction shifted because we began to see that we did not have the tools to help all of the Aarons or all of the Children of the Storm. We had some money to buy school supplies, but how could we, in a week's stay, make a difference for people who had lost all worldly possessions? How could we build anything apart from a temporary castle in the sand?

Some kids reached out for a hug. One sat and cried. Others watched warily. They are kids, after all. Some played and laughed while others poked and teased each other, marched down the hallway in their new uniforms. (Williams-Boyd, Journal, September 21, 2005)

Though always a team, we each embarked upon our own distinct personal journeys, not knowing the final destination or what lay around the next corner. One constant stood out, and that was the emotion engendered by the expressions and the gratitude given when human contact was offered.

Their eyes and silent faces speak the things that are left unsaid. They have lost all material things, these Children of the Storm. They fill this school. We shopped to purchase some of the basic needs of classroom teachers and their students. Five "Project Backpack" shirts shopping in Wal-Mart give rise to questions. People thank us—all of us, seen and represented—for caring about them, for thinking about the people of Louisiana, for heeding the call for help. We only begin to touch the surface. (Williams-Boyd, Journal, September 21, 2005)

We intended to stay until Friday, but Hurricane Rita's approach prompted Governor Blanco to ask all visitors to leave Baton Rouge and our Dean called and expressed concern.

We are fleeing to save our own lives. But we are leaving thousands of people who have already fled to this place as their last hope of refuge. The storm is no longer Katrina. It is Aaron, Diamond, Stephanie . . . (Williams-Boyd, Journal, September 23, 2005)

We left with a hurry none of us anticipated or desired. We were returning to Michigan hoping to find the tools that we needed to disentangle our own thoughts and questions.

How are our lives to intertwine with the people of Katrina and Rita? Where is the intersection of social agency and moral imperative? How do charity and justice collide or merge? How can we work for empowerment and avoid enablement? Do we seek liberty or liberation?

We have been challenged by the resilience and compassion of a people who, in the face of grave disaster, have lived experiences none of us can even partially comprehend. We do not pretend to understand the complex struggle of these new friends. What we do know is that they are not now and never have been "the Other," an objectified, nameless, faceless, group that deserves pity and simple charity. In truth, what we do know is that these People of the Storm are not they; they are us. (Williams-Boyd, Journal, September 23, 2005)

Three weeks later, Team Two left for New Orleans and the bayous, going with even more uncertainty, lacking a known place to sleep but reassured that a semi-truck load of backpacks filled with school supplies would finally reach Terrebonne Parish and the New Orleans Metairie school district.

The second team reflected Eastern Michigan University's desire to teach students to be agents for social action and, hopefully, social change. One professor from Team One and three graduate students traveled to Lakeview, that part of New Orleans hardest hit by the broken levee.

We quietly stepped out of the van and began to slowly walk down empty, battle-worn streets, void of human life. Everywhere we looked rubble, broken dreams, abandoned cars, houses, hopes. The profound silence was broken only by the occasional bird. And there was no one there.

Crushed CD cases, broken glass, a water-soaked book lay open, its pages arbitrarily fluttering in the brief wind. An upside-down doll carriage, a single tennis shoe baked into mud, a twisted cell phone, a boom box, rugs, pieces of clothing, a young child's graded homework, a never-filled-out change-of-address card, a page from the September 23, 2005 *Times Picayune Newspaper,* peek out from under layers of dead leaves, misshapen tree branches, piles of dried palms, and heaps of barely recognizable furniture, appliances, photo albums, antiques, and cherished memories are mounded up everywhere. And there was no one there.

The noise of the crunch of dried mud under my feet as I slowly walked down the one-time sidewalk sounded like the crackling of a winter's fire. A car door stood open as if casually awaiting someone who never came. The smell of mold was everywhere. And there was no one there.

As we stood in the middle of a deserted, dust-blown ghost town, a place once occupied by $300,000–$500,000 homes, we tried to make sense of what we were feeling. The students began to ask questions, and for 45 minutes talk continued, as we stood with our arms around each other. There were tears and husky voices in our little band, tears born of disillusionment and the realization of the fragility of life.

How could we really understand what went on here? What is really important in life if what we save for and work for can be lost in a moment? What ought we to do with our lives to ensure lasting value? How can we help our own students to more fully realize their own potential in life, to help them discover that for which they have been created, to nurture their understandings of self-efficacy, advocacy, and fulfillment of one's own destiny? (Williams-Boyd, Journal , October 12, 2005).

The brown-caked silt of the floodwater's remains began to coat our shoes as we walked along silent streets and breathed dust that would later create a phenomenon called "Katrina Cough." Graduate students who had begun the journey as young people on a mission began to view their work as teachers in profoundly different ways. They found themselves caught in the conundrum of contemporary education in that the innocence of the world which they had been taught to trust was erased by their knowledge of possibilities for horrific acts, totally devoid of social consciousness or human decency. Like the first team, Team Two heard repeated pleas for simple tools with which to rebuild lives. No one had prepared the students for what they saw, and as professors, we, too, had remained blissfully ignorant of the turmoil of a world turned inside out and of a people rejected by a society that does not like its ugly secrets exposed.

When do teachers leave the tidy confines of their classrooms and enter the messy social arenas that provide them with opportunities to model acting upon moral imperatives informed by social need? Penny Gleason, Coordinator of Titled Programs for Terrebonne Parish and life-long resident of the bayous, repeatedly told us, "All my life well-meaning people have sent much-needed things following hurricanes. But you are the first people to ever come down here." Why was this so significant? Why have we allowed the walls of our classrooms to dictate the confines of our teaching? How could the experience of the professors and graduate students who traveled South after Katrina and Rita be replicated for other students so that the antiseptic world of the traditional institutional setting could be raised to a level of increased consciousness, one rooted in definitions and uncertainties emergent in multiple realities?

It could be argued that in the age of objectified accountability, we have lost sight of much of what it means to be a teacher who teaches to the whole person. How could we measure what the students learned that fall afternoon in Louisiana? Likewise, we, as teacher educators need to find new tools to use in a broken society. Our children face a world rooted in confused ideologies and uninterrogated philosophies, while our own work and our 'products' are under scrutiny by the state. The Ivory Tower has begun to feel the strain of the accountability movement's call for excellence, and now, we, too, will be judged as being "effective" institutions solely on the basis of our teacher graduates' success in the field.

This raises fundamental questions. What is it that ethically centered teacher educators are bound to do? What tools do we need to equip our future teachers? How impoverished have we become in a society that devalues the very institutions which taught them the skills needed for their own vocations? Do we still have enough credit of our own in this world to support our ethos, or is our validity constantly denied by a system which declines to legitimate what we know to be morally centered and pedagogically sound? How can we balance the need to graduate teachers who can meet the technical demands of the state, while safeguarding their civic awareness and willingness to act against oppressive social actions? Why have we so easily given up our own convictions? When did we stop focusing on education as the focal point for improving life in the world and step into the arena of making sure that standards and benchmarks are reflected properly in lesson plan writing? How many of our students would be willing to set their lives aside and step into the fray when a community issue demands their attention and action? How many of them will rise up and go? How many of them could say with Marliese from Team Two:

> How can we get other people to understand what we have seen here? How can we share with them this perspective and how it changes so many things? . . . "I felt we were doing such a good job. Now as I'm standing here (in Lakeview, La.) in comparison to the magnitude of the destruction, I feel we have done so little." "You're right, Marliese, but we have done something." (Williams-Boyd, Journal, October 12, 2005)

Just as the commission that investigated government actions in the wake of Katrina exposed tremendous failings, so do we find ourselves severely lacking in preparing our teachers for the exigencies of the lived life of educators. In this sense, we challenge standard teacher preparation programs and find them too often to be boilerplate programs, devoid of the passion that drives and informs effective pedagogical practice. Our concern is that intellectually and emotionally we have to recognize the need to interrogate the basic assumptions that tell us that knowing how to use computer software is more important than opening classroom discussion to sociopolitical debate.

As a result of an extremely litigious society, we have perhaps fallen into a dominant realm of safety. We fear "getting too personal" because we might offend sensibilities. We might be called to task by a conservative referendum driven by structural functionalists' fear of change and Plato's notions of absolute truths.

Today, we "train" teachers rather than prepare educators. Dogs are "trained" to do tricks or small children are trained to eat with utensils rather than fingers, but these are mechanical acts. Educating is an act that touches the core of humanity's center. To be an educator is to be a moral participant, to develop an ethical frame, to center the heart around community while supporting the individual, to see the whole as well as the part, and to know that the work done in the classroom is fundamentally a way of working not only with society's people but with society itself.

In this sense, teacher preparation programs have as their center a commonality of focused philosophical discourse. Those who study to be educators learn to think of rebuilding hope and refashioning communities that are centered upon the premises of common moral and ethical values. A connected sense of "we" is resurrected, one which draws upon those functions of trust, shared beliefs of human goodness and possibility, and confidence in the kind of social responsibility which can set us all in pursuit of something far greater than ourselves alone.

It is unthinkable in Katrina's aftermath for us to take the route of denying blame, for we, too, share it on several levels. Students and teachers disengage from the monotony and lack of connectivity that pervade so many classrooms in schools across the nation today. Too many teacher educators have become behaviorally driven, focused on meeting the cognitive demands of methodology while ignoring the affective demands of caring through which community is built. Students studying in far too many teacher education institutions remain ignorant of the full scope of their work because we have perhaps chosen to ignore the full content that should be taught.

If we simply teach the methodology of writing lesson plans, behavioral objectives, differentiating curriculum, and other elements that constitute segments of good teaching, we have left out a significant part of what is needed for the emergence of learning. When we do not educate the whole student, that is, the technical, practical, and emotionally emancipated, caring person, we reduce that individual to a person who stands in front of students proclaiming someone else's truths but who is unaware of the demands presented by the issues of the students who sit in that classroom and of the social world beyond. In this sense, we have not equipped them with the tools to effectively engage in the messy discourse of interrelationships, the stuff of teaching that challenges each person to work with heart in worlds of possibilities linked to a milieu of disparate challenges and impediments.

As teacher educators, we have to ask ourselves hard questions. The People of the Storm whom we met in Baton Rouge, in New Orleans, in Houma, and in the bayous survived and thrived despite prohibitive ecological, economical, cultural, and sociopolitical factors. As we prepare teachers today, can we say with confidence that we will equip each of them with the tools needed in order to understand a contextual environment of overlapping ecological spheres, to peel away layers of subjectivities fraught with the complexities of mores, values, perceptions, meanings and interactions resonant, and often dissonant, in the interweaving of multi-disciplined epistemologies?

The essence of much of our work lies in educating people in building communities. However, we must first nurture that community within our own work.

Do we remember who we are? Did we ever really know? How often do we follow Maxine Greene's directive to awaken to full agency in the social world as intellectuals, educators who willingly accept the moral imperative needed so that we can encourage our students to move beyond teaching from the textbook to educating the world instead?

The people of the bayous have learned about community through common struggle. Dawn LaFont, the inspirational principal of Pointe-Aux-Chenes Elementary School, told the team, "Our needs far outweigh our differences." The team commented on the warmth and openness of the bayou people, to which a Terrebonne Parish Schools administrator said, "We are taught humility through our common vulnerability." Perhaps candor becomes the norm and simple truths become more easily expressed when all is lost except that which is most important: one's dignity and communal life.

Both of these comments move teacher educators to an important pedagogical moment. While we have become a country which prizes individuality above justice for all, where we have defined the protection of an ill-conceived liberty at the cost of the greater good, where we have expressed democracy through competition in isolation, the People of the Storm have learned community, once again, brought together by collective loss and communal outpourings of both grief and hope. This is significant in that in a community-referenced agenda, communitarians maintain that there is no individual freedom without group and community participation.

When we speak of community, we speak of a community of mind which is characterized by its understandings of shared meaning, shared values, shared conceptions, shared purposes, and shared obligations. In order for disjointed schools to become true communities of learners and learning, students and staff join together, trusting in the validity of each group, fundamentally bound in an engendering sense of intellectual and social identity.

The People of the Storm took solace in being able to go to schools even where paint peeled off the walls, where mold grew on ceiling panels, where running water did not exist, and where the suffocating heat of mid-day sucked the air out of rooms without air-conditioning. Here, they found their commonality of spirit; here they began to create a community for at least seven hours of the day. Then most of the students and teachers boarded buses or walked to over-crowded shelters where they or their caregivers might try to clean the clothes they had worn that day for re-use on the next. They did not complain; they did not demand, and they did not give up. They rose up and persevered because it is human nature to fight to survive, and they did it with dignity.

They found resiliency in their renewed sense of community and the familiarity of the constructs of school. At the same time, teachers in the reopened schools for evacuees used the experience of Katrina to build a curriculum in a situation where textbooks did not exist.

> As we looked into a classroom, we saw the assignment written on the board. Write an essay answering these questions: Where were you when the storm hit? What happened to you and your family? How did you feel? Who helped you? What happened after the storm? How do you feel now? What plans do you have for the future?

Why not question what lay behind the haunted eyes of everyone there? Why not discuss experience so that it need not be repeated? Why not ask for the tools to understand what was still beyond comprehension? Why not invite discursive practices which lead to the sorts of respectful argument and debate that encourage the emergence of new regimes of truth? How can we not change? Indeed, how can we not have been changed, having seen that nothing remains immune from outside forces?

This sense of urgency was part of the power that emerged during Katrina's aftermath. Whereas all too often we "have sought to solve the problems of poverty simply by segregating the poor into ghettos" (Bellah et al., 1987, p. 247) or, in the case of Katrina, into football stadiums, we now know that we are morally bound to educate our students to teach the poor by illuminating the tools that can be used to invite them to join the greater social milieu, regardless of their points of entry. Rather than being trapped in self-denying social pathologies which breed alienation and the loneliness of which Durkheim wrote, we see the need to speak of our experiences, to share our stories, to maintain our ties to the bayou schools, and to challenge our students to believe and invest in the social values which speak to hope and connectedness. Kemmis argues, "What makes values shared and what makes them politically powerful is that they arise out of the challenge of living well together in hard country" (1993, p. 283).

Curriculum is an ongoing discursive practice that revolves and shifts and changes constantly given the demands of the society in which it exists. If a curriculum remains static, it is ineffectual and eventually will be swept out by a typical reform movement which usually offers a rehashing of an old idea rather than offering anything truly new. As teacher educators, we see the need to share what we have learned from our Katrina experience with our students. What will we teach?

We must resurrect the notion of schools as symbols for reestablishing community and the role of the educator as community advocate. We must prepare educators who think of ways to rebuild hope that engenders a burgeoning social trust needed for us to rebuild and refashion communities. This trust is based on the premises of common moral and ethical values, rooted in the penultimate human condition facing us all, regardless of our social position, culture, ethnicity, or other hermeneutically constructed definitions. This means that teacher educators will focus upon creating a connected "we," centered upon those functions of mutual obligations supported by common purposes of trust, shared belief, and shared hope and possibility that draw people together.

Our thinking arises out of the very insistence of a human definition that demands a call to truth. This is a truth that will be ongoing and freed of the bonds of time, a truth which speaks the Politics of Reclamation, a truth whose epistemology is stimulated by the provocative insights that emerge from the re-creation of a new social identity. It presents a schema for adaptation and regeneration that is based on a dialogical confrontation with presumptions of what dominant society envisions what power is and the consequent interactions that revolve around issues of faith, trust, belief, and shared vision.

We do not presume as teacher educators to hold the keys to enlightenment for our students, nor do we believe that we will hand them out to the deserving few who rise to our expectations, as defined by the Academy. This is to deny the validity of individual human identity and human agency.

Rather, we reach for a form of empowerment that is the property of those Giroux (1981) termed transformative intellectuals, i.e., those who arise from a sort of teacher education that is rooted in principles of social agency and is totally divorced from any sense of benevolent hierarchical bestowment that is the result of gracious goodwill. Instead, we see this process as a moment of recycling power in that we advocate restoring what was once owned and then denied. It is opening a sphere of influence for voices that have been silenced by hierarchical formations that fear the truths they might expose.

As teacher educators, we do ourselves and our students a grave disservice if we sit complacently and acquiesce to the demands of the state while ignoring the needs of the greater social whole. It is no longer acceptable, nor was it ever for us to deny or silence the validity of the voice of the marginalized on the basis of our own privilege, one born out of a guise of elevated professional educational expertise.

Having seen the changes in ourselves after the immediate disaster and resulting political debacle of Hurricane Katrina, we have stood long enough in the eye of the storm.

> As we turn our van toward home, we leave friends in new places. Our journey has been powerful, our travels both across much land and deeply within ourselves. We have been taught the greater lessons of life. We have seen that which can disappear in a moment. We have felt that which will last a lifetime. (Williams-Boyd, Last Journal Entry, October 14, 2005)

If we do not change our ways, we will lose our schools, and we will see our students and teachers fall into a moral abyss where the wants of the individual transcend the needs of the whole. To avoid this moment, we advocate a fundamental shift in our work and in our ways of looking at the world.

This is a philosophical shift in position, a recognition of the place of the Other, a recognition of one's own place in an ever-changing world, an unveiling and unfolding recognition of one's power and responsibility to step up and act, and, if needed, to act out. It is a shift founded in true educational reform which is seen as a conjunctive, relational, and contextual reality that lies in opposition to the existential, voiceless, and marginalized discourse of the present. It is reform which speaks of community, reform which frees us to see true possibility and gives us the courage to find it within. Most importantly, it is reform that allows us to step into Ernst Bloch's world of the not yet (1995). It is integration rather than alienation, coalition rather than polarization, interdependence rather than dependence, and emancipation rather than submission.

If we were to advocate less, we would deny our students the very tools that Aaron needed so desperately. These are the tools that educate for self-respect, the tools needed to construct castles on the rock, to build something new, something better, and, quite literally, something that can weather the storms we will all face.

REFERENCES

Bellah, R., Madsen, R., Sullivan, W., Swidler, A., & Tipton, S. (Eds.). (1987). *Individualism and commitment in American life*. New York: Harper & Row.

Bloch, E. (1995). *The principle of hope,* Vol. I. (N. Plaice, S. Plaice, & P. Knight, Trans.). Boston, MA: The MIT Press.

Foucault, M. (1975). *Discipline and punish: The birth of the prison*. London: Penguin Books.

Giroux, H. (1981). *Ideology, culture, and the process of schooling*. Philadelphia, PA: Temple Press.

Kemmis, D. (1993). The last best place: How hardship and limits build community. In S. Walker (Ed.), *The Graywolf ten: Changing community*. Saint Paul, MN: Graywolf Press.

Williams-Boyd, P. (2005, September 20–25). *Notes from Natchez, Team One*. Message posted to College of Education, Project Backpack, archived at http://www.emich.edu.

Williams-Boyd, P. (2005, October 10–14). *Notes from Natchez. Team Two*. Message posted to College of Education, Project Backpack, archived at http://www.emich.edu.

■|■|■

CHAPTER 13

Creating World-Class Teachers

Prospects for Katrina Recovery and Beyond

SHARON PORTER ROBINSON & PENNY ENGEL

"We see an opportunity to do something incredible."
Kathleen Babineaux Blanco, Governor of Louisiana in signing a
bill allowing the state to take over most of the schools in New Orleans
November 2005

In the wake of Hurricanes Katrina and Rita in 2005, major disaster areas were declared along the United States Gulf Coast. In New Orleans, the largest city affected by the catastrophe, Katrina destroyed most of the public education system. Fewer than 20 of the 120 school buildings of the central city's Orleans Parish remained usable, and all students, teachers, and administrators were forced to evacuate. The city's parochial schools, which educated 40% of its students, were also devastated. It was predicted that large numbers of teachers were unlikely to return until jobs became available, and many who found posts elsewhere would never come back (Hill & Hannaway, 2006).

Seven months after Katrina, only 20 public schools had reopened in New Orleans, and most buildings required significant environmental remediation. The open schools were overcrowded and becoming more so as the daily return of students sought spaces where none existed. The New Orleans Public School system announced in early 2006 that it would lay off 7,500 employees and terminate their health benefits. Teachers faced continued uncertainty about their homes and livelihoods. While one school system in the region arranged for staff to live on school property in trailers, other teachers whose homes were destroyed left their communities to seek job opportunities elsewhere. (Miller, 2006)

Almost a year after Hurricane Katrina struck, an intriguing quandary faced the city and the nation. If education leaders were to begin from scratch—with few limitations imposed by the former establishment of education institutions, bureaucracies, policies, or practices to restrict their vision of the future—what was the optimal education system they could create? What would a system of public education look like if all decisions were guided wholly by students' learning needs?

▪|▪|▪

"We have an opportunity of a lifetime: out of adversity to create a school system that would be the envy of people around the country."
Scott Cowan, President of Tulane University, Chair of the
Education Subcommittee, Bring New Orleans Back Commission

▪|▪|▪

Even before the hurricane, the New Orleans Public Schools were acknowledged to be among the worst in the nation. Multiple reforms had been tried, but with little success. A total overhaul was needed. The reconstruction imperative following Katrina provides a unique opportunity, as Tulane's Scott Cowan said, to create a new school system that will be the envy of the country. In fact, many of the nation's best known reformers have responded to the call for help, undoubtedly drawn to the prospect of effecting change in a living laboratory under extreme pressure, with the support of the state and the nation. These are exactly the unique circumstances that could propel progress—not only for the benefit of New Orleans, but also for that of the nation.

▪|▪|▪

"New Orleans might pioneer new ways of organizing public education in cities nationwide. It is not the only city with rapidly changing total enrollments, many low-performing schools, transient populations, teaching forces unprepared to meet students' instructional needs, and facilities in the wrong places. In fact, almost every large school district in the country fits that basic description."
Hill & Hannaway, 2006

■|■|■

The Bring New Orleans Back (BNOB) Commission's Education Subcommittee, which Cowan chairs, has recommended a decentralized Education Network Model as a framework for beginning the rebirth of the city's public schools. To "attract, develop, and retain the best teachers and educational leaders for New Orleans" is near the very top of the Commission's vision statement (BNOB Commission, 2006).

The Importance of the Teacher

As representatives of teacher preparation programs across the nation, we agree strongly with the importance the BNOB Commission has placed on finding the best teachers. As Hill and Hannaway (2006) noted, the new schools in New Orleans will need "exceptionally good principals and teachers"—the city "cannot afford to be a magnet for weak school providers, teachers, and principals who have failed elsewhere."

Evidence supporting the primary importance of the teacher to student learning has been accumulating over the last 15 years. Many of the most highly respected members of the research academy, as well as top economists and prestigious think tanks and commissions, support this finding.

- The Carnegie Corporation of New York (2001, p. 1) stated, "New and convincing evidence that teaching is more important for school children than any other condition has been stunning in its clarity and exciting in its implications."
- The National Academy of Education's Committee on Teacher Education (Darling-Hammond & Bransford, 2005, p. 14) said, "Although many have assumed that students' backgrounds such as income, parent education, and other family factors are the major reasons for wide differences in student achievement, some studies have found that the quality of teachers can have an effect at least as large."
- The Teaching Commission (2004, pp. 14–15) reported, "Quality teachers are the critical factor in helping young people overcome the damaging effects of poverty, lack of parental guidance, and other challenges . . . The effectiveness of any broader education reform including standards, smaller schools, and choice is ultimately dependent on the quality of teachers in the classroom."

Support for these conclusions is based on analyses of thousands of pupil records in many cities and states. Ferguson (1991) studied the importance of teachers' expertise measured by their scores on a certification exam, master's degrees, and experience on student achievement. He found that, in nearly 900 Texas school districts, the large disparities in achievement between Black and White students were almost entirely accounted for by differences in the qualifications of their teachers. Strauss and Sawyer (1986) reported, after controlling for school and student background factors, that a 1 percent increase in the quality of the North Carolina teachers studied was associated with a 3 percent to 5 percent decline in the proportion of students failing state competency tests.

The Tennessee value-added assessment studies (Sanders & Rivers, 1996) found about a 50-percentile-point difference in achievement on standardized tests between students who attended classes taught by high-quality teachers and those taught by low-quality teachers for three consecutive years. Further, Hanushek, Kain, and Rivkin (1998) reported that effective teachers increased their students' learning by a full grade level beyond that attained by students taught by less effective teachers. Replacing an average teacher with a very good one nearly erased the gap in math performance between students from low-income and high-income families.

Exceptional Teachers

Knowing how important exceptional teachers are to student learning and to the hurricane recovery compels reformers to identify their traits—so that more such teachers might be recruited to the task. We need masterful teachers who turn kids on to learning; who know special ways to teach every student, regardless of background; who genuinely care about each child; who will never give up on a child; ultimately, who are world-class teachers, whose students achieve.

To immediately find exceptional teachers amidst the Katrina crisis is no small task, and identifying such teachers requires easily quantifiable factors for quick evaluation of teacher candidates. Fortunately, from a growing and impressive research base and from judgments from practicing professionals, a strong consensus and clear vision of teacher quality are emerging. Effective teachers are, and should be, caring, competent, and qualified; knowledgeable about learners and about how they learn and develop; cognizant of the subject matter and skills to be taught; and understanding of teaching in terms of the content and learners being taught (National Council for Accreditation of Teacher Education, 2002; Darling-Hammond & Baratz-Snowden, 2005).

More specifically, research and professional judgment tell us that teachers should have acquired the following knowledge, skills, and dispositions necessary to help all students learn:

- Basic literacy skills in reading, writing, and math. Several studies have correlated teachers' test scores on basic-skills tests and college entrance exams with their students' scores on achievement tests (e.g., Ferguson, 1991; Ferguson & Ladd, 1996; Strauss & Sawyer, 1986). These studies found that high-scoring teachers are more likely to produce significant student achievement gains than their lower-scoring counterparts.

- Deep knowledge of the content they will be teaching, appropriate to the levels of their students. The work of Monk (1994) supports this contention, finding particularly on the part of math and science teachers that teachers' content knowledge has a positive impact on student achievement. (See also Goldhaber & Brewer, 1997; Monk & King, 1994; Rowan, Chiang, & Miller, 1997.) This knowledge is best acquired through a broad liberal arts education and, for secondary-level teachers, an undergraduate major in the subject they plan to teach.

- A foundation of professional knowledge upon which to base instructional decisions. This foundation includes a firm understanding of the varying ways in which students develop and learn; of how to translate curriculum objectives into the correct content and instructional techniques; of appropriate interpretation and utilization of assessment data; of effective methods of teaching students who are at different developmental stages, have different learning styles, and come from diverse backgrounds; and of research-derived knowledge of best practice (Center for Teaching Quality, 2004; Darling-Hammond & Baratz-Snowden, 2005; National Commission on Teaching and America's Future, 2003; National Council for Accreditation of Teacher Education, 2002).

- Pedagogical knowledge and skill, both generic and content-specific. Teachers must understand how to teach—that is, how to create positive learning environments, effectively manage and discipline a classroom of students, motivate children to learn, integrate modern technology into curricula, and align their content to state standards. (See Darling-Hammond & Youngs, 2002, and Monk, 1994.) In addition, however, teachers must be able to teach by translating their hands-on knowledge into skills that they actually apply in real classrooms with real students. Rice (2003) reported that pedagogical coursework contributes to teacher effectiveness at all grade levels, and a near-universal consensus exists in support of extended clinical practice to develop and hone hands-on skills (Darling-Hammond & Baratz-Snowden, 2005; Darling-Hammond & Bransford, 2005).

- Dispositions conducive to helping all students learn. Highly effective teachers show commitment to their practice and to its continuous improvement. They participate with enthusiasm in the professional growth and development of the learning community of which they are a part. They exhibit high expectations toward the learners in their charge and consistently encourage them to greater achievement. They treat all students and adults fairly and with respect and behave responsibly and honorably as members of the teaching profession (Interstate New Teacher Assessment and Support Consortium, 1992; National Council for Accreditation of Teacher Education, 2006; Sparks, 2003).

The Preparation of Exceptional Teachers: Escalating the Transformation

Teachers who possess all the attributes just described are not average teachers, but *exceptional, world-class* teachers. These are the teachers typically missing from urban-area public schools such as those of New Orleans, a situation that a system rebirth must unquestionably rectify. Frankly, it should not take a disaster to provide such teachers for districts all across the land but especially for districts with the neediest students and fewest resources.

The science of preparing teachers is slowly being transformed. Traditional, collegiate-based teacher preparation, dominated by classroom lectures, textbook-based coursework, institutional credits, and degrees—with "student teaching" tacked on at the end—is changing. Traditional programs are not so "traditional" anymore as they adapt to incorporate the findings of research, adjust to students' needs, and integrate new technologies.

Perhaps in the adversity of Katrina, the rebirth of New Orleans will also serve to escalate the transformation of teacher preparation for the good of the entire nation.

The National Academy of Education (Darling-Hammond & Baratz-Snowden, 2005) has reported the common features of teacher preparation programs whose graduates have a strong sense of preparedness and are most highly rated by employers:

- *A common core curriculum* grounded in knowledge of development, learning, subject-matter pedagogy, and assessment, taught in the context of practice
- *Well-defined standards of practice and performance* used to guide the design and assessment of coursework and clinical work
- *Extended clinical experiences* (at least 30 weeks) that are interwoven with coursework and are carefully mentored
- *Strong relationships between universities and schools* that share standards of good teaching that are consistent across courses and clinical work

- *Relating teachers' learning to classroom practice* through the use of case studies, teacher research, performance assessments, and portfolio examinations

Good models exist for many of these key features. A well-established model of clinical experience, the professional development school (PDS), continues to evolve and expand. The PDS concept now has a set of standards, model exemplars, and a 1,000-member national association in which both university and school-based faculty are active participants. Other examples of good clinical experience are embraced by Harvard's Project for the Next Generation of Teachers, the Carnegie Corporation of New York's Teachers for a New Era, and New York Teaching Fellows. Another model of these characteristics, the Urban Teacher Academies, is illustrated by the master's degree program at California State University–Long Beach that takes place totally on-site at a local elementary school. Clearly, expanded clinical experience is recognized as critical to effective preparation programs, both traditional and alternative.

A plethora of new preparation providers and alternate routes to teaching are emerging—due in large measure to the increased diversification in age and background of many new teacher candidates. In addition to newly minted education school graduates, growing numbers of applicants are returning teachers, career-switchers, or arts and sciences graduates who have decided to go into teaching. To meet the needs of this new population, preparation programs now more frequently offer condensed, intensified summer sessions in collaboration with school districts experiencing teacher shortages. These programs often extend faculty engagement with the novice into the K-12 classroom through a teacher's induction period.

In fact, successful alternative preparation programs can be found in many institutions of higher education, often designed and delivered in cooperation with elementary or secondary schools. These innovative programs provide professional training for prospective teachers and have the same standards and expectations of competence as traditional teacher education programs. The fundamental differences between an alternative and traditional program are the target audience, the training design, and the length of training—not the program's content, rigor, or expected outcomes.

Some of the "fast track" routes to teaching are of questionable value, however, placing unprepared novices in classrooms to learn as they go, sink or swim—to their detriment and that of their students. However, there is clearly a need for accelerated and high quality, preservice education paths to address critical shortages, such as those of New Orleans. The profession must endeavor to ensure that the rebirth does not bring forth what failed in the previous life and, in the haste of the moment, reinstitutionalize a failed system for posterity.

It is important that non-collegiate-based alternative programs operate on parity with collegiate-based teacher preparation programs in certain basic areas. Alternative programs should have the same five features noted above that the National Academy of Education recommends for traditional programs.

Furthermore, all programs should prepare candidates to teach all the children who will be attending our nation's schools. All programs should model effective, evidence-based practices. In addition, all programs must be accountable for documenting the quality of candidates and for measuring their effects on student learning. We must not sacrifice standards on the backs of underprivileged children in our neediest schools—such as those of New Orleans—and we must not perpetuate the placement of insufficiently prepared teachers in their charge, regardless of the source of the preparation.

Lessons that derive from adversity can be profound. In this instance, we can clearly learn lessons that could escalate the transformation of teacher preparation. We know the importance of more constant and continuous engagement among our faculty, our teacher candidates, and the faculty and students in K-12 schools. The profession knows it needs to integrate new technologies and new pedagogies into collegiate teaching and prepare new teachers to do so in their schools. The determined efforts of New Orleans institutions to literally emerge anew from the flood are powerful examples of innovative pedagogy designed in response to the circumstances and needs of the learner.

The total devastation of Dillard University by Katrina illustrates the point. Dillard's president, Marvelene Hughes, testified in April 2006 before Congress that the campus was under 8 to 10 feet of water for three to four weeks. All facilities were damaged, three residence halls were destroyed by fire, and all of the buildings had been gutted. Losses were in the hundreds of millions of dollars. Students and faculty were living and learning together in a Hilton Hotel, dubbed "The Dilton" (Hughes, 2006). Surely, some of the students and faculty at The Dilton were in teacher preparation programs, and we can imagine the synergies of learning this amazing cohort of learners might have experienced.

Xavier University offers another scenario. Deborah Bordelon, the education chair, had left New Orleans when Katrina brought 8 feet of floodwater to the campus. When she returned several months later, Bordelon found herself grappling with turning graduate education classes—once taught face-to-face in classrooms—into interactive, on-line courses for displaced Xavier students (Hawkins, 2006). The adversity of Katrina thus propelled an innovation that can expand the reach of Xavier's teacher preparation program well beyond its current borders, and well into the future.

In his best-selling globalization study *The World Is Flat,* Tom Friedman (2005) writes about companies, but we can substitute "education schools" and the point still applies: The best [education schools] are those who are the best collaborators. In the "flat" world, Friedman explains, more and more work will be done through collaborations with and between organizations. The interconnected layers of value creation are becoming so complex that no single organization will be able to master them alone. That is why collaboration is so important.

The lesson of collaboration, and the lack of it, was taught to us firsthand in the aftermath of Katrina. It is a good lesson for all, but particularly for the profession that is preparing world-class teachers for the new millennium. We take it to heart and to our work.

The rebirth of New Orleans can serve to escalate the transformation of teacher preparation for the good of the entire nation. What is needed is known but not yet widely practiced. We know the critical importance of the teacher. We know what constitutes exceptional teachers and how they can be developed, and we know the essential elements of accelerated preparation. Now is the time to put that knowledge to work.

> *"Life doesn't always take you in a predictable direction, but it's important to understand where you start and to have some sense of how to get to where you want to go."*
>
> Former President William J. Clinton
> Commencement address, Tulane University,
> New Orleans, Louisiana
> May 13, 2006

REFERENCES

Bring New Orleans Back Commission, Subcommittee on Education. (2006, January). *Rebuilding and transforming: A plan for world-class public education in New Orleans.* New Orleans, LA: Author.

Carnegie Corporation of New York. (2001). *Teachers for a new era: A national initiative to improve the quality of teaching.* The corporation's program announcement. New York: Author. http://www.carnegie.org/sub/program/teachers_announcement.html.

Center for Teaching Quality. (2004). *Unfulfilled promise: Ensuring high-quality teachers for our nation's students. No Child Left Behind: A status report from Southeastern schools.* Chapel Hill, NC: Author. Retrieved June 8, 2006, from http://www.teachingquality.org/pdfs/NCLB_PublishedReport.pdf.

Darling-Hammond, L., & Baratz-Snowden, J. (Eds.). (2005). *A good teacher in every classroom: Preparing the highly qualified teachers our children deserve.* Sponsored by the National Academy of Education, Committee on Teacher Education. San Francisco: Jossey-Bass.

Darling-Hammond, L., & Bransford, J. (Eds.). (2005). *Preparing teachers for a changing world: What teachers should learn and be able to do.* Sponsored by the National Academy of Education,

Committee on Teacher Education. San Francisco: Jossey-Bass.

Darling-Hammond, L., & Youngs, P. (2002). Defining "highly qualified teachers": What does "scientifically based research" tell us? *Educational Researcher, 31,* 13–25.

Ferguson, R. F. (1991). Paying for public education: New evidence on how and why money matters. *Harvard Journal on Legislation, 28*(2), 465–498.

Ferguson, R. F., & Ladd, H. F. (1996). How and why money matters: An analysis of Alabama schools. In H. F. Ladd (Ed.), *Holding schools accountable: Performance-based reform in education* (pp. 265–298). Washington, DC: Brookings Institution Press.

Friedman, T. (2005). *The world is flat:. A brief history of the twenty-first century.* New York: Farrar, Straus and Giroux.

Goldhaber, D., & Brewer, D. (1997). Why don't schools and teachers seem to matter? Assessing the impact of unobservables on educational productivity. *Journal of Human Resources, 32,* 505–523.

Hanushek, E. A., Kain, J. F., & Rivkin, S. G. (1998). *Teachers, schools, and academic achievement.* Working paper. Cambridge, MA: National Bureau of Economic Research.

Hawkins, B. D. (2006). The Katrina stories. Washington, DC: Reading First Teacher Education Network. Retrieved June 8, 2006, from http://www.rften.org/content/KatrinaStories/KatrinaStories.html? PHPSESSID=fe371a4425c59100b78a7c085b45e85f

Hill, P., & Hannaway, J. (2006, January). *The future of public education in New Orleans.* (In the series After Katrina: Rebuilding opportunity and equity into the *new* New Orleans.) Washington, DC: The Urban Institute.

Hughes, M. (2006, April). Testimony before the House Committee on Education and the Workforce at the Hearing on the Gulf Coast recovery: Facing challenges and coming back stronger in education, April 26, 2006. http://edworkforce.house.gov/hearings/109th/fc/gulfcoastrecovery 042606/hughes.htm.

Interstate New Teacher Assessment and Support Consortium. (1992). *Model standards for beginning teacher licensure and development: A resource for state dialogue.* Washington, DC: Council of Chief State School Officers.

Miller, G. (2006, April). *Democratic proposals to open and rebuild Gulf Coast schools and colleges.* A report presented by The Honorable George Miller, Senior Democratic Member, Committee on Education and the Workforce, U.S. House of Representatives.

Monk, D. H. (1994). Subject matter preparation of secondary mathematics and science teachers and student achievement. *Economics of Education Review, 13*(2), 125–145.

Monk, D. H., & King, J. A. (1994). Multilevel teacher resource effects in pupil performance in secondary mathematics and science: The case of teacher subject-matter preparation. In R. G. Ehrenberg (Ed.), *Choices and consequences: Contemporary policy issues in education* (pp. 29–58). Ithaca, NY: ILR Press.

National Commission on Teaching and America's Future. (2003). *No dream denied: A pledge to America's children.* Washington, DC: Author.

National Council for Accreditation of Teacher Education. (2002). *Professional standards for the accreditation of schools, colleges, and departments of education.* Washington, DC: Author.

National Council for Accreditation of Teacher Education. (2006). *NCATE unit standards revision.* Retrieved June 8, 2006, from http://www.ncate.org/public/0511_stdRevision.asp?ch=150

Rice, J. K. (2003). *Teacher quality: Understanding the effectiveness of teacher attributes.* Washington, DC: Economic Policy Institute.

Rowan, B., Chiang, F.-S., & Miller, R. J. (1997). Using research on employees' performance to study the effects of teachers on students' achievement. *Sociology of education, 70,* 256–284.

Sanders, W. L., & Rivers, J. C. (1996). *Cumulative and residual effects of teachers on future student academic achievement.* Knoxville: University of Tennessee Value-Added Research and Assessment Center.

Sparks, D. (2003). We care, therefore they learn. *Journal of staff development, 24*(4), 42–47.

Strauss, R. P., & Sawyer, E. A. (1986). Some new evidence on teacher and student competencies. *Economics of Education Review, 5*(1), 41–48.

The Teaching Commission. (2004). *Teaching at risk: A call to action.* New York: Author.

■|■|■

PART THREE

The Social Dynamics
of Education Reform

■|■|■

CHAPTER 14

Tikkun Olam

ARTHUR E. LEVINE

Other chapters in this volume speak to the overwhelming educational needs of the children of New Orleans, the profound challenges facing the city's schools, and the extraordinary opportunity to reinvent urban public education in a historically weak school system. This essay is about a different group of children attending different schools, who have also been left behind by Katrina. It is about the challenges and opportunities Katrina poses for all of America's children attending all of the nation's schools, particularly those physically untouched by the storm.

This essay is the product of a conversation with a group of community college students, conducted as part of a study of today's undergraduates—their attitudes, values, and experiences. We asked the students what social or political events most influenced their lives, noting that if they had been born in the 1920s they might have said the Depression, or Pearl Harbor if they had been born a decade later or the death of John Kennedy if they were born still later. As might be expected, the most powerful event in their lives the September 11 attacks, but they named Katrina and the war in Iraq as weak seconds.

What was striking was the meaning the students attached to the hurricane. They focused on the ineptness of federal, state, and local officials. They were critical of politicians, politics, and government. Katrina was seen by one as a sign of the impending decline of the United States, pointing to the Roman Empire as a comparison.

Katrina could have affected the students in many ways. It could have been a lesson in service, the need to help those whose lives were upended by the storm. It could have been a means for learning about the wide gap between the most advantaged and disadvantaged Americans in health care, income, housing, and safety. It might have been a call to a vocation—government, medicine, or meteorology—as Watergate was to journalism. It could have been any of these things or a host of other possibilities, but it was not.

For the group of students I interviewed, the lessons of Katrina were negative and disaffecting. It said to them that they needed to look out for number one. No public person or organization was going to be there for them; no one cares. As a matter of fact, their conversation on Katrina was interspersed with discussion of price gouging by oil companies and oil being the reason for the Iraq war.

A Teachable Moment

If all that children have been learned from Katrina is cynicism, we failed them. There are special moments that are given to schools and teachers, families and parents, government and politicians, churches and ministers, and all of the other social institutions and their leaders who make up our lives. These are the times that make it possible to teach powerful lessons. Katrina is one of them. It offers an extraordinary opportunity to teach citizenship and the fundamental elements that compose it—hope, responsibility, justice, and efficacy.

Hope

The nineteenth-century political and literary thinker William Hazlitt wrote: "Hope is the best possession. None are completely wretched except those without hope" (*Characteristics*, 1823, p. 35). The kind of hope our children must possess is not a rosy-eyed or sugar-coated view of reality. It is something much simpler—a belief in promise. Tomorrow can be better than today.

Our children need to be taught that Katrina was a terrible, terrible event. They need to understand the extent and depth of the toll that was left in the hurricane's wake. It was a human disaster. Well over 1,000 people died. The evacuation of the New Orleans resulted in a diaspora of its population to all 50 states. Still uncounted numbers of homes and possessions of a lifetime were lost. Katrina was an environmental disaster. One hundred and ninety-three thousand barrels of oil and petrochemicals leaked into the Gulf of Mexico. Katrina was an economic disaster. Over $50 million a day were lost in tourist revenue. The closure of Mississippi River gambling casinos cost approximately half a million dollars a day. More than 80 percent of port operations were closed. Tens of thousands of jobs disappeared. It was a national security disaster as 47 percent of the nation's oil refinery production was slashed. It was a municipal disaster as the population of New Orleans fell from 462,000 to 250,000 during the daytime and 60,000 to 70,000 at night (*The World Almanac and Book of Facts 2006*, p. 6).

At the same time, though, despite the billions of dollars reconstruction will cost and the continuing years of pain it will entail, our children need to understand that there is reason for hope. New Orleans was not the first city in America to be devastated by natural disaster. Chicago was destroyed by fire in 1871; Galveston was the victim of a hurricane in 1900; and San Francisco was devastated by an earthquake in 1906. Each of these cities was rebuilt and revitalized and New Orleans and the Gulf coast can be too.

Disasters can be lessons that can be woven into the curriculum of our schools via studies of history, literature, and science. It is instruction that can be the theme of sermons delivered by our clergy. It is something parents can talk about with their children. It is the stuff our government officials can highlight in their public addresses. We are being presented with an extraordinary opportunity to teach our children about hope. It would be a terrible thing to miss it.

Responsibility

The Gospel of Luke tells us that "unto whomsoever much is given, of him shall much be required" (Luke, 12:48). The children of the United States are as a group advantaged in comparison to their peers around the world. Those who were spared the fury of Katrina are privileged as well. They have an obligation to serve those who are less advantaged and less privileged. This is a tenet of most world religions. In the Jewish religion, it is called "tikkun olam." Jews are commanded to improve the human condition by their deliberate acts.

All of our children need to be taught the secular version of "tikkun olam." They have an obligation to improve the human condition. This does not mean that they are individually responsible for repairing the entire world, but that they have an obligation to make better the part of the world within their reach—volunteering to work in a hospice, helping to clean up the local pond, or tutoring a child in mathematics. The essential lesson is that to help one person is to repair the world.

Katrina offers extraordinary examples of individuals who demonstrate this lesson. Dr. Lisa Aptaker is an example. She said:

> I was in my apartment in New York City, and on days two and three, I distinctly remember watching the news and seeing faces of desperation of all ages—young and old–just crying out for help. I just could not stand (the sight of suffering). I ended up through phone calls finding two other guys who were going down to New Orleans—one of them was a paramedic—who wanted to do the same thing. We rented an SUV and drove down, literally from Brooklyn, New York all the way, straight to Louisiana. (as cited in Dyson, 2006, p. 2002)

These volunteers are all around us. We need to bring them to our classrooms, religious services, and award ceremonies to show our students why they did what they did, what difference their acts made, and how they felt after carrying them out. Students need to learn such people are no different from any of the other people in their lives. Anyone is capable of repairing the world, if they wish to.

Justice

Nearly half a century before the birth of Jesus, Cicero said "It is the function of justice not to do wrong to one's fellow man ("De Officiis," 44 B.C., 1:28:99). Our children need be educated to achieve Cicero's vision of justice. To accomplish this goal, they have to be able to distinguish right from wrong, justice from injustice. This task requires they be equipped with the skills and knowledge to sort through the various messages they hear each day—to determine which of those messages are based on facts and which are opinion, which are statements of ideology and which are empirically based. They need to understand the gradations of justice—what is good, what is better, and what is best. What is absolute and what is relative? Our children need to learn about what happens to minorities in America—those who hold minority opinions, those who are members of minority groups, those who are advocates for unpopular positions. They need to understand the history of justice in society— the evolving meaning of the term and its impact on national life.

Katrina is a superb vehicle for teaching these things. The hurricane placed a spotlight on injustices in American life. Blacks and poor people were disproportionately affected by the storm. While 54% of whites in New Orleans lived in flooded areas, 80% of minorities resided in those areas. When it came to evacuation from the city, 17% of poor whites lacked access to cars versus 53% of poor blacks.

Cars were the primary means for leaving the city. There were comparable disparities in health and property insurance (Dyson, 2006, pp. 9, 31, 145).

Our children should be asked to confront these realities. They should be asked to examine questions of right and wrong. For instance, was stealing wrong? Is it always wrong? Can it ever be right? The executive director of the New Orleans Housing Authority, Dr. Nadine Jarmon, described why her organization resorted to looting.

> We ran out of food and water, just like everybody else. So we ventured down and we went into one of the stores. People don't understand. When you are desperate, you've got to be resourceful. We tried to get some food. So we looted. (Dyson, 2006, p. 140)

Our children could also be asked who was to blame for the poor response to the hurricane. Perhaps a better question is what was wrong and what needs to change—the condition of the poor, the condition of the city, the condition of disaster relief? Darlene Mathieu, a Katrina survivor, raised the question this way.

> The things that happened are unbelievable. And they're saying it was FEMA's (Federal Emergency Management Agency) fault, it was the governor's fault, it was the mayor's fault. . . . Why didn't they rescue the people? Why didn't they save the people? Why'd the people have to go through what they went through? Why did those people suffer? (Dyson, 2006, p. 108)

Our children can be asked too to examine whether how much organizations and people should be rewarded for helping out in disasters. The practice by corporations of demanding premium prices at times of great public need is called "disaster capitalism." FEMA awarded contracts of more than $1.5 billion in the weeks following Katrina for rescue, support, and recovery. For instance, it paid the Carnival Cruise Line twice their usual ticket price to house Katrina evacuees on three nearby ships. Is this just? Under what circumstances could it be just? What should happen?

Katrina provides compelling case studies, which permit our children to differentiate fact from fiction, distinguish absolute from relative values, determine gradations of justice, and learn about the place of minorities in America. Schools can use these cases from the earliest grades, starting with stories for our youngest children. Religious institutions, social organization, and government should take advantage of the power of stories.

Efficacy

Robert Kennedy frequently told audiences: "Some men see things as they are and say why. I dream things that never were and say why not" (Salinger, Guthman, Mankiewicz, & Seigenthaler, 1993, p. 3). Kennedy offers us a definition of efficacy, the sense that one has the power to make a difference.

Our children need to learn that no matter what it is they choose to do—butcher, baker, or candlestick maker—they will make a difference. They will touch scores of lives—family, friends, neighbors, co-workers, clients. For bad or for good, they will make a difference in each of those lives. Making a difference is their birthright. No one can take that away from them. They must not give it away.

These skills are best taught experientially. Children need opportunities to engage in service. These activities must be meaningful, age appropriate, have a great likelihood for success, and incorporate excellent mentoring. Too often these activities are overly ambitious, demanding too much from participants. The result is frustrated volunteers, who feel they failed, having been unable to eliminate poverty in a semester or end environmental pollution by working for two hours a week.

For these reasons, our children also need to be taught the limits of efficacy, the barriers that need to be overcome, what is possible and what is less possible. Biography is critical. Children should read about people like Martin Luther King, Rachel Carson, Thomas Edison, Emile Zola, Ralph Nader, and Edward R. Murrow, who had great successes and great failures. They need to know that people as a seamstress named Rosa Parks can change the world.

Katrina provides accounts of both the successes and the failures. It is filled with stories of teachers, firefighters, engineers, doctors, and a cornucopia of others who gave their time and made a difference in people's lives. It is a story of charity and giving. Americans wrote checks to help other troubled Americans. The Salvation Army raised more than $220 million to provide water, shelter, food, and other essentials to more than 600,000 people. The Red Cross collected more than $1.3 billion dollars, which supported 963,000 families, provided 8.1 million overnight stays in shelters and hotels all over the country for hurricane victims and served more than 20 million hot meals (*World Almanac,* p. 6).

Katrina also provides lessons on the failure of service which students need to learn. Perhaps the most telling are the small ones, like that of Dr. Mark Perlmutter, an orthopedic surgeon from Pennsylvania, who came to Louisiana as a volunteer. He was stopped from giving chest compressions to a dying woman by a federal official because he was not registered with FEMA. Perlmutter was the only doctor available. He watched people dying all around him, unable to help them in any way. If our children are to make a difference, they need to understand why Dr. Perlmutter could not and be prepared to overcome comparable barriers.

Conclusion

Perhaps the greatest gift anyone can receive is the ability to look in the mirror every day and be proud of the sight. We have the capacity to provide that gift to all of our children. We can teach them hope, responsibility, justice, and efficacy. Hurricane Katrina provides a unique vehicle for accomplishing this. If we succeed, engagement can triumph over cynicism.

REFERENCES

Dyson, M. E. (2006). *Come Hell or high water: Hurricane Katrina and the color of disaster.* New York: Basic Books.

Salinger, P., Guthman, E., Mankiewicz, F. & Seigenthaler, J. (Eds.). (1993). *An Honorable Profession: A Tribute to Robert F. Kennedy.* New York: Doubleday.

The World Almanac and Book of Facts 2006. (2006). New York: World Almanac Books.

■|■|■

CHAPTER 15

Wastebasket Kids and Katrina

Reflections from a "Jim Crow" Child

DIANNE SMITH

I teach undergraduate and graduate students curriculum theory and cultural diversity at a Midwestern urban university. Embedded within the school of education's conceptual framework are values that are visible on hallway walls, syllabi, listservs, online Web sites, and so on. It is my responsibility, as a faculty member, to ensure that the students enrolled in the classes that I teach are familiar with these values. For the purposes of this reflection, I want to note two of the five values that will help guide me through this writing project: a belief in "democracy and social justice," and "creating a safe and caring environment." I agree with these principles that will move pre-service and in-service educators to teach "other people's children" (Delpit, 1995) as if they were their own. For me a more telling metaphor for my idea is encased in Thich Nhat Hanh's (1995) thought:

> When you hammer a nail into a board and accidentally strike your finger, you take care of the injury immediately. The right hand never says to the left hand, "I am doing char-

itable work for you." It just does whatever it can to help—giving first aid, compassion, and concern. In the Mahayana Buddhist tradition, the practice of *dana,* generosity, is like this. We do whatever we can to benefit others without seeing ourselves as helpers and the others as the helped. This is the spirit of non-self. (p. 66)

This is a clear way of understanding the importance of teaching other people's children regarding democracy and social justice, and creating a safe and caring environment. Another link to this concept is that educators should not see themselves as "missionaries" who are arriving to save the "souls" of students (Freire, 1970), but should envision their purpose as education for the practice of freedom and transgression (hooks, 1994). In the wake of Hurricane Katrina, I was glued to the television. My reflections are about remembering watching the images of Black faces. In particular, I focused on the faces of Black children struggling to survive in the midst of Katrina's wrath and after "she" left the city of New Orleans. For two days, I cried and became angry that we live in a country that espouses democracy but, in essence, does not practice a true democratic ideal. I also wondered about what happened to the safe and caring environment for our Black children.

I asked myself, "Will they go to preschool, Head Start, public school?" "Will other teachers in other cities want to teach them?" Did others watching the news see "the oppressive role of a broader white supremacist culture in undermining the human potential of" (Duncan, 2005, p. 213) Black children? What are their stories to tell now, and later in life about being cared for beyond their families' bosoms? So, what I hope to do in this essay is to discuss a brief history of the "uncaring" for Black children and schooling in this country; Jim Crow schooling, as Irons (2002) calls it. Hopefully, I will follow this with Geneva Gay's (2000) treatise regarding the importance of creating a safe and caring environment in schools for Black children to be vibrantly successful in schools. In other words, I think that I can link Gay's discourse with the notion that we need to see present-day schooling for Black children as a "new form of Jim Crow" regarding uncaring environments. Included in this, I am sure, are other questions about "generosity, concern, compassion, and an ethic of care."

Jim Crow Schooling: An "Ethic of Uncaring" in Schools

I was born, raised, and schooled in South Carolina during the 1950s and 1960s. This was the era of Jim Crow schooling, or, as I knew it, segregated schooling. I attended all-Black schools until the eleventh grade. It was 1968 when *Brown vs. Board of Education,* 1954, became real. That said, I was an avid reader; however, I did not have access to the public library due to Jim Crow rule regarding segregation of Black and

White folks. Once I went to Foster Chapel Elementary School, I remember that the books available to me were used raggedy textbooks that had been handed down from the White schools. White kids' names were printed in them and I also learned about the goodness of Dick, Jane, and Sally; in essence, I learned about the purity of Whiteness.

I want to add here that while I began to understand the "unimportance" of my existence, as a Black child, I felt cared for by the Black teachers in my schools. (To be honest, there were other issues surrounding social class and skin color that were apparent, but that is the topic of another essay.) Therefore, for the sake of this writing, I am using Gay's (2000) definition of caring:

> Caring interpersonal relationships are characterized by patience, persistence, facilitation, validation, and empowerment for the participants. Uncaring ones are distinguished by impatience, intolerance, dictations, and control. The power of these kinds of relationships in instructional effectiveness is expressed in a variety of ways by educators, but invariably the message is the same. Teachers who genuinely care about students generate higher levels of all kinds of success than those who do not. They have high performance expectations and will settle for nothing less than high achievement. Failure is simply unacceptable to them, so they work diligently to see that success for students happen. (p. 47)

I felt validated and empowered in Mrs. Sartor's first-grade class, as a four-year-old Black girl. I wanted to read more and please her because the "instructional effectiveness" was "expressed in a variety of ways" by her. In the second grade, Mrs. Young taught me the importance of storytelling and imagination. During the ninth and tenth grades, I practiced using my imagination as I learned French and dreamed of visiting Paris, France, one day; a dream that came true for me as an adult. These are wonderful recollections as I write this essay. However, I must name that I did not feel cared for in Mr. Morrow's history class, at the white school. He used the word "nigra" when talking about enslaved Blacks. Nigra is an old-fashioned White way of saying "nigger."

Thus, at the time, I did not understand that "Knowledge should be examined not only for the ways in which it might misrepresent or mediate social reality, but also for the ways in which it actually reflects the daily struggle of people's lives . . ." (McLaren, 2003, p. 211). McLaren continues by stating that "knowledge (truth) is socially constructed, culturally mediated, and historically situated" (p. 210). I now know that my "truth" (knowledge), in the Jim Crow schools was being historically situated and socially constructed for me. It is hard for me to name, but, I now know that while Mrs. Sartor cared for me; Jim Crow schools were "wastebaskets for Black children." This is what I saw in the faces of the Black children in the New Orleans Superdome; the "dome" became a wastebasket for Black children.

I am referring to a broader social, cultural, and historical context than that on which McLaren (2003) draws. What follows provides a clearer image of what I mean regarding a social, cultural, and historical context:

> At the end of the week, we left for New Orleans, the place of our final destination, which we reached in two days. Here the slaves were placed in a negro-pen, where those who wished to purchase could call and examine them. The negro-pen is a small yard, surrounded by buildings, from fifteen to twenty feet wide, with the exception of a large gate with iron bars. The slaves are kept in the buildings during the night, and turned out into the yard during the day. (Brown, 1847, p. 41)

Brown's imagination of a ""negro-pen" resonates with my notion of the "dome" and schools for Black children as a wastebasket for them/us to maintain an imposed existence.

Another historical referent of an ethic of uncaring for Black children in this country is offered by my 95-year-old aunt. As I prepared this essay, I became curious about her schooling, some eighty-nine years ago. She said, "I went there (school) for a long time. I came up on the rough side of the mountain. We walked and sometimes that dog ice would be on the ground and by the time I got to school, my foots was froze" (Personal conversation, 2006).

I was sitting in her living room, and she had her eyes closed as she remembered her schooling experience. It seemed to me that my aunt felt her frozen feet all over again. My interpretation of her story is that she knew that an ethic of uncaring existed in her schooling. Gay (2000) would suggest that my aunt's physical, emotional, and academic abilities were not supported and protected. A second aspect of our conversation helps me to understand that my aunt, today, knows of her marginalization as a Black woman in this country. I asked her how long has she lived in her apartment: "Twenty-seven years. Once water came up to my porch. I told him (manager) if White folk lived here, you would fix it but cause I'm Black you don't give a damn."

I employ Brown's, my aunt's, and my memories as mechanisms for bringing forth " . . . how knowledge gets constructed the way it does, and how and why some constructions of reality are legitimated and celebrated by the dominant culture while others clearly are not" (McLaren, 2003, p. 196). For example, during my schooling I did not read Brown's "slave narrative" nor was it important for me to know about my aunt's Jim Crow schooling, which is linked to my own Jim Crow schooling. Brown's reality was not legitimated in the ""negro-pen"; my aunt's reality was not celebrated while walking to school with frozen feet, and mine was not legitimated as I read about "pure little White (an oxymoron) children and their goodness in the world."

This leads me back to our Black children who attend schools that are uncaring wastebaskets for them to be thrown into on a daily basis. Caruthers and Smith

(2006) suggest, quoting Young, that the structure and organization of schooling often cast poor and culturally diverse students as the "other." To be cast as other means "to experience how the dominant meanings of a society render the particular perspective of one's own group invisible at the same time as they stereotype one's own group and mark it out as the other" (Young as cited in Caruthers & Smith, 2006, p. 122).

According to our state's Department of Elementary and Secondary Education (DESE, 2003), 70.66 percent of my community's school district are Black. It is largely segregated, what I term the "new Jim Crow schools." Caruthers (2005) says it best in that fifty-plus years after *Brown,* public schools for Black children are emboldened with low-academic tracking practices, low teacher expectations, watered down and fragmented curriculum, and low expectations for parent participation. Land (2005) speaks of education for Blacks being much like warfare: education is "the basis of life and death" and "the way to survival or extinction." Throughout the years, African Americans have suffered many casualties of this "war": the dropouts, push-outs, the racially tracked, the psychologically oppressed, the voiceless, etc. (p. 106)

What pains me about Caruthers' and Land's speculations is that I know of what they speak. I have spent time in our local urban schools and witnessed the effects of uncaring, wastebasket ideological positioning. I have seen and heard teachers yell and scream at our Black children; I have seen classrooms without a teacher; I have seen chronic teacher absenteeism; I have watched as our Black children were not expected to read and write at grade level; and I have seen black four-year-olds sitting in the principal's office waiting to be punished. Subsequently, I am led back to the imagery of Brown's negro-pen; my aunt's frozen feet; pure little white Dick, Jane, and Sally (See Spot run. Run, Spot, run.); and the Black faces of the children at the dome (the massive wastebasket).

While I have painted a fairly bleak picture of schooling in the United States for Black children, historically and socially, I want to revisit Thich Nhat Hanh's (1995) offering of hope:

> The right hand never says to the left hand, "I am doing charitable work for you." It just does whatever it can to help—giving first aid, compassion, and concern . . . We do whatever we can to benefit others without seeing ourselves as helpers and the others as the helped. This is the spirit of non-self. (p. 66)

As I conclude this section on uncaring in schools, I want to tell you, my readers, that there is always hope. We should do whatever we can to benefit others. bell hooks (2002) asserts that hope is strongly connected to "'that which can be,'" or possibility (Simon, 1988). Roger Simon supplies a quote that I use often in my writings:

> An education that empowers for possibility must raise questions of how we can work for the re-construction of social imagination in the service of human freedom . . . the proj-

ect of possibility requires an education rooted in a view of human freedom as the understanding of necessity and the transformation of necessity . . . Beyond its emphasis on deconstruction of dominant knowledge forms and social identities, a project of possibility requires practices that do not simply advocate possibility but also enable it. (p. 2)

What follows next is my interpretation of a project of possibility, namely caring in schools (Gay, 2000), which facilitates a re-construction of social imagination.

Burning the Wastebasket: Caring and Hope for Black Children in Schools

As I reflect on generosity, human freedom, and transformation, Miss Ella Baker comes to mind. Robert Moses (2001) quotes Miss Ella Baker in his book, *Radical Equations: Civil Rights from Mississippi to the Algebra Project*:

In order for us as poor and oppressed people to become a part of a society that is meaningful, the system under which we now exist has to be radically changed. This means that we are going to have to learn to think in radical terms. I use the term radical in its original meaning—getting down to and understanding the root cause. It means facing a system that does not lend itself to your needs and devising means by which you change the system. That is easier said than done. But one of the things that has to be faced is, in the process of wanting to change that system, how much have we got to do to find out who we are, where we have come from and where we are going. . . . I am saying as you must say, too, that in order to see where we are going, we not only must remember where we have been, but we must understand where we have been. (p. 3)

I agree with Miss Ella Baker's position in that changing a system, public schools, is easier said than done. Specifically, changing schools that will embrace the cultural, historical, and social contexts of which Black children bring to school takes work and deliberate thought. However, the wastebasket can be burned.

Geneva Gay (2000) offers one solution: "Conventional wisdom, personal experience, theoretical assertions, research findings, and best practices attest to the effect of genuine teacher caring on student achievement" (p. 46). Gay continues by positing that caring is "manifested in the form of teacher attitudes, expectations, and behaviors about students' human value, intellectual capability, and performance responsibilities. Teachers demonstrate caring for children as *students* and as *people*" (p. 45). This is a "radical" way of thinking about educating Black children, particularly, as I reflect on where we have been in the process of educating our children.

Valerie Ooka Pang (2005) dances with Gay's steps by indicating that an ethic of caring becomes evident through culturally relevant pedagogy. What this means, according to Pang, is that teachers

> know how to connect the students' prior knowledge with the academic content being taught. Culturally relevant teachers understand their students' value systems and act as *cultural mediators* in situations where the behaviors and values of children conflict with mainstream expectations. (p. 10)

The dance, as I call it, can be choreographed in such a way that teaching and learning become smooth, graceful, energizing, and beneficial for all involved. In essence, "Culturally relevant teaching can be a powerful force in learning" (Pang, 2005, p. 11).

The dance can be imagined in Gloria Ladson-Billings' (1994) research on culturally relevant pedagogy. She writes that "Culturally relevant pedagogy empowers students intellectually, socially, emotionally, and politically by using cultural referents to impart knowledge, skills, and attitudes" (p. 18). Ladson-Billings notes the following:

> For example, let us examine how a fifth-grade teacher might use a culturally relevant style in a lesson about the U. S. Constitution. She might begin with a discussion of the bylaws and articles of incorporation that were used to organize a local church or African American civic association. Thus the students learn the significance of such documents in forming institutions and shaping ideals while they also learn that their own people are institution-builders. This kind of moving between the two cultures lays the foundation for a skill that the students will need in order to reach academic and cultural success. (p. 18)

This is similar to my own teaching of curriculum at my urban university. I try to show how content can be meaningful for school children, especially Black children in the urban core. I use the "American Revolution," which is a prescribed subject in U.S. schooling. I say to pre-service and in-service teachers that we can radically change the concept by erasing the word "American" and focusing on "Revolution." I think that it is radical because socially constructed "truth" (knowledge) informs teachers that the word "American" has to be the primary focus. This leads me back to McLaren's (2003) summation about what knowledge is affirmed and legitimated.

The hope is that by removing the word "American" brings about a transgressive (hooks, 1994) approach to thinking about and experiencing curriculum and lived experiences. That is, my definition of revolution might differ from another's definition. For example, the 1992 Los Angeles uprising can be viewed as a revolution in some ways rather than a riot. This viewpoint creates opportunities for students to question why the Boston Tea Party is named a "party" and not a "riot." I argue that it is a practice that opens the dance floor to many ways of doing the two-step. As Ladson-Billings (1994) suggests, "This kind of moving between the two cultures lays the foundation for a skill that the students will need in order to reach academic and cultural success" (p. 18).

As I bring this short reflection to a close, I must admit that as I sat and watched Katrina's uncovering of the blatant racism and social class divide within this "wealth of a nation," I have asked myself: "What have I done to assist in the eradication of such abject poverty and oppression? Have I done enough to insure that a caring and safe environment is real for our Black children? How many bathrooms do I need in my home to be comfortable? How many more left-overs am I going to throw away?" These are the questions that haunted me last August and September. I watched as other people's children needed water, cleanliness (which is next to godliness, they say), safety, food; and most of all, I think, an ethic of caring.

I am tired of hearing that change takes time. Thich Nhat Hanh (1995) says, "When you hammer a nail into a board and accidentally strike your finger, you take care of the injury immediately" (p. 66). In 1990, I wrote that

> To live in a world which is not yet, we must engage in a language of critique that contributes to the establishment of a just and compassionate community within which a discourse of possibility becomes the guiding principle for a new social order. A language of critique meshes with a language of possibility and this language of possibility creates a passion for that which can be. And in order to do this we must constantly raise new questions. (Smith, 1990, pp. 123–124)

I say that it is time to take care of the injury; it is time to be radical; it is time to name the many frozen feet that exist; it is time to understand what the negro-pen means today; it is time to claim culturally relevant pedagogy as transgressive and hopeful (hooks, 2003); IT IS TIME TO BURN THE WASTEBASKET!

REFERENCES

Brown II, C. & R. Land (Eds.), *The politics of curricular change: Race, hegemony, and power in education* (pp. 211–229). New York: Peter Lang.

Brown, W. W. (1847). *Narrative of William W. Brown: A fugitive slave.* Boston: Published at the Anti-Slavery Office, No. 25 Cornhill.

Caruthers, L. (2005). The unfinished agenda of school desegregation: Using storytelling to deconstruct the dangerous memories of the American mind. *Journal of Educational Studies,* 37(1), 24–40.

Caruthers, L., & Smith, D. (2006, Summer). Re-living dangerous memories: On-line journaling to interrogate spaces of 'otherness' in a multicultural course. *Journal of Curriculum Theorizing,* 121–136.

Delpit, L. (1995). *Other people's children: Cultural conflict in the classroom.* New York: The New Press.

Duncan, G. (2005). Race and change in education: Toward a semiotics of curriculum. In M.

Freire, P. (1970). *Pedagogy of the oppressed.* New York: Continuum.

Hanh, T. N. (1995). *Living Buddha, living Christ.* New York: Riverhead Books.

hooks, b. (1994). *Teaching to transgress.* New York: Routledge.

hooks, b. (2003). *Teaching community: A pedagogy of hope.* New York: Routledge.

Land, R. (2005). Wounded soldiers in the classroom: Qualifying black teachers' experiences. In M. C. Brown, II & R. Land (Eds.), *The politics of curricular change: Race, hegemony, and power in education* (pp. 105–127). New York: Peter Lang.

McLaren, P. (2003). *Life in schools.* (4th ed.). Boston: Allyn and Bacon.

Moses, R. (2001). *Radical equations: Civil rights from Mississippi to the algebra project.* Boston: Beacon Press.

Pang, V. O. (2005). *Multicultural education: A caring-centered reflective approach.* (2nd ed.). Boston: McGraw-Hill.

Simon, R. (1988). For a pedagogy of possibility. *Critical Pedagogy Network, 1,* 1–4.

Smith, D. (1990). *A social and political construction of child abuse: A study of Afra American women teachers.* Unpublished doctoral dissertation. Ohio University, Oxford, Ohio.

CHAPTER 16

Can You Hear Me Now?

Transforming Today's Challenges to Position America for the Future

MARY HATWOOD FUTRELL

"The more I cover foreign affairs, the more I wish I had studied education in college, because the more I travel, the more I find that the most heated debates revolve around education."

Thomas Friedman, columnist
The Washington Post

When we reflect on the last decade, especially the last year, it is very obvious that we, the United States, are currently experiencing one of the most profound periods of change within the history of America—change that impacts our economic and political systems but also the very foundations of our education system. The challenges we face as a nation, and especially as educators, are largely shaped by this change— on a local, national, and global level. Allow me to reflect on two examples of change that made national headlines this year and how they will redefine whom we educate and how we go about it. Then, let us look forward to some of the challenges we face as part of our increasingly global society and the role of education in helping America address those challenges. Finally, I will point out three inherent advantages that America should rely on and improve upon as it faces the future.

At the start of the 2005–2006 school year, we all witnessed the devastating effects of Hurricane Katrina. Thousands of people were affected, many tragically, and the catastrophic damage led to massive disruptions and displacements. Families lost their homes, their jobs, and their communities. Over 372,000 elementary and secondary children in the Gulf Coast region were displaced from public and private schools; hundreds of schools were so badly damaged they had to be closed indefinitely.

While the hurricane's force was felt primarily in Alabama, Louisiana, and Mississippi, its impact was felt across the nation. Children and their families dispatched by the storm have been scattered all over the country. Schools in at least 25 states have been impacted as a result of efforts to accommodate children from the Gulf Coast region whose schools were closed. Efforts are underway to rebuild the affected communities, especially to re-open those schools. Fellow Americans from all across the nation have contributed time, effort, and/or money to help repair damaged schools and build new ones, and have donated textbooks, technological equipment, and other instructional materials.

At the higher education level, over 70,000 college students were forced to relocate because 15 of the colleges and universities in the region had to be closed after the storm—all are still trying to re-establish themselves. As a result, colleges and universities throughout the nation opened their doors to admit students who were displaced by the hurricane.

For some, recovery will be relatively easy; for others, it will be a slow, tedious process. As educators and human services providers serving the nation, we are faced with a choice about how to respond to these students' needs. We can simply provide makeshift services, or we can use this as an opportunity to build a model system of education that provides a quality education for every child throughout the region. We can consider this an opportunity to strengthen and better align education at all levels, including higher education; an opportunity for researchers, practitioners, students, parents, and community leaders to work together to build a system that guarantees every person a quality education, not just for today, but for the future; and an opportunity to exemplify the highest levels of educational excellence and to create a model for how we can transform education systems in other parts of the country.

Many of the families displaced by the hurricane also have had to adjust to new environments and new communities—communities in which they may be viewed differently based on their race, class, or culture. The challenge of inclusiveness, a significant one for schools and universities even in the best of times, is great and will become even greater as communities continue to change.

This observation brings me to the second example of America's current period of social change. In 2006, immigration has risen once again to the top of America's *political* agenda, as it has intermittently done for two centuries. We are witnessing the transformation of our communities, especially in our workplaces and schools, as more immigrants from Latin America, Asia, Africa, Eastern and Central Europe, and the Middle East come to our shores. We are seeing small Midwestern towns, urban and suburban centers, and even the foothills of Virginia become more culturally, linguistically, and religiously diverse.

Some communities have welcomed their new neighbors; others are quietly watching; and still others are resistant to change. However, let us not forget our history. We have been down this road before—a road that Michael Powell of *The Washington Post* describes as "a road well traveled"—when the Germans, the Irish, the Italians, and Jewish immigrants came to America. Many came fleeing the Holocaust, seeking safety; others came looking for economic security; others sought freedom and democracy, and still others simply came because they wanted to be in America, the land of opportunity. Some, including the Chinese, were refused the right for many years to come here, and some immigrants arrived against their own free will.

The transition was not always easy. Many refused to learn to speak English; others hyphenated their names. However, our willingness to set aside our differences, build on our commonalities, and live by the principles that define America has enabled us to become an even stronger, more united nation. Today, an America that embraces diversity and unity is the only America that will succeed in an increasingly interconnected, multicultural global society—a society which is to a greater extent bilingual, even multilingual, not monolingual.

As we look to the future and reflect on America's role in the world, we need to understand that the global village will continue to evolve and will be very different five, even 10, years from now. We need to acknowledge that we are already living in that global society and have been for several decades. It has just become more obvious now—in the marketplace, through the impact of rapid transportation, and through information technologies that allow us to communicate anywhere in the world at any time on any given day.

When many of us "baby boomers" were born, our competition was our next-door neighbor. Today, our competition may be somewhere in Brazil, South Africa, China, India, Russia, or Saudi Arabia. We are now and will continue to be competing with everyone else in the world, from industrialized to developing countries.

The three issues I have discussed intersect with one another. Rebuilding the educational infrastructure in the Gulf Coast region, the new era of immigration, and globalization's impact on our economy, national security, and democracy are three examples of why it is becoming increasingly necessary for Americans to understand the transformation occurring throughout our nation and the world, and, as we approach these challenges, we do so with three very powerful advantages upon which we must rely and improve in order to succeed.

First, the United States is already one of the most diverse, if not the most diverse, countries in the world. We need to continue efforts to build on that diversity by welcoming new arrivals and helping them to become acculturated into our society. At the same time, we need to build on the linguistic and cultural attributes that our newcomers bring to the country. We must enhance their knowledge and skills so that we may further strengthen our nation's social, economic, and political stature.

Second, America's universal education system is one of the fundamental foundations of our democratic society and of our economic system. I believe that our education system—P-20—has played a major role throughout our history in making it possible for immigrants to become part of American society. We must ensure that our schools continue to play that role—for all racial, ethnic, and economic groups.

However, we also live in a changing world—a world in which highly educated citizens will be in great demand at every level. We therefore need to ask ourselves a question: "Why do we educate?" By educate I do not mean simply teaching the basics, even though that is a critical component of the educational process, but for what purpose do we prepare citizens, leaders, and workers, whatever their vocation or profession? What do citizens need to know to be viable players in this complex, multi-cultural, highly competitive global society? As Thomas Friedman, author of the book, *The World Is Flat,* said, "The more I cover foreign affairs, the more I wish I had studied education in college, because the more I travel, the more I find that the most heated debates revolve around education." Rightfully so. The question is not whether each one of us will be part of that debate, but rather, if we will be prepared to actively engage in it.

Yes, we need to learn more about science, math, and technology, but that will not be sufficient. We need to expand, not narrow, our curriculum to ensure that all Americans better understand the rest of the world. Unfortunately, reports are showing that because of the No Child Left Behind Act, many school districts are doing just that—dramatically narrowing their curriculum to teach to the adequate yearly progress requirements outlined in that legislation. Instead, schools and school districts need to align curricula, content, and instructional standards so that all children are assured the educational foundation they need to demonstrate not only mastery of the subjects they are taught but how to use what they have learned to further educate themselves. In order to achieve this goal, the curriculum should be enriched, not depleted.

For example, we need to start in primary school, certainly no later than middle school, to teach our children to speak another language (i.e., Chinese, Arabic, Spanish, Russian, and Hindi) and teach them to understand the geography and culture of other nations. In other words, we need to ensure that our students are equipped with the "tools" to be independent workers, as well as have the communicative, social, and education skills to be team players, whether it is at home or abroad.

As Carnevale and Desrochers (2002) said in their paper, *The Missing Middle: Aligning Education and the Knowledge Economy,* "Access to good jobs and earnings in the American system are driven by the complementarities between soft skills such as general reasoning, problem solving, and behavioral skills, general education beyond high school, occupational preparation, and the resultant access to learning and technology on the job." We need to ensure, first of all, that all graduates have those skills and, second, continue to enhance them as they move up the educational ladder. Every citizen, in order to be a viable player in the America of tomorrow, will need to constantly build on their knowledge and skills and be prepared today for a future whose hallmarks will be continued change and adaptability.

To achieve these goals, educators at all levels of the educative process need to be willing to change. We need to break down the silos that currently define our education system. Thus, a key question for those of us at the university level, particularly our schools, colleges, and departments of education, is whether we are preparing educators, especially teachers, for the knowledge-based, global society in which we now live, or whether we are still preparing them for the industrial era that is long past.

The model of schools as cubicles—in which teachers teach their classes in isolation using the didactic method, or where subjects are taught as isolated disciplines—is no longer the most practical or most effective way to teach and learn (Futrell, 2006). Today, students need to understand the interdisciplinary relationship between, for example, technology, English, history, and biology. Such courses could be taught by teams of teachers using strategies like block scheduling or mediated learning to allow more time for students to develop strong social and academic foundations, and to learn how to learn together. In these environments, students would discover how to ask real world questions and research, synthesize, and effectively communicate the answers. Thus, they would have more opportunities to become self-motivated and inquisitive and to become leaders in their learning environment. Throughout their educational experiences and beyond, students will be able to draw upon these valuable skills.

America has a third powerful advantage, which is an extension of the second one: our higher education system. Its strength and the wide range of opportunities it provides have served as magnets for American students and students from countries throughout the world. These students, in turn, have gone on to make major contributions both to the United States and to other countries.

Our colleges and universities have played a major role in strengthening equality of educational opportunity in the United States by enabling young people from a wide range of economic, racial, and ethnic backgrounds to participate in American society at the highest professional levels. The challenge is to ensure that our policies, both fiscal and social, make it possible for colleges and universities to continue—and to increase—the educational opportunities they provide to diverse student populations.

As we prepare for the challenges of the future, we need to ensure that more people are prepared for and have access to higher education. As Friedman (2005) said, "The flatter the world gets the more critical tertiary education becomes because technology and other sources will be churning over old jobs and spawning more complex ones much faster than during the transition from the agricultural era to the industrial one."

It is projected that enrollments at the higher education level of our education system will grow by three million additional students—from 13 to 16 million by 2015—at the undergraduate level alone. Of those three million new students, it is anticipated that 80 percent will come from racial and language minority groups (i.e., African American, Hispanic, or Asian/Pacific Islander) (Institute for Higher Education Policy, April 2006). At the same time, it is also projected that more Americans 30 years of age and older will be pursuing a postsecondary education. The question is will they be prepared for and will they be able to afford a postsecondary education, whether at a two- or four-year college or university? Put another way, can we afford not to educate more Americans and educate them better than any previous generation?

We need to transform our education system—pre-kindergarten through graduate school—to guarantee every American access to quality education and to ensure that they are prepared to be lifelong learners. Our ability and determination to fulfill that transformation have now become a national priority. For example, the critical role of education in defining and shaping the future of America is reflected in the federal government's decision to conduct two major studies of education. One is a study of all schools of education. By calling for a study of teacher preparation programs, Congress is acknowledging the vital role of schools of education in ensuring that America remains one of the most socially, economically, and politically advanced countries in the world. The results of that study are to be presented to Congress during the spring of 2007.

The second federal study is of higher education in general. That study, The Secretary of Education's Commission on the Future of Higher Education, was designed to create a dialogue about what needs to be done to ensure that the system continues to meet the nation's needs for an educated and competitive workforce in the twenty-first century. Today, 80-plus percent of the fastest growing jobs require at least some postsecondary education. Whether we are preparing policymakers or policemen, corporate leaders or salesmen, astronauts or artists, counselors or chefs, or educators or engineers, a quality education for all is the key to ensuring that the United States will continue to be a primary leader in our global society. Thus, the Commission is exploring ways to ensure that college is affordable and accessible and is assessing how well institutions of higher education are preparing our students to compete in the new global economy. The final report is due in August 2006.

Whatever the results of these two studies and others that may be underway, two things are very clear: (1) education—P-20—has become a national concern, and (2) we need to transform our education system in order to better align and communicate the expectations that citizens will be required to meet in a knowledge-based global economy. We also need to redefine the curricula to reflect the content, skills (including academic, interpersonal, and problem-solving), and experiences that more accurately and realistically reflect the intercultural world in which we live. In other words, the education citizens receive today should enhance their quality of life, help them adapt in a constantly changing society, and help define what type of society we want.

The issue of education is not simply an American debate. In country after country, leaders recognize the importance of education in preparing their citizens to face the challenges of tomorrow. They have developed a better understanding of and appreciation for the inevitable link of aligning education, the demographic realities of their countries, and the knowledge economy that is transforming the world. The strongest nations will be those that invest in education to build on the interrelationship between human potential and the political, economical, and social viability of their people. It is about understanding who we are as a people, as a society, and what knowledge and skills are needed to survive, to grow, to make a difference for the public good.

At times like these, individuals who have been prepared at the university level bear a particular responsibility to help others respond to the mosaic of changes and challenges in our society. To successfully address any of these issues requires commitment and courage on the part of each of us.

The challenges before us—institutional, professional, and personal change—are neither new nor did they just recently bubble to the top of the pot. In addition, we are not simply talking about a once-in-a-lifetime catastrophe like Hurricane Katrina.

What happened in the Gulf Coast region could happen anywhere in America, for there is no part of this country that is totally safe from a natural disaster. Furthermore, the appearance of millions of immigrants in our neighborhoods is not a new issue. These natural and cultural changes simply reiterate the defining characteristics of America, both in its past and in its future. On the international level, globalization is a reflection of the continuous evolution of who we are as a people, as a society, as a world. Again, the challenges we face are not unique to any one particular part of our country or the world, but nevertheless impact each of us and all of us.

However, we should not need a disaster or demographic revolution to understand the need to transform our education system to continually expand access to and enhance the quality of education. Education is neither stagnant nor should it take a crisis to force us to understand that our educational system, like other parts of our infrastructure—whether political, social, or economic—suffers wear and tear, and, thus, needs constant monitoring and refinement. Education is vibrant; it is constantly evolving. It defines who and what we are as a people and as a nation. On the one hand, it must be protected, but it also must be cultivated to meet the changing social, economic, and political needs of our society. This process requires careful planning, nurturing, and hard work from all of us.

As I have stated throughout this chapter, how well we sustain the viability of our nation will be a reflection of how well we understand the role of education in positioning the United States to be a key player in defining and shaping the continuous evolution of our global village. For almost three decades, we have had national conversations about reforming our education system. While those conversations have been ongoing, they have been fragmented and hotly debated, and have not brought about transformative results (change has been incremental, not comprehensive). At the same time, we recognize that much of what we have accomplished as a nation has occurred because education is a major foundation of our democracy and, in particular, our economy.

Educating our people has enabled us to successfully address the myriad challenges that changed us from an agrarian to an industrial and now to a knowledge-based society In addition, we have committed ourselves to just that—continuing to educate the peoples of America. This means colleges and universities, as well as pre-K-12 school personnel; federal, state and local policymakers; members of the respective professions and their professional organizations; the business community, parents, students, and other key players need to work together not simply to rebuild or correct deficiencies but to truly transform our education system to more effectively educate all of the nation's citizens, particularly all our children regardless of their heritage, for they are the future of America.

We are experiencing the convergence of an era of enormous change. The question is whether we are prepared for those changes, especially as they increasingly define our quality of life, and who we are as a people and as a society. Our response must be, "Yes, we hear the call and we understand the message." We are prepared for some of the changes, but it is becoming overtly obvious that we have much more to do to prepare for the changes already on the horizon and for those yet to emerge. The United States must transform its infrastructure, especially its education system, so that at every level we are providing each American with the educational foundation to fulfill his or her responsibilities, as well as to realize their dreams as a citizen of this country and of the world.

REFERENCES

Carnevale, A., & Desrochers, D. M. (2002, April). *The missing middle: Aligning education and the knowledge economy.* Princeton, NJ: The Educational Testing Service.

Carnevale, A. P., & Fry, R. A. (2000). *Crossing the great divide: Can we achieve equity when Generation Y goes to college?* Princeton, NJ: Educational Testing Service.

Committee for Economic Development. (2006). *Education for global leadership.* Washington, DC: Author.

Friedman, T. L. (2005). *The world is flat: A brief history of the twenty-first century.* New York: Farrar, Straus and Giroux.

Futrell, M. H. (2006). For what purpose do we prepare teachers? In the *Handbook of research on teacher education. Teacher education: Enduring issues in changing contexts.* New York: Teachers College Press.

Institute for Higher Education Policy. (2006, April). *CONVERGENCE: Trends threatening to narrow college opportunity in America. A project of the Institute for Higher Education Policy.* Washington, DC: Author.

Powell, M. (2006, May 8). U.S. immigrant debate is a road well traveled. *Washington Post,* A1, A4.

■|■|■

CHAPTER 17

A Continuing Katrina
for At-Risk Children

How We Can Make It Right

ARTHUR E. WISE & JANE A. LEIBBRAND

Hurricane Katrina brought with it a renewed awareness of the disparities between the haves and have-nots in our society. Americans looked on in horror as thousands of people were trapped in the center of New Orleans—for the most part, those who did not have the means to leave for higher ground. So it is that millions of children are trapped in schools where they do not learn to a proficient or even basic level. In spite of desegregation rules, busing, demonstration projects, and some equalization of property tax structures, children in inner cities are trapped just as surely as were the hurricane victims. They can't get out. Just as it occurred in the aftermath of Katrina, new resources must be brought to where these children are, and a structure for these resources must be built into the districts where the children reside.

Recent polling data reveal that the majority of the public is willing to invest more in public education. More than 83 percent of the public favor higher salaries for teachers, even if it means higher taxes. Fully 88 percent favor eliminating the practice of hiring unqualified teachers. When asked about the qualities of good teachers, by a vast majority the public agreed that good teachers "are well trained and knowledgeable about how to teach," and "understand how people learn." Teaching is the public's number two most respected profession, behind the clergy. The public's top priority in education is teacher quality; its lowest priority is focusing solely on standardized test scores.

The public's interest in hiring qualified teachers is unfortunately not always implemented at the state and local level, as states lower teaching standards by allowing those with no preparation to enter the classroom and possibly even be called 'highly qualified.'

Currently, low performing urban schools are experiencing the brunt of the increase in unqualified personnel. Over the past three decades, more women and persons of color gained new employment opportunities and moved into managerial and other professional ranks. For example, no longer are women consigned to nursing or teaching. As a result, teacher shortages are now a chronic condition, which can only be termed a crisis in at-risk schools. These schools are forced to hire unprepared and inexperienced "teachers," some of whom are the products of alternate certification programs of a few weeks' duration. The results are predictable. Low performing children remain low performing. Sixty percent of the teachers are gone within three years. The schools are forced to replace them with new unprepared and inexperienced teachers. With this passing parade of teaching temps the cycle of low performance continues. According to National Assessment of Educational Progress data, the average scale score in reading for eighth-grade students of American Indian, Hispanic, or Black origin has actually declined in the last two years, and the score for those eligible for free/reduced price lunch has remained the same—at 23 to 25 points below those of White/Asian/Pacific Islander students. In eighth-grade math, the scale scores of American Indian, Hispanic and Black children remain 34 points below that of White and Asian/Pacific Islander groups, even though scores of all groups have increased slightly. Results of those eighth grade math students eligible for free/reduced price lunches are about the same as for the non-White groups. (http://nces.ed.gov/nationsreportcard/)

What affirmative steps can we take to ameliorate this longstanding achievement gap once and for all? Increasing rigor in teacher preparation and licensing, to ensure that all teachers are highly qualified, and building new structures for the education of teachers to familiarize them with students in at-risk schools and learn to work with them successfully, are two important strategies we can and should move forward.

Increasing the Rigor of Quality Assurance in Teaching

In the established professions, practitioners move through three distinct phases of preparation and development. First is graduation from a professionally accredited program of study. Next, in all of the "helping" professions, in addition to some of the others, novice professionals practice under close supervision for an extended period—usually at least one year—before being granted a degree or a professional license to practice. Finally, practicing professionals enhance their skills by studying for board certification in their field.

The three phases of preparation and development correspond to three quality assurance mechanisms—professional accreditation, state licensing, and advanced certification—which the established professions have used to assure public trust in those who are licensed to practice.

The profession of teaching has been hard at work during the last decades of the twentieth century and the start of the twenty-first to develop such a system. NCATE, as the profession's preparation arm, the Interstate New Teacher Assessment and Support Consortium (INTASC), through the Council of Chief State School Officers, and the National Board for Professional Standards, are three organizations which have worked together for almost two decades to develop a coherent and consistent set of standards and assessments in the areas of preservice preparation, licensing, and continuing professional development.

There is growing recognition among policy makers and educators that preservice preparation is the initial phase of educator preparation, but a teacher's development continues throughout his or her career. Preservice preparation grounds the future educator in subject matter knowledge and pedagogical knowledge. Some policymakers are recommending that teachers simply take a test of subject matter knowledge and be assigned a mentor to begin teaching. While professional development is necessary, it cannot substitute for or replace an entire foundation of knowledge. The National Academy of Education recently released a report that sets forth a common core of knowledge and skills that a beginning teacher should possess. The common core of knowledge correlates with NCATE standards for teacher preparation.

Licensing

More and more states are developing tiered licensing systems, with a novice license designation for beginning teachers. The novice license provides the opportunity for an extended clinical period of education for new educators. This designation has begun to emerge as a legitimate aspect of teacher preparation and development. By extending initial preparation and development, education decision makers recognize that the beginning teacher needs a great deal of support and assistance—not only to ensure more successful teaching, but also to help retain the new teacher for the following year. Mentoring programs and extended clinical practice settings such as professional development schools increase teacher retention (Teitel, 2004).

Professional teachers continue to learn from new advances in research and practice and engage in continuing professional development to enhance teaching knowledge and skill. With more available data on student achievement, teachers more easily see results, leading to a focus on continuous improvement in practice. Advanced certification now provides formal recognition of advanced skill, which translates into salary enhancements and leadership opportunities.

Parts of an emerging system of quality assurance are in place, while others are still taking shape. Standards have been developed for P–12 students through national standards projects and state efforts. NCATE has overhauled its accreditation standards and uses a performance-based system. Accreditation standards now incorporate P-12 student standards and INTASC model state licensing standards. Advanced certification of teachers, indicating special competence in a discipline, is now a reality.

Alignment of Assessment with Standards

Licensing tests were not common until two decades ago, and private companies initially developed them with minimal input from the field. The Higher Education Act of 1998, which required states to make public the candidate pass rates on teacher licensing examinations, encouraged all states to develop teacher licensing examinations. NCLB, with its emphasis on student testing, reinforced the use of teacher licensing examinations. In 2002, NCATE initiated an effort to ensure that the teaching profession's standards are the basis of teacher licensing examinations. Educational Testing Service is collaborating with NCATE-member specialty professional associations to ensure that standardized assessments are aligned with the profession's standards. ETS now invites representatives of specialty associations to review test specifications as well as the assessments themselves and provide feedback and advice. The alignment ensures that a common body of knowledge that all teachers should know is included in the assessments. The profession is now exploring the development of benchmarks in the various disciplines to help clarify professional expectations for beginning teachers. Benchmarks would also provide greater consistency to on-site accreditation teams as they review candidate performance on state licensing examinations.

Thus, those in the profession are now integrally involved in creating the licensing examinations, in critiquing them, and in validating them. The collaboration will bring a new professionalism to teaching in the twenty-first century. It will provide evidence that teaching is a profession with a base of knowledge that licensed teachers know and apply. The revised examinations are better measures of teacher knowledge than we have had in the past, because they reflect current professional consensus on important subject content and teaching knowledge. Recognizing that no knowledge base in the professions is static, the precedent has now been set for alignment between licensing examinations and professional standards for teacher preparation.

Advances in Assessment

During the decade of the 1990s there were several other developments in the assessment of new teachers and teacher candidates. The National Board for Professional Teaching Standards moved the entire field forward with the development of standards and assessments for experienced teachers. The teaching profession is reaping the benefits of the work of NBPTS, which has advanced the state of the art in assessing teaching performance. The assessments created by the National Board are instruments used to certify accomplished teachers, but the methodologies the Board has developed, some of which drew on even earlier work in Connecticut, have provided models for assessing the practice of teaching (in contrast with knowledge about teaching) that had not previously existed. INTASC has applied these methodologies to design "portfolio" assessments specifically for teaching content fields. The intent has been to create models that states could align with their own teacher standards and student standards and that would be administered during an initial teacher's first or second year of experience. Moreover, following the lead of INTASC, some states are creating portfolio assessments for preservice use that select from, and adapt, the INTASC portfolios. An important element of the portfolios is a focus on student learning in the classroom of the teacher or candidate who is completing the assessment. If these portfolio assessments come into general use they will fill a critical gap in teacher licensure testing—the current lack of evidence that the new teacher can teach effectively—and meet the needs of children with diverse educational needs, so that all students learn.

In addition, INTASC licensing standards and NCATE performance-based accreditation standards are aligned with National Board standards for experienced teachers and have been built in part on the work of the National Board in developing ways to assess teaching performance.

NCATE has provided leadership in encouraging institutions to redesign advanced master's degrees to incorporate the standards of the National Board for Professional Teaching Standards. This move is strengthening existing master's degrees. New and revised programs focus on improving teaching skills in specific subject areas. This dramatic change in master's degree programs aligned with NBPTS standards means increased professionalism and competence among experienced teachers. As more teachers become acquainted with the standards of the NBPTS, more will seek Board certification. As accredited institutions revise their programs to align standards with those of the National Board, they will be prepared to help teachers who wish to move toward Board certification.

In summary, NCATE has provided leadership in aligning accreditation standards with P-12 student standards, with licensing standards, and with advanced certification standards.

Two Different Directions . . . To What End?

While the professionalism movement was beginning to mature, a countermovement mushroomed in the first years of the twenty-first century. Several annual reports from the Secretary of Education said teacher education had "failed." Alternate routes to teaching, many that bypass teacher preparation at institutions, were encouraged. Complete deregulation of state licensing has been recently touted by several scholars and groups, including Checker Finn and the National Council for Teacher Quality. NCATE was seen as a monopoly. The U.S. Department of Education recognized a second accrediting body for teacher preparation, the Teacher Education Accreditation Council. TEAC was formed by the Council for Independent Colleges, a group of independent college presidents. It audits individual programs that wish to be accredited and measures the results according to individual program goals. The National Council for Teacher Quality, formed from Checker Finn's Thomas B. Fordham Foundation, has been a vocal critic of teacher preparation and NCATE. A new organization, the American Board for Certification of Teacher Excellence, (ABCTE), supported heavily with federal funding, is promoting a "passport to teaching" test to make it easier for teachers to move from state to state; it is also competing with the National Board to certify teachers at the advanced level. Alternate mechanisms have been created to those the profession established or strengthened in the 1990s.

States have followed the two routes somewhat simultaneously—48 out of 50 states developed and continued their partnerships with NCATE, which encouraged professional accreditation of colleges of education. At the same time, many states developed alternate routes to teaching, some of which bypass graduation from any teacher preparation program—much less an accredited one. Some cities, e.g., New York, have taken a middle route—hiring Teach for America graduates and other non-licensed individuals but requiring them to earn a master's degree to gain professional licensure status. All of this dual activity has had an effect of watering down the profession's movement to upgrade teaching as a profession. To clarify who indeed is "highly qualified," I propose the following definition for "highly qualified" and "professional" teacher: an individual who has graduated from a professionally accredited program of study and who is fully licensed. Others who are teaching without this core fund of knowledge may be designated as residents, interns, or provisionally licensed teachers.

Which of the two directions will become predominant in the field of teaching? Only time will tell. If we deregulate state licensing and deprofessionalize teaching by foregoing adherence to professional standards, we will most certainly exacerbate the two-tier education system. If we follow a path toward professionalization, all children could be taught by qualified teachers—even the children of Katrina.

Teacher Preparation Standards: New Expectations for Colleges of Education

Policymakers are searching for ways to scale up school and higher education reforms that are happening in small pockets across America. The U.S. Department of Education and private foundations fund reform projects at P-12 schools and institutions; some of those reforms take hold; others disappear once the funds are gone. The hope, of course, is that reforms that make a difference in student learning will be integrated into the culture of the P-12 classroom—and in higher education. Creating lasting change is a huge challenge. The advantage of the NCATE system is that it serves to institutionalize reforms. NCATE is creating new norms of behavior around reform ideas and concepts in teacher preparation. In this way NCATE is not merely an accrediting agency—it is a force for the reform of teacher preparation.

Performance-Based Accreditation

Traditionally, specialized professional accreditation has focused a great deal on the curriculum and on inputs, including adequate resources to conduct the programs. While these factors are very important, not enough attention has been paid to the ultimate outcomes of the programs. Information on curriculum and other inputs, such as faculty qualifications, does not answer the most pressing question: Are the programs at NCATE accredited colleges of education effective in producing teacher candidates who know the subjects they plan to teach and who can teach effectively so that students learn? Answering that question is now central to NCATE's performance-based accreditation system.

In NCATE's performance-based system, accreditation is based on results—results that demonstrate that the teacher candidate knows the subject matter and can teach it effectively so that students learn. In the NCATE system, it is no longer good enough for a faculty member or a teacher candidate to say, "I taught the material." The focus is on providing evidence that the candidate can connect theory to practice and be effective in an actual P-12 classroom. Performance-based accreditation answers the question: "Is the institution preparing candidates with appropriate knowledge, teaching strategies, and professional dispositions to teach students so that they learn and achieve P-12 standards?"

Subject Matter Knowledge

The foundation of knowledge rests with each subject area/discipline. As knowledge is defined and codified, educators in each discipline come together to decide what should be emphasized, given the structure and tools of the discipline.

Defining what P-12 students should know and be able to do in each discipline is the first step on the road to higher student achievement. NCATE standards prepare teachers who can help students meet P-12 student standards, because NCATE's teacher preparation standards are built on what P-12 students should know and are able to do.

There are various ways that the P-12 student standards are embedded into the fabric of teacher candidate preparation at accredited institutions. Specialty professional associations in the teaching disciplines set standards for P-12 students in the relevant discipline, as well as parallel standards for teacher preparation. NCATE expects those standards, or state standards that are aligned with them, to be used in the design and delivery of teacher preparation programs at accredited institutions.

NCATE's Standard 1, *Candidate Knowledge, Skills and Dispositions,* expects the education unit (school/college/department of education, or organization) to ensure that candidates meet professional, state, and institutional (or organizational) standards (NCATE, 2002). The professional standards are those set by NCATE and its member specialty associations. Thus, the unit helps ensure that programs meet professional standards.

Subject matter knowledge may be assessed by PRAXIS II or another similar licensing test, and this information will be used in the accreditation decision. However, other measures of candidate content knowledge are required as well. A candidate's ability to synthesize the content to help P-12 students understand it is also assessed. One important measure of candidate knowledge is how an institution fares on NCATE's program review process.

The review of individual programs is a critical part of the NCATE performance-based accreditation system. These reviews feed directly into the analysis of NCATE's Standard 1 on candidate knowledge and skills. Institutions must meet all standards to be accredited without conditions.

Program Review

The new program review system was first implemented in early 2005 by institutions that agreed to pilot the process. Much was learned from the pilot, and the inevitable bumps in the road are being smoothed out.

NCATE's program standards answer the question: what must teachers and other educators know and be able to do? The standards are developed by 19 specialized professional associations representing the various disciplines of teaching. They are recognized by NCATE's Specialty Areas Studies Board for use in NCATE's performance-based accreditation system.

NCATE's 50 state partners have either adopted NCATE's program standards or have closely aligned their state standards with these program standards. Thus the program standards developed by education professionals in their respective fields, along with public members and state representatives, have become de facto national program standards to a considerable degree.

For an example of what is contained in the standards, let's consider the secondary mathematics standards. These standards are divided into three subsets: process, pedagogy, and content. Process standards require candidates to "reason, construct, and evaluate mathematical arguments," to "use varied representations of mathematical ideas to support and deepen students' mathematical understanding," and "use technology as a teaching tool" among many other competencies. In terms of content, as an example, one standard focuses on algebra: "Candidates must emphasize relationships among quantities including functions, ways of representing mathematical relationships, and the analysis of change." There are five more content standards as well as a standard on pedagogy.

NCATE's new method of reviewing individual programs at institutions is an example of reform in action. The review answers the question: What is the evidence concerning what teacher candidates know and can do? NCATE expects all candidates in an individual program (mathematics, English, social studies, and so on) to undergo six to eight common assessments developed by the institution. Curriculum is guided by the standards, as are the common program assessments.

Faculty must first attend to the standards in order to develop the assessments. Faculty development of common assessments requires collaboration among faculty within the school of education, and between faculty in the school of education and the relevant arts and sciences department, such as math or science.

The common assessments must include key elements. Two of the assessments must be on content knowledge. If the state requires a licensure test, data from the test(s) are the first assessment. In addition, the institution must provide one other assessment of content knowledge, such as a test developed by the institution. The program must provide two assessments of pedagogical knowledge and skills—one that demonstrates that candidates can plan effective instruction and design appropriate assessments, and another that demonstrates that candidates can teach effectively. Institutions must also develop an assessment of candidate effects on P-12 student learning.

NCATE's use of national professional standards developed by the teaching disciplines integrates a number of disciplines under one accreditation umbrella. An electronic format saves time and resources, while specialists in the various disciplines ensure quality and integrity in the review of individual programs. This process is at the heart of NCATE's performance-based system and provides much of the data on which an accreditation decision is made.

Through NCATE's state partnerships, state and professional expectations have been integrated, providing increased rigor to standards for teacher preparation. For institutions that use state program standards for the NCATE review, NCATE examines the program standards, through the mechanism of state partnership protocols, and has found them to be substantially aligned with the specialty association program standards.

Assessment System and Unit Evaluation

In addition, the college must have a system in place to assess its candidates. This system must include assessments at entry, throughout the program, and upon exit. Benchmarks for acceptable learning must also be set, and institutions must have evidence that candidates who are recommended for licensure have performed at acceptable levels. NCATE has established rubrics for institutions to use to help them determine satisfactory levels of performance. Criteria for the development of assessment systems by programs or units are on NCATE's Web site in the Resources section under "Articles."

Sound assessment systems are integrated with learning experiences throughout the teacher candidates' development and are not merely a series of "off-the-shelf" measures. They are embedded in the preparation programs and conducted on a continuing basis. Candidate monitoring is planned in response to faculty decisions about the points in the program best suited to gathering performance information. Typically such information is gathered at candidate entry, in coursework, in field experiences, prior to the start of practice teaching, and at completion of the program. Examples of types of program assessments (which can be used for unit assessment purposes) include end-of-course evaluations; teacher work sample methodology; student teaching evaluations in the various discipline areas, and other such methods. Information from the program can be complemented by performance data originating from external sources. Examples are candidate performance evaluations during induction years and follow-up studies, and performance on state licensing exams that assess candidates' knowledge of subject matter and pedagogy. Together, the unit can draw on all information about candidates for continuous evaluation of candidate progress and program success.

Clinical Practice and Field Experiences

NCATE 2000 standards have served as an impetus for change in the area of clinical practice. The NCATE standards expect the school of education to develop a collaborative partnership with the cooperating P-12 schools where candidates are learning to practice. In the old student teaching model, one teacher, who had no real connection to the college or university, supervised the candidate; the university supervisor came to the site two or three times to observe. The concept of "partnership" does not exist in this model. NCATE has spearheaded change so that candidates have experiences in P-12 schools early in their programs, so that true collaboration between the college and P-12 personnel can be built, with P-12 teachers often serving as adjunct faculty. The accredited institutions and P-12 personnel now collaboratively plan the candidates' clinical program of study.

Technology

An emphasis on technology is woven throughout the accreditation standards. NCATE expects schools of education to prepare teachers who can effectively integrate technology into instruction and to model this integration within the school of education.

Diversity

The college of education must provide curriculum and experiences that help candidates develop the knowledge and skills necessary to help all students learn. Candidates must have field experiences with diverse learners, including learners with exceptionalities and students of different racial/ethnic backgrounds. The United States is a pluralistic and multicultural society, and candidates are expected to be able to work with children from all types of backgrounds that they will undoubtedly encounter in a teaching career.

Faculty Performance

The faculty performance standard expects faculty to model the best professional practice. The standard also expects faculty performance and its effect on candidate performance to be evaluated. Tying faculty performance to candidate performance raises the expectations for this standard significantly.

Unit Governance and Resources

To summarize, NCATE requires the education unit to use multiple assessments from internal and external sources and to collect data from applicants, candidates, recent graduates, and faculty. NCATE expects the institution to regularly compile, summarize, and analyze the data to improve candidate and faculty performance.

NCATE's expectations weave many of the reforms of the 1980s and 1990s into one piece of cloth—the concepts embedded in professional development schools; the measures of effective teaching in specific subject areas created by the National Board standards; the alignment of licensing examinations with teacher preparation standards; making teacher preparation a "real world" experience.

A powerful sign that these concepts are now embedded into the expectations of the field is that the language of the NCATE unit standards has been adapted or adopted as state standards for teacher preparation in more than half the states.

Professional Development Schools

One entity conceptualized in the 1980s and brought to life in the 1990s is the professional development school, or PDS. These are restructured and re-staffed schools operated by districts and universities to prepare new teachers to work effectively in hard-to-staff settings. Were they to become the norm for teacher preparation and staff development in a city, there is evidence to suggest that student achievement will increase, new teachers will be more effective, and many of those teachers will remain teaching in urban schools longer.

Both school district and university must be willing to commit resources, share responsibility, and be held accountable for outcomes. Regional, state, and private universities as well as city-based universities could work together in partnership. This collaboration can expand the pool of teacher candidates to include those coming from outside the city.

The PDS is to teacher preparation as the teaching hospital is to physician preparation, i.e., a new institution to provide high quality service to students while preparing new generations of teachers. Children in the PDS have the benefit of expert teachers and university faculty present and focusing on their needs. At the same time these experts are mentoring and supervising candidates who are learning to practice effectively.

The district could recruit and select the best teachers in the city to be mentors and master teachers and compensate them accordingly. It is essential that senior staff be specially selected and prepared for assignment in a PDS. Expertise in teaching must be accompanied by skills in mentoring and supervision. This is, and should be viewed as, a prestige assignment for which appropriate and significantly enhanced compensation is provided.

Districts could require that all new teachers spend their induction year in a PDS and demonstrate that they can teach so that students learn before they are assigned to other schools in the district. If about 10 percent of the schools in a district are PDSs, then all teachers new to the district can be accommodated for a year as members of a cohort of interns or induction-year teachers.

The district could create a management system that ensures that a mentor teacher is responsible for the achievement of every P-12 student and that every intern is trained and supervised by qualified mentors. Cohorts of candidates can be integrated into teaching teams led by mentors and master teachers. A team structure can provide time for mentor teachers to work with candidates and for candidates to have reduced teaching schedules to allow time for professional preparation.

As in a teaching hospital, the curriculum should be developed by school and university faculty and be built around identifying and meeting the needs of the students in the school. The PDS professional learning model provides opportunities built into the structure of the day for observations, conferences, participation of candidates in schoolwide and team meetings, and seminars with mentors focused on student work.

There are many options for funding strategies. One possibility is for districts to pay half salary for candidates with the other half covered by Title I funds. In this way candidates do not have to forego a year of salary while they are training. Using Title I funds to supplement the candidates' salary also frees up district funds to compensate mentors and master teachers. Recently retired, highly qualified teachers might be recruited as mentors or master teachers, compensated appropriately but on a part time basis. District and university can share salaries for PDS coordinators.

REFERENCES

National Council for Accreditation of Teacher Education. (2002). *Professional standards for the accreditation of schools, colleges, and departments of education.* Washington, DC: Author.

Teitel, L. (2004) *How professional development schools make a difference: A review of research.* Washington, DC: National Council for Accreditation of Teacher Education.

AFTERWORD

Children Drowning in Our Tears

LYNN HUNTLEY

In the 1980s, I had occasion to travel to the African nation of Mozambique and visit a farm established for the rehabilitation of children orphaned by the rebel group called "Renamo." In its quest for power, the leaders of Renamo had brutally killed thousands and created legions of "child soldiers," who were forced/incited into committing shocking acts of violence and cruelty. The children had become what the adults who exploited them taught them to be.

At the farm, throngs of orphaned children freed from Renamo's grip came forth to greet me and other well-fed and well-intentioned Americans as we left our bus to visit. Most of the children had stomachs distended from hunger and the faded blond hair characteristic of malnutrition. They gave us flowers and sang brave little songs of welcome. Though they were in the sunlight, their eyes had a sadness in them that was deeper than the darkest night.

Later, as we visitors talked with officials of government about the plight of the children, some of us were moved to tears by what we had seen. Graca Machel, then the wife of the president of Mozambique, seeing these tears, said pointedly: "We don't want your tears. We could drown in your tears. We want your help."

The children of Mozambique came to mind as I watched scenes of the devastation wrought on the Gulf Coast by Hurricane Katrina. If the children of the Gulf Coast are, as adults, illiterate, disturbed, underdeveloped, destitute, and marginalized, it won't be because of the storm. It will be because the failures of the public schools to which the children have been sent for "education."

The children of the Gulf Coast don't need our tears. They need our help.

■|■|■

"If America is to remain a first-class nation, it cannot have second-class citizenship."
—Martin Luther King, Jr., 1959

Education really is the "great equalizer," as Horace Mann said so many years ago. Talent doesn't repose in any one group of people. Our country needs and should have a public education system that does not doom some children to failure and help other children to success based on arbitrary factors such as proximity to a storm or poverty or race. We need a public education system that can help *all* of the children have fair chances to develop their talents to the fullest and contribute to the common good. That is what the promise of democracy is all about.

Although the one-year anniversary of Hurricane Katrina has pass, we do well to pause and consider the storm's aftermath and how far from adequate efforts to reconstruct public education on the Gulf Cost have thus far been. No one who reads this volume can or should be pleased. Though the papers point to streams of sunlight and progress in a few places and positive things that could be done to improve education in others, the fact is that we have miles to go before even the basic improvements in public education the children of the Gulf Coast need and deserve are in place.

The chapters in this volume provide a taxonomy of education issues. Though framed in the context of the Gulf Coast, much of what is said pertains to other pockets of poverty around the nation.

The Gulf Coast states are part of the American South, a region where forty percent of the nation's low-income people reside. It is a place of concentrated poverty, underachievement, underinvestment in education, slow progress, and deep economic, political and social inequality. A new majority of the students in the region's public schools, including rapidly growing numbers of children from immigrant families, are poor. A majority! Consider the following:

- The Gulf Coast states affected by Hurricane Katrina—Mississippi, Louisiana, and Alabama—are among the poorest in the nation, ranking 49th, 50th, and 41st among all of the states in the nation in terms of per capita income Mississippi, Louisiana, and Alabama have levels of per pupil spending in public education far below the national average: 47th in Mississippi; 34th in Louisiana; 41st in Alabama.

- Abundant reports document that low-income students in these states and others in the South attend, by and large, the least well equipped schools, and have the least access to technology, the fewest advanced placement courses and counseling services, the most inadequate libraries and are taught by the least experienced teachers.

- Dropout rates are dysfunctionally high, portending ill for the future tax base, earnings and quality of life for millions of students and their families that they will establish in the future. The rates for Mississippi, Louisiana, and Alabama are 41%, 37%, and 40%, respectively.

- Levels of educational achievement are for these low income students significantly below those of more affluent counterparts. Low income students' test scores lag demonstrably behind those of more affluent students in Mississippi, Louisiana, and Alabama. Indeed, the average test scores of the best students in these states, as a group, lag behind those of their counterparts.

- State and federal need-based financial aid is grossly inadequate in relation to the number of potential college students from low-income families.

- Historically Black colleges—Xavier University, Southern University at New Orleans, and Dillard University—like the predominantly White colleges, such as Tulane, have sustained massive damage and face major reconstructive challenges and a potential decline in future student enrollment.

- Less than 23% of the adults in the states of Mississippi, Alabama, and Louisiana have college degrees, a prerequisite in today's skills-driven, competitive global marketplace.

Put another way, when Hurricane Katrina decimated the Gulf Coast, displacing thousands of families and students at all levels, destroying homes and livelihoods and creating an uncertain future, it negatively impacted an already broken public education system in Mississippi, Louisiana, and to a lesser extent, Alabama. More than that, it stressed public school systems in states where displaced students were relocated. Reports are just beginning to come forth documenting the adjustment and achievement problems that such students are experiencing.

In the chapters in this volume, the question of accountability for the inadequate and unfair public education *status quo* looms large. The situation is complex.

There are many layers of responsibility for discrete elements of the restorative effort in the Gulf Coast and many constituencies and stakeholders with diverse interests and duties. This diffusion of responsibility for the quality of the whole of the public education system is one of the gravest barriers to surmount. The failure of the many pieces of this puzzle to come together to address the tasks at hand is a commentary on the lack of or inefficacy of extant leadership and coordination from the federal level on down.

Even if the state and local officials in Louisiana and Mississippi, the two states most severely affected by the storm, had the will to make significant improvements in public education and redesign a first-rate new system, they can't and won't succeed without significant amounts of additional federal funds. Archbishop Desmond Tutu once said that "It is difficult to awaken a man pretending to be asleep." There are many positive and good things that can be done to create a quality system of public education in the Gulf Coast region, but there is a lot of snoring going on.

Of course, resources are not all that is required, but resources are a necessary predicate to systemic change and improvement in public education in the Gulf Coast (and elsewhere). One recent estimate suggests that it would take close to 80 percent of the extant public education budget in Mississippi just to reconstruct the schools decimated by the storm. The state budget in Louisiana faces yawning shortfalls, yet it is the primary revenue source for state public education.

If those of us who care about improving public education allow reconstructive half-steps that result in Gulf Coast public schools with fewer resources than they had before the storm, we will have undercut equity efforts in the South for years to come. A message will be sent, loud and clear, that the public education of low income students isn't important to the nation.

At present, the public debate over reconstruction in the Gulf Coast region is dominated by concerns with physical infrastructure—housing, roads, bridges, levees, sanitation, health, and other basic services. However, without an effective, high quality public school system and dramatically improved schools, the South, including the Gulf Coast, will remain at the bottom of the economic ladder, as will its people. The best way in a modern economy to promote growth is to have highly skilled people to generate innovation, knowledge, and attract jobs that pay livable wages. How can the public be mobilized to come to real terms with this reality?

Too many people see public education as an individual benefit and not an indispensable social good. Many of the seventy-five percent of taxpayers who don't have children in the public schools do not see that the health and well-being of the region—its tax bases, capacity to attract capital, develop jobs and maintain infrastructure, health of its people, social safety net, and future—depend upon helping young people develop today the skills and sensibilities that they will need to be productive and caring adults tomorrow.

The chapters in this volume suggest some of the efforts underway to restore and improve education on the Gulf Coast. If the good judgment and commonsense reflected in these papers were heeded, fulsome, high-quality restorative measures would be already well underway.

The children in Mozambique whom I visited so many years ago showed remarkable resiliency in the face of all that they had lost. Given a fair chance, so, too, would the children of the Gulf Coast. However the key, whether in Mozambique or Mississippi, Alabama, and Louisiana is more and better education. Important work lies ahead.

■|■|■

About the Editors

SHARON PORTER ROBINSON is president and chief executive officer of the American Association of Colleges for Teacher Education in Washington, DC. Dr. Robinson is a nationally known leader in education rights for disadvantaged students. She is former president of the Educational Testing Service's Educational Policy Leadership Institute. While at ETS, she also served as senior vice president and chief operating officer, as vice president for teaching and learning, and in the State and Federal Relations Division.

Before joining ETS, Robinson was assistant secretary of education with the U.S. Department of Education's Office of Educational Research and Improvement. She also held a variety of leadership positions at the National Education Association, including director of the National Center for Innovation, NEA's research and development arm, and she recently served as interim deputy director of the National PTA's Programs and Legislation office. A lifelong civil rights activist, Robinson has waged a personal crusade to realize the moral and professional responsibility to develop strategies for educating and maximizing the potential of minority and dis- abled students in rural and inner-city districts.

Dr. Robinson received her bachelor's and master's degrees from the University of Kentucky, where she also later earned a doctorate in educational administration and supervision. She has also completed the renowned Harvard Business School Advanced Management Program. Her business interests include serving on the board of directors for Management & Training Corporation, a private company that operates Job Corps centers and prisons, and for Sable Uplink Communications, a private company that operates independent satellite uplink communication trucks.

Dr. Robinson also serves on the board of trustees for Alfred Harcourt Foundation; on the Supplemental Education Task Force of Columbia University; and on the board of directors for Jobs for America's Graduates, Strategic Planning Committee. She is past chair of the Diversity Issues in Measurement Committee, National Council for Measurement in Education. Among her many awards are an honorary doctorate from the University of Louisville, the Award of Appreciation from the National Head Start Association, the Founders Award from the National Commission for African American Education, the Pinnacles of Excellence Award by Helping Hands Enrichment & Leadership Foundation, the Teach for America Award, and the Girl Scouts' Woman of Distinction Award.

M. CHRISTOPHER BROWN II is vice president for Programs and Administration at the American Association for Colleges of Teacher Education. He oversees the management and support of the Association's research, programs, convenings, pub- lications, and internal technology. He was previously director of social justice and professional development for the American Educational Research Association (AERA), as well as former executive director and chief research scientist of the Frederick D. Patterson Research Institute of the United Negro College Fund.

Dr. Brown is on a continuing leave of absence from his appointment as associ- ate professor of education and senior research associate in the Center for the Study of Higher Education at The Pennsylvania State University. Prior to joining the Penn State faculty, he successfully developed a nationally ranked higher education program at the University of Illinois at Urbana-Champaign.

Dr. Brown began his career as an elementary school teacher in Orangeburg, SC. He has earned a national reputation for his research and scholarly writing on edu- cation policy and administration. His research addresses issues of leadership and governance, postsecondary statutory and legal concerns, institutional history, and diver- sity. He is especially well known for his studies of historically Black colleges, educa- tional equity, and institutional culture. Brown has lectured and/or presented research in various countries on six continents—Africa, Asia, Australia, Europe, North America, and South America.

Dr. Brown is the author or co-author of more than 90 journal articles, book chapters, monographs, and publications related to education and society. His books include *The Quest to Define Collegiate Desegregation* (1999), *Organization and Governance in Higher Education* (2000), *Black Sons to Mothers* (2000), *Equity and Access in Higher Education* (2002), *Studying Diverse Institutions* (2003), *Black Colleges* (2004), and *The Politics of Curricular Change* (2005). He has received research support from the Lumina Foundation, Spencer Foundation, AT&T Foundation, the Pew Charitable Trusts, the Sallie Mae Fund, as well as other foundations and corporations.

Dr. Brown received his B.S. in Elementary Education at South Carolina State University and the M.S.Ed. in Educational Policy and Evaluation from the University of Kentucky. He received a Ph.D. in Higher Education from the Pennsylvania State University with a cognate in public administration and political science.

Dr. Brown received the 2001 American Society for Higher Education's Promising Scholar/Early Career Award and the 2002 AERA Committee on Scholars of Color Early Career Contribution Award. He is also a former AERA—Spencer Foundation Fellowship recipient.

Contributors

SISTER JUDITH BRUN, CSJ, is a career educator with her most recent experience being at St. Joseph's Academy in Baton Rouge, Louisiana. During her tenure there, SJA was recognized three times as a national school of excellence and received national recognition for integrating technology into instruction. She received a master of arts degree in educational administration from Louisiana State University. Currently, she is the Director of Advance Baton Rouge, a community-supported initiative founded to support raising the performance of the children in the public schools through systemic change.

T. ELON DANCY II is completing the doctor of philosophy degree program at the Louisiana State University with a major in Higher Education Administration. His research and scholarly writing consider the intersection of race and gender in colleges and universities. More specifically, his agenda focuses on identifying the strategies for improving the social and academic experiences of African American men in different college contexts, as well as understanding African American male constructions of manhood and sense making. Additionally, careful attention is paid to assessing African American male persistence and outcomes. He has authored forthcoming manuscripts based on original data collection in *American Behavioral Scientist* and co-authored forthcoming empirical work that considers the scholarly productivity of faculty of color. Additional manuscripts are also forthcoming that review extant scholarship including topics of curricular change and in texts concerned with the socio-historical nature of schooling such as *Black Issues in Higher Education.* Furthermore, his published research and commentary on African American male experiences and engagement have appeared in other periodicals *Black Issues in Higher Education.* He has presented at several national conferences.

LINDA DARLING-HAMMOND is Charles E. Ducommun Professor of Education at Stanford University School of Education, where she serves as principal investigator for the School Redesign Network and the Stanford Educational Leadership Institute. Her research, teaching, and policy work focus on educational policy, teaching and teacher education, school restructuring, and educational equity. She is the founding executive director of the National Commission on Teaching and America's Future which produced the 1996 widely cited blueprint for education reform *What Matters Most: Teaching for America's Future.* Among her more than 200 publications is *The Right to Learn,* recipient of the 1998 Outstanding Book Award from the American Educational Research Association and *Teaching as the Learning Profession,* awarded the National Staff Development Council's Outstanding Book Award in 2000. She began her career as a public school teacher and has co-founded several schools, including a charter high school in East Palo Alto, CA.

JAMES EARL DAVIS is a professor in the Department of Educational Leadership and Policy Studies at Temple University with affiliate appointments in African American Studies and Women Studies. Dr. Davis has a B.A. in sociology from Morehouse College, a Ph.D. from Cornell University, and he has completed a postdoctoral fellowship in the Division of Education Policy at the Educational Testing Service, Princeton, New Jersey. His research focuses on the academic and social experiences of students placed at-risk for underachievement and school disengagement, particularly African American boys and men. His work has appeared in various research journals, including *Gender & Society, Urban Education, American Journal of Evaluation, Peabody Journal of Education, Evaluation Review,* and *Educational Researcher.* Dr. Davis is author of *African American Males in School and Society: Policies and Practices for Effective Education* (with Vernon C. Polite) and *Black Sons to Mothers: Compliments, Critiques, and Challenges for Cultural Workers in Education* (with M. Christopher Brown). A former National Academy of Education/Spencer Foundation Postdoctoral Fellow, Professor Davis has taught at the University of Delaware and Cornell University. He has also been a visiting scholar in the Institute for Research of Women and Gender at the University of Michigan-Ann Arbor and in the Center for Education Research, University of Wisconsin-Madison. His work has been funded by the Spencer Foundation, the National Science Foundation, Marcus Foundation, and the U.S. Department of Education.

LINDA SCHAAK DISTAD is the associate dean for Education Programs at the College of St. Catherine in St. Paul, Minnesota. She has been involved with teacher preparation for over twenty years, at the local, state, and national levels. She is the former president of the Minnesota Association of Colleges for Teacher Education and she is currently on the Board of Directors for the American Association of Colleges for Teacher Education. Her areas of expertise are reflective practice, technology use in education, and teacher leadership.

PENNY ENGEL is assistant director for research & policy at the American Association of Colleges for Teacher Education in Washington, DC, where her research and writing address a variety of teacher preparation issues. She was previously at Educational Testing Service, Mathematical Policy Research, Educational Projects, Inc., and University Research Corporation. Ms. Engel holds a Master of Arts degree in education from George Washington University.

M. JAYNE FLEENER is the E. B. "Ted" Robert Professor and Dean of the College of Education at Louisiana State University. She has a Ph.D. in Curriculum and Instruction, an MAT in mathematics, and an M.A. in philosophy, all from the University of North Carolina. Her undergraduate degree is in philosophy from Indiana University. Dr. Fleener's teaching and research have been in the areas of philosophy, computer science, mathematics education, and curriculum inquiry. She has taught mathematics and computer science at the pre-collegiate level in North Carolina. She has numerous national and international publications including her recent books *Curriculum Dynamics: Recreating Heart* and *Chaos, Complexity, Curriculum, and Culture: A Conversation* (edited with Doll, Trueit, and St. Julien).

KASSIE FREEMAN currently serves as the dean for Academic Advancement at Bowdoin College. Previously, she was the dean of the Division of Educational and Psychological Studies and professor of education at Dillard University. Her research interests include cultural considerations related to African Americans and college choice and comparative/international issues in higher education and the labor market and Black populations in the diaspora. She is the author or editor of three books titled, *African Americans and College Choice: The Influence of Family and School* (SUNY Press), *African American Culture and Heritage in Higher Education Research and Practice* (Praeger), and *Black Colleges* (with M. Christopher Brown, II). She is the former president of the Comparative and International Education Society.

SUSAN FUHRMAN was recently named president of Teachers College, Columbia University. For the past seven years, Dr. Fuhrman has served as dean and George and Diane Weiss professor of education of the University of Pennsylvania's Graduate School of Education. She was at Rutgers's Eagleton Institute of Politics and a professor of education policy before joining the University of Pennsylvania. In addition to her deanship and teaching, Fuhrman has been chair and director of the Management Committee of the Consortium for Policy Research in Education (CPRE) since 1985. She is editor of *From the Capitol to the Classroom: Standards-Based Reform in the States* (2001) and *Rewards and Reform: Creating Educational Incentives that Work* (1996). Fuhrman is a former vice president of the American Educational Research Association, a member of the National Coalition on Asia and International Studies in the Schools, and she serves on the board of the Fund for New Jersey. She has a B.A. and M.A. from Northwestern University and a Ph.D. from Columbia University.

MARY HATWOOD FUTRELL is the dean of the George Washington University Graduate School of Education and Human Development (GSEHD). A professor of education and co-director of GW's Center for Curriculum, Standards, and Technology, Dean Futrell specializes in education reform policy, professional development, and diversity issues. She is chair of the Holmes Partnership Board and is a member of the Boards of the National Society for the Study of Education, the Kettering Foundation, Horace Mann Insurance Company, and Lynchburg College. From 1989 to 1995, she served as a senior consultant for Quality Education for Minorities Network. Prior to becoming dean of GSEHD in 1995, Dr. Futrell was president of the National Education Association (NEA) for an unprecedented six-year term and, before that, served as president of the Virginia Education Association (VEA). In 2004, she completed her term as president of Education International (EI), a global federation of 30 million educators from 152 countries that works with governmental and non-governmental organizations in advocating education for all. She also is the former president of the World Confederation of Organizations of the Teaching Profession. First and foremost a teacher, Dean Futrell is an advocate for human and civil rights and improved education worldwide. She has received over 20 honorary degrees from universities and colleges and has won numerous awards. Some of her honors include the American Association of Colleges for Teacher Education David G. Imig Award for Distinguished Achievement in Teacher Education (2002), the NEA Foundation Award for Outstanding Service to Public Education (2003), and UNESCO's Jan Amos Comenius Medal (2004).

VIVIAN L. GADSDEN is Director of the National Center on Fathers and Families (NCOFF) and Associate Professor of Education at the University of Pennsylvania. From 1990 through 1996, Dr. Gadsden also served as Associate Director of the National Center on Adult Literacy at the University of Pennsylvania. She received her doctorate in developmental psychology and education with a specialty in policy from the University of Michigan. Dr. Gadsden's research focuses on family development and literacy across the life-span and within multiple cultures, primarily African American, Latino, and American Indian families, and families living in poverty. Her work examines the nature of persistence and consequences of intergenerational learning within families and explores issues of race, class, and gender within the home, school, and social contexts. Dr. Gadsden's current research projects are: (1) a multigenerational study of 25 African American families, (2) a parent-child Head Start project with African American and Puerto Rican families, and (3) a project with adolescent and young mothers and fathers. Dr. Gadsden has published several articles and book chapters on issues related to families, literacy, and culture and is currently completing two book-length volumes: (1) a single authored work from her multigenerational study and (2) a co-edited volume, entitled *In Our Father's Image, In Our Mother's Heart: Life Notes on Families, Race, and Gender.* A third volume, co-edited with Daniel Wagner, *Literacy among African American Youth: Issues in Learning, Teaching, and Schooling,* was published in 1995 as part of the literacy series by Hampton Press. Her work has appeared as book chapters and as articles in journals such as *Theory into Practice,* for which she edited a special issue entitled "Literacy and the African-American Learner: The Struggle between Access and Denial."

KRISTY HEBERT has been an educator of 25 years who received her Ph.D. from Louisiana State University in educational leadership. The roles within which she has participated during her career include: middle and high school teacher in Louisiana; Teach for America support staff; middle school administrator in Rhode Island; professor of educational leadership at Southern Connecticut State University in New Haven, Connecticut; and senior vice-president of Edison Schools, overseeing all charter schools in the state and city of New York. She currently serves as the Educational Partnership Director who oversees a multi-million dollar grant from the Bill and Melinda Gates Foundation. This grant allows for the building of an autonomous school network (modeled after the New York City Empowerment

Schools) within the largest urban public school district in the state, East Baton Rouge Parish Schools.

LYNN HUNTLEY is president of the Southern Education Foundation—a public charity that advances strategies to ensure equity and excellence in Southern education, from preschool through higher education. An honors graduate of Barnard College and Columbia University Law School, where she was a member of the Law Review, Ms. Huntley has served as program director at the Ford Foundation, staff attorney at the NAACP Legal Defense and Educational Fund, and section chief in the United States Department of Justice, Civil Rights Division, among other positions. Ms. Huntley has worked nationally and internationally on issues of social justice and civil rights. She serves on the Boards of CARE USA, the Interdenominational Theological Center, the American Constitution Society, and Grantmakers for Education, among other organizations.

JACQUELINE JORDAN IRVINE is Charles Howard Candler Professor of Urban Education in the Division of Educational Studies at Emory University. Professor Irvine's specialization is in multicultural education and urban teacher education, particularly the education of African American students. Her books include *Black Students and School Failure* (Greenwood), *Growing up African American in Catholic Schools* (Teachers College Press), *Critical Knowledge for Diverse Students* (AACTE), *Culturally Responsive Lesson Planning for Elementary and Middle Grades* (McGraw-Hill), *In Search of Wholeness: African American Teachers and Their Culturally Specific Pedagogy* (Palgrave), and *Educating Teachers for Diversity: Seeing with the Cultural Eye* (Teachers College Press). *Black Students and School Failure* received the Outstanding Writing Award from the American Association of Colleges of Teacher Education and was selected as an Outstanding Academic Book by the American Association of College and University Research Librarians. In addition, she has published numerous articles and book chapters. She has received the Distinguished Career Award from the SIG on Black Education of the American Education Research Association, an award from the Association for Supervision and Curriculum Development for exemplary contributions to the education of African American children, the 2000 Dewitt-Wallace/AERA Lecture Award, the 2001 AACTE Hunt Lecture, and the 2003 AACTE Lindsey Award for Distinguished Research in Teacher Education. At Emory University's 2000 Commencement ceremony, Professor Irvine received the Thomas Jefferson Award, the highest award given to an Emory University faculty member for service and research. A renowned educator, in 2004 Professor Irvine received the prestigious *Crystal Apple Award* for Excellence in Graduate Teaching. At the 2005 meeting of the American Educational Research Association, she was presented with AERA's *Social Justice in Education Award* for her efforts to advance social justice through education research.

GLORIA LADSON-BILLINGS is the Kellner Family Professor of Urban Education in the Department of Curriculum & Instruction at the University of Wisconsin-Madison and the 2005–2006 president of the American Educational Research Association. Ladson-Billings's research examines the pedagogical practices of teachers who are successful with African American students. She also investigates Critical Race Theory applications to education. She is the author of the critically acclaimed book, *The Dreamkeepers: Successful Teachers of African-American Children, Crossing over to Canaan: The Journey of New Teachers in Diverse Classrooms,* and many journal articles and book chapters. She is the former editor of the *American Educational Research Journal* and a member of several editorial boards. Her work has won numerous scholarly awards including the H. I. Romnes faculty fellowship, the Spencer Post-Doctoral Fellowship, and the Palmer O. Johnson Outstanding research award. In 2002 she was awarded an honorary doctorate from Umeå University in Umeå, Sweden, and in 2003–2004 was a fellow at the Center for Advanced Study in the Behavioral Sciences at Stanford University. She is the 2004 recipient of the George and Louise Spindler Award for ongoing contributions in educational anthropology, given by the Council on Anthropology & Education of the American Anthropological Association. In the spring of 2005 she was elected to the National Academy of Education.

JANE A. LEIBBRAND serves as vice president for communications of the National Council for Accreditation of Teacher Education. Ms. Leibbrand plans and directs media relations, outreach to numerous target audiences, market research, communications, and publications development on behalf of the Association. She created and produces a national newsletter highlighting trends and issues in teacher preparation. She has directed NCATE's public relations since 1991, helping to bring NCATE to the fore as a major contributor to standards development and education reform, as portrayed in national and trade press coverage. From 1989 to 1991, Ms. Leibbrand served as Director of Off-Campus Programs for the George Washington University, where she marketed and managed master's degree programs at 14 off-campus locations. From 1984 to 1989, she served as director of communications and marketing for the American Association for Adult and Continuing Education where she conducted a national public relations campaign culminating in a national awards ceremony on Capitol Hill for adult learners. She has an M.A. in English from the University of Georgia, an M.Ed. from the University of Virginia, and a B.A. cum laude in English from Wake Forest University. Leibbrand has authored numerous chapters and articles on education in professional publications. She previously taught English at the high school and college levels.

JACQUELINE LEONARD is an associate professor of mathematics education at Temple University in Philadelphia. She earned her Ph.D. in the Department of Curriculum and Instruction at the University of Maryland at College Park in 1997. As a former elementary and middle school science and mathematics teacher, her research agenda is focused on learning environments, broadly defined as reform-based mathematics instruction, culturally responsive teaching, computer-based instruction, and university collaborations with professional development and charter schools. Dr. Leonard has worked in the field of education for 25 years, published 20 articles, and presented 40 papers at national and international conferences. She currently has a contract with Lawrence Erlbaum to author a book entitled *Culturally Specific Pedagogy in the Mathematics Classroom.*

ARTHUR E. LEVINE is the sixth president of the Woodrow Wilson National Fellowship Foundation. Before his appointment at Woodrow Wilson, he was president and professor of education at Teachers College, Columbia University. He also previously served as chair of the higher education program, chair of the Institute for Educational Management, and senior lecturer at the Harvard Graduate School of Education. Dr. Levine is the author of dozens of articles and reviews. His most recent book is *When Hope and Fear Collide: A Portrait of Today's College Student* (with Jeanette S. Cureton). Among other volumes are *Beating the Odds: How the Poor Get to College* (with Jana Nidiffer), *Higher Learning in America; Shaping Higher Education's Future; When Dreams and Heroes Died: A Portrait of Today's College Students; Handbook on Undergraduate Curriculum; Quest for Common Learning* (with Ernest Boyer); *Opportunity in Adversity* (with Janice Green); *and Why Innovation Fails.* Much of his research and writing in recent years has focused on increasing access to higher education and improving equity in the schools. Dr. Levine's numerous opinion editorials appear in such publications as *The New York Times; The Los Angeles Times; The Wall Street Journal; The Washington Post;* and *The Chronicle of Higher Education.*

Dr. Levine has received numerous honors, including a Guggenheim Fellowship and a Carnegie Fellowship, as well as the American Council on Education's "Book of the Year" award (for *Reform of Undergraduate Education),* the Educational Press Association's "Annual Award" for writing (three times), and 17 honorary degrees. In 1998 *Change* magazine listed him as "One of the Most Outstanding Leaders in the Academic Community." He currently sits on the Boards of Blackboard, Inc., DePaul University, and All Kinds of Minds. He is a member of the American Academy of Arts and Sciences.

Dr. Levine was also previously President of Bradford College (1982–1989) and Senior Fellow at the Carnegie Foundation and Carnegie Council for Policy Studies in Higher Education (1975–1982). He received his bachelor's degree from Brandeis University and his Ph.D. from the State University of New York at Buffalo. Dr. Levine formally joined the Foundation staff in September 2006.

IRA LIT, a former elementary school teacher, is the Director of the Teachers for a New Era initiative at Bank Street College of Education. Prior to joining the faculty at Bank Street College, Dr. Lit served as the Associate Director of the Stanford Elementary Teacher Education Program. His book exploring the experiences of minority students in a voluntary desegregation program is entitled *The Bus Kids* and will be published by Yale University Press.

P. RUDY MATTAI is professor, Educational Foundations, SUNY-College at Buffalo, Buffalo, New York, and has recently served as founding dean, School of Education, SUNY-Old Westbury, Long Island, New York. He is currently President (2006–2009) of the Global Federation of the Associations for Teacher Education (GloFATE) and immediate Past President (2006–2007) of the Association for Teacher Educators (USA); serves on the board of the following organizations: National Association for Ethnic Studies (NAES); International Society for Educational Planning (ISEP). He is the editor of *Child Studies Journal*. He serves as an external examiner for graduate programs at the University of the West Indies at St. Augustine, Trinidad. His research areas include race and ethnic issues in education and urban education and, he has published widely in both areas. He is co-editor of *Culturally Responsive Teacher Education: Language, Curriculum and Community* (Lawrence Erlbaum, 2006). He has received numerous awards and consults nationally and internationally on diversity issues and program development and evaluation.

VERNON C. POLITE is the dean of the College of Education at Eastern Michigan University (EMU). EMU is the largest producer of professional educational personnel in the nation with 8,000 candidates in pursuit of one or more of 49 degree initial and advanced programs offered. He is the founding dean of the School of Education at Bowie State University. Prior to serving at Bowie, Dr. Polite was the Dr. Euphemia Lofton Haynes Professor of Educational Administration at the Catholic University of America in Washington, DC. He earned his doctor of philosophy degree in the areas of Educational Administration and Sociology from Michigan State University. Dr. Polite has published more than 30 articles in such scholarly journals as *Secondary Education Today*, the *Journal of Curriculum Studies;* the *Journal of Negro Education;* and *Urban Education.* He has also contributed several book chapters to well-known edited volumes. Most recently he released an important and timely work, *African American Males in School and Society: Practices and Policies for Effective Education* (1999, Teachers College Press). In addition to teaching and writing, he has received numerous grants from the U.S. Department of Education, the Edna McConnell Clark Foundation, and W. Kellogg Foundation through the National Education Association, and the National Association of Secondary School Principals.

DIANNE SMITH is a native of Jonesville, South Carolina, who now resides in Kansas City, Missouri. She attended Foster Chapel Elementary School, Sims High School, and she graduated from Jonesville High School in 1970. Dr. Smith continued her postsecondary education at Spartanburg Methodist College (A.A. in Early Childhood Education), Winthrop University (B.S. in Special Education and M.Ed. in Educational Administration and Supervision), and Miami University-Ohio (the Doctor of Philosophy in Curriculum Theory and Cultural Studies). She is an author of numerous educational and research publications that focus on curriculum theory, feminist pedagogy, and cultural studies. Dr. Smith is Division Chair and Associate Professor of Urban Leadership and Policy Studies in Education, University of Missouri-Kansas City (UMKC). The UMKC School of Education celebrated its 50th anniversary in October, 2004, and Dr. Smith is the first black woman to hold the position in the history of the School. Such recognition is important due to the fact that 2004 was the 50th anniversary of the landmark desegregation case, *Brown v. Board of Education Topeka* (1954).

PAMELA K. SMITH is an assistant professor in the Department of Teacher Education at Eastern Michigan University. Prior to joining Eastern Michigan's Curriculum and Instruction program, she worked more than 30 years as a teacher and administrator for one of Ohio's small urban school districts. Dr. Smith also spent 17 years working as a Visiting Assistant Professor at Miami University in Oxford, Ohio, where she also earned her doctorate through the Department of Educational Leadership. She focuses primarily on curriculum theory, with the intent to merge it with the social and cultural issues confronting members of all educational settings in the past, present, and conceivable future.

JON SNYDER is currently Dean of the Graduate School of Education at Bank Street College. He has worked as a researcher and a teacher educator at the University of California, Santa Barbara, Teachers College Columbia University, the National Center for the Restructuring of Education, Schools, and Teaching, and the National Commission on Teaching and America's Future. He remains engaged in researching teacher learning, conditions that support teacher learning, and the relationships

between teacher and student learning. His current position allows him the opportunity to explore these issues with his colleagues in the context of an exemplary stand-alone professional school of education.

JACQUELINE M. WILLIAMS is currently completing an Ed.D. in Curriculum and Instruction with an emphasis on the Gifted and Talented. She has been an instructor in Exceptional Education in public schools in New York and Florida and has taught in both traditional and nontraditional classrooms. She currently serves in the capacity of Practice Administrator/Vice President; Advanced Rehabilitation Medical Services (ARMS), Charlotte Harbor, Florida. She is actively engaged in school board administration and pursues research activities in the area of the gifted and talented. Her current research for completion of her dissertation is *The Perception of Teachers Regarding the Identification and Participation of Students of Color in Gifted and Talented Programs: A Case-Study of the United States of America, the Netherlands, and the United Kingdom.* She has received numerous academic awards including the Certificate of Excellence Award and a Minority Fellowship Award, SUNY-College at Buffalo, Buffalo, New York.

PAT WILLIAMS-BOYD is professor of education at Eastern Michigan University. She has received numerous scholarships, grants, and awards, including Teacher of the Year during her twenty-seven years in public school, and the Outstanding Teaching Award for the College of Education during her ten years at EMU. Williams-Boyd holds a doctorate in ethnomusicology and a doctorate in curriculum and instruction. Her publications and presentations address issues such as poverty and full-service schools, critical thinking, excellence in middle grades teaching and learning, qualitative research and educational leadership. She has been an invited speaker throughout the United States and Europe and an invited professional development coach who intensively works with K-12 schools as they embrace best practices on behalf of all students.

JERRY WILLIS is Associate Dean for Research in the College of Education at Louisiana State University. His Ph.D. is in child clinical psychology from the University of Alabama, and his areas of scholarly interest include the philosophical foundations of social science research, qualitative research methods, interpretive and critical theories of education, and the integration of technology into constructivist learning environments.

ARTHUR E. WISE is President of the National Council for the Accreditation of Teacher Education (NCATE). During his career, Art has worked toward teacher quality and professionalism, school finance reform, and the advancement of educational research. At NCATE, he has directed the design of performance-based accreditation, a new approach, and led efforts to develop a system of quality assurance for the teaching profession. He is co-author of *A License to Teach,* which is a blueprint for the professionalization of teaching. Art first came to national prominence as the author of *Rich Schools, Poor Schools: The Promise of Equal Educational Opportunity.* That 1968 book conceived the idea of the school finance reform lawsuit. Since then, a majority of state supreme courts have ordered the equalization of state school finance systems, boosting spending in poor districts and narrowing the disparity with affluent districts. His 1979 book, *Legislated Learning,* anticipated the call for teacher professionalism. As senior social scientist and director of the RAND Corporation's Center for the Study of the Teaching Profession, he proposed education policies concerned with teacher licensing, teacher evaluation, and teacher compensation. Many of these proposals have been incorporated into state laws and regulations. Long active in federal education policy Art was associate director for research, National Institute of Education, Department of Education and Welfare. Subsequently, at the Office of Management and Budget, he helped to create the separate cabinet-level U. S. Department of Education. On a number of occasions he has testified before Congress on policies to improve education and educational research. Art's previous positions include: Associate dean and associate professor of education at the University of Chicago, and captain in the U.S. Army and assistant director of research at the U.S. Military Academy, West Point and Visiting Scholar, ETS. He is a graduate of the Boston (Public) Latin School, Harvard College, and received an MBA and a Ph.D. in education from the University of Chicago. He has made hundreds of presentations, published scores of articles, and has been the recipient of numerous awards.

EBONI M. ZAMANI-GALLAHER is an Associate Professor in Higher Education Administration in the Department of Leadership and Counseling at Eastern Michigan University. She coordinates the Graduate Certificate Program in Community College Leadership at EMU. She has previously held appointments as a faculty member at West Virginia University and doctoral fellow for Mathematical Policy Research, Inc., and ACT, Inc. Her areas of teaching expertise largely include Analysis of Research in Educational Leadership, The Community College, Educational Leadership in a Pluralistic Society, Introduction to Higher Education, Policy Analysis in Higher Education and Women in Leadership. Her research and consulting activities primarily concentrate on adjustment and transition of underrepresented collegians at two- and four-year institutions of higher learning; diversity initiatives in higher education, and institutional policies impacting work and family balance.

3 5282 00636 1474